Financing without Bank Loans

Jiazhuo G. Wang · Juan Yang

Financing without Bank Loans

New Alternatives for Funding SMEs in China

Springer

Jiazhuo G. Wang
School of Business
College of Staten Island
City University of New York
Staten Island, New York, NY
USA

Juan Yang
HSBC Business School
Peking University
Shenzhen, Guangdong
China

ISBN 978-981-10-0900-6 ISBN 978-981-10-0901-3 (eBook)
DOI 10.1007/978-981-10-0901-3

Library of Congress Control Number: 2016936416

Printed on acid-free paper

This Springer imprint is published by Springer Nature
The registered company is Springer Science+Business Media Singapore Pte Ltd.

Preface

On June 3, 2013 at a finance summit in Shanghai, Jack Ma of Alibaba "opened fire" on the commercial lending provided by the large state-owned commercial banks in China, criticizing the fact that their loans earned 80 % of all profits, but only served 20 % of the market's fund demand. Ma claimed that the financial industry should not be a "self-entertained" circle; instead, it needs to well serve the "outsiders" of the financial industry, allow the entry of external "intruders", and take steps toward financial reform and innovation.[1] As can be expected, Jack Ma's comments triggered enormous debate in the media, both inside and outside financial industries, on the whole basket of related financial issues. The most salient question was as to who comprised this lucky 20 % and who were the 80 % who were "leftovers?" Why could these "20 %" easily obtain the abundant funding they demand, and sometimes even beyond what they need, from large banks, but such funding barely covered the remaining 80 % who could not even secure much smaller amounts of money that they badly need? What can the Chinese financial industry do to address these issues, and will the long-waited financial reform take a real step forward? And, finally, will China's financial industry truly open the door for private capital and non-state-owned small- and medium-sized enterprises (SMEs)? These were all questions that burgeoned from Jack Ma's ostensible comments on June 3.

In China, there is a tacit understanding among participants in the financial industry that the very few, and very large, state-owned commercial banks are the primary legal fund suppliers in the financial market, and have been for many decades. It is also known that the primary recipients of the funds provided by these large commercial banks are the same state-owned, very large companies, which typically represent these lucky "20 %," as described by Jack Ma. On the other hand, the low income individuals and the small- and medium-sized enterprises (SMEs) that make up over 99 % of the total number firms in China become the "leftover 80 %," and have to struggle and compete for the remaining 20 % of funds in the loanable fund market. It should be no surprise, then, that the most of these latter

[1]http://money.sohu.com/20130604/n377910523.shtml.

companies and individuals end up with nothing in hand, and have to turn to "shadow banks" for funding—the fund market which, for the most part, are filled with the illegal underground fund providers charging extremely high interest rates, such as over 50 %, on an annualized basis. As a result, SMEs' struggle for financing has become a tremendous challenge, greatly impeding the growth and development of SMEs in China.

Historically, the role played by SMEs in China's economy was considered somewhat insignificant. Under the existing ownership structure, the majority of SMEs are privately owned firms that were either set up as a private one since their inceptions or transferred from state-owned during the period of time of ownership reform in 1990s. Compared to large state-owned corporations and their roles as the dominant force in the economy, SMEs were typically perceived as relatively trivial entities whose primary functionality is to fill market niches and cover the few segments uncovered by large state-owned corporations. As a result, SMEs and the financing of SMEs were not perceived as a top priority issue on the agenda of China's economic development.

However, that page of the China's economic growth has been turned over. After more than three decades of high-speed growth, China's economy is now at a crossroads, and SMEs stand near, if not at, the center. Overconsumption of non-renewable energies, and increasingly polluted land, water, and air have been the cost of rapid expansion. In addition, China's heavily investment and export-driven economy and competition based only on inexpensive labor make continued growth in the same vein unsustainable. The 2015 third quarter GDP growth rate, as recently released by China's State Statistical Bureau, fell below 7 % for the first time in the past 35 years.[2] The figure is a clear indicator of the changing diagram of the Chinese economy. So the question truly is: what new growth model will allow China to remain on track for the forthcoming decades?

History has repeatedly demonstrated that progress in economic growth is simply and persistently the result of "creative destruction," as Joseph Schumpeter pointed out several decades ago.[3] Innovation from the market place internally drives the growth of the economy, while entrepreneurs are the initiators and executors of such innovations. In trying to achieve the goal of sustainable economic growth, China cannot be an exception in this regard. Innovation-driven growth, along with the participation of entrepreneurs and millions of SMEs, will be the key to breaking the vicious cycle.

The participation of SMEs in innovation is certainly important for improvement in economic inclusiveness. However, their impact can go far beyond that. SMEs not only make up the majority of the total number of firms in an economy, and can conduct innovations in many areas that larger corporations cannot cover, but they also have stronger motivation to innovate in the first place. By nature, innovations—especially the fundamental ones—are changes or destructions in existing product

---

[2]State Statistics Bureau of China: http://www.gov.cn/xinwen/2015-10/20/content_2950474.htm.

[3]Schumpeter J., 2006, Capitalism, Socialism and Democracy, New Edition, Routledge, London.

and market structure, and the larger firms typically benefit more from the status quo. As a result, large corporations, usually, may tend to be less motivated to innovate than SMEs. Kodak, for example, was widely considered a classic case of a large corporation in a monopolistic position, who resisted new digital technology innovation due to a conflict of interest with its traditional film business, and eventually filed for bankruptcy. Therefore, SMEs are widely expected to play a much more critical and strategic role, instead of a niche one as before, in China's sustainable economic growth in the coming decades.

However, despite the new tasks that SMEs have been expected by the market to undertake, obtaining adequate funding to support innovation and entrepreneurship has been a difficulty for many such small and medium companies. In a monetary economy, conducting innovation without funding would be like driving a car without gasoline or electricity. The difficulties in financing SMEs under the traditional financial system in China remains a huge hurdle that companies must overcome before the Chinese economy can emerge from a nonsustainable growth model to a sustainable one. As a result, a financial innovation would be a necessary condition for a successful economic transition in China.

To be fair, the lack of sufficient funding for SMEs in China cannot be entirely attributed to lack of enthusiasm on the part of large state-owned commercial banks. It is more so that the characteristics of SMEs and the inherited risk associated with SME financing are difficult for such large banks to ignore. First, compared with large state-owned corporations, there appears higher degree of asymmetric information. In general, the outsiders of a company always know less than the insiders about what actually goes on at a firm, but the level of the imbalance would be more severe for SMEs, due either to cost considerations or protection concerns. As a result, SMEs are typically perceived as enterprises with much higher degree of uncertainty and risk.

Second, in addition to less disclosure to the general public, the financial information reported by the SMEs is, usually, less likely to be standardized in a format that is in compliance with the generally accepted accounting principles. Due to limited resources, SMEs usually cannot afford to hire financial professionals to prepare their financial documents, or contract public accounting firms to audit their financial statements. As a consequence, even when SMEs consent to providing their documents, not much of the information can be actually used by financial institutions when they make financing decisions toward SMEs' funding.

Third, because SMEs are smaller firms, the amount of assets that they can use as collateral for bank loans are typically less. When compared against the financing values that most SMEs request, the collaterals they possess are usually not adequate to meet the collateral requirements of most large banks.

Fourth, SMEs typically lack adequate credit records. However, credit records and credit history of the borrowers are what commercial banks commonly use as the critical point of reference when making financing decisions. Because many SMEs do not have any history of borrowing money from banks, thanks to the difficulties in securing bank loans in the first place, they are usually rejected for bank loans due to the lack of credit history. This creates what is apparently a vicious cycle. If an

SME does not have adequate credit history, it would not be able to get credit; but if it cannot get credit, it is almost cyclically banned from ever being able to obtain a loan.

Fifth, given the inherent risk associated with SMEs financing, there lacks the economies of scale needed as an incentive for financial institutions. From the perspective of commercial banks, regardless the size of the firm that requests the loans, the bank needs to take, at least, the same amount of effort and procedure to clear that firm for lending, such as application reviews, credit assessment, comprehensive analysis, on-site investigation, and final release of funds, all of which are a heavy consumption of time and resources. Given the relatively smaller size of SME loans, compared to those requested by larger corporations, it is difficult for the commercial banks to achieve the same economies of scale when lending to SMEs. Needless to say, commercial banks, on the whole, prefer larger corporations.

As a result, financial innovation in China requires alternative financing methods for SMEs. In addition to indirect financing with traditional bank loans and focus on the large amount of funding as provided by large state-owned commercial banks, infrastructure for direct financing and funding for smaller amount of financing request also needs to be in place. Felicitously, enormous financial innovations have emerged in China's financial market in recent years, including direct financing such as the bond and equity market, funding vehicles focused on the smaller amount of funding such as micro/small loans, innovative methods of funding SMEs without tangible collateral such as chattel pledge and supply chain financing, and financing through the Internet such as P2P online lending and crowdfunding. This book intends to analyze all these remarkable progresses in the financing of SMEs in China, and summarize some key takeaways for the readers and observers of Chinese economy, in general, and of SME financing, in particular.

This book covers all the primary innovations in SME financing in China from the past decades, including debt financing such as micro and small loans, guarantee and mutual guarantee, bond issuance, P2P online lending, chattel pledges, supply chain financing, financial leasing, and equity financing such as private equity, reversal merger, New Third Board, and crowdfunding. The book analyzes in detail the business models that were developed by each individual financing method, the method of operation and cash flow generation, as well as the risks intrinsic to each method and risk control. Each alternative method of financing is analyzed with actual SME financing case studies, and the prediction for their future development is also discussed. Some alternative ways of SME financing, such as pawn, are not included, as they are currently not in the main stream of new alternative financings, and are also less likely to be in the future. On the other hand, given the increased role that SMEs will play in China's economy in the coming decades, large state-owned commercial banks have also started to design and provide financing products for SMEs. Since state-owned commercial banks are still the dominant financing providers in China's financial market today, we added one chapter at the end to introduce some of the new financial products these large state-owned banks have designed for SMEs, in addition to some services that also involved in SMEs as discussed in other debt financing chapters; however, given the consideration of economies of scale, what additional "percentage" these large banks can serve in addition to the current "20 %" still remains to be seen.

As a book that covers all the important financial innovations in SME financing, and which combines theoretical analysis and real world practices in China's financial market, it could be of interest and value to a variety of readers, including, but not limited to, the following:

First, institutional and individual investors both inside and outside China may find this topic relevant and intriguing. Financial institutions such as security firms, investment banks, private equity funds, venture capital firms, commercial banks, other financial intermediaries, and individual investors including angels could gain a better understanding about the financing of SMEs, which covers 99 % of the Chinese business community. In particular, SME financing involves many smaller amount financial transactions, which will provide investment opportunities for smaller investors who may not be able to participate under the traditional financial regime.

Second, Chinese SMEs that are looking for financing should also be interested in this topic. As China adapts its growth model into a more innovation-oriented one, obtaining adequate funding becomes a critical prerequisite for success. Understanding what is available, and which method of financing can best meet SMEs' needs and match the nature of their business, would be of tremendous value for SMEs that are operating in China. For example, debt financing may better fit the working capital needs, while equity financing may be more appropriate for R&D and start-ups.

Third, investors and professionals who are running alternative financial entities, such as online platforms, may take an interest in this topic. Like the running of any other financial operation, running an alternative financing entity not only provides an innovative business opportunity for the parties that are engaged, but also exposes the alternative financial operators to the new risks associated predominantly with these new financial services. As a result, they would have an urgent need to supplement their knowledge and understanding about this changing industry, especially its risks and the potential downfalls, in order to maximize their bottom line returns and mitigate risk. Therefore, this book will indubitably be an important reference tool for them.

Fourth, bankers in traditional financial institutions might be interested in this book as well. New alternative ways of financing, especially Internet-related innovations, can be reasonably considered as both a formidable challenge and a lucrative opportunity for traditional financial institutions. Opening the door for private equity and the integration of finance and Internet has been recognized as both an indomitable and irresistible trend, and the "anywhere, anytime, anyway, customer experience" has become fundamental to all service industries, including finance. As this trend grows at an increasingly high pace, the question facing the traditional commercial banking system is how traditional banks can promptly meet this challenge, and in a more competitive market environment besides. Gaining thorough understanding of the status quo of the current financial market and new alternative financial innovations will become a priority item for traditional commercial bankers and their major shareholders, domestic and international. This book would certainly provide an important reference for that purpose.

Fifth, members of regulatory agencies could find value in this book as well. In China, the financial industry is strictly regulated, and any new "innovations" will be closely "watched" by regulatory agencies. Even though more explicit legislation regarding certain new alternative financing methods, such as P2P online lending and crowdfunding, has not been fully delineated yet, it is merely a matter of time before regulatory agencies bring the hammer down; this is true especially because the general public has become increasingly exposed to the risks associated with new alternative methods as the public gains more knowledge and understanding about these "innovations." The major dilemma in government regulation, however, is always the extent or degree to which regulations should be set up and implemented. While overregulation can unnecessarily hinder the innovations needed for business development and economic growth, underregulation may fail to control the risks that will damage said business development and economic growth. As a result, a comprehensive analysis and understanding about the new alternative financing is a prerequisite for the regulators, in order to help them achieve the optimal balance between regulation and market innovation. This book could offer some valuable insights.

Sixth, academics inside and outside China could be interested in this book as well. Because the growth model of the Chinese economy has fundamentally changed, and even more changes are expected down the road, the role of SMEs in Chinese economic growth in the next decades has been redefined, and SMEs' status has been repositioned. Understanding how SMEs can be financially funded so that they can survive and succeed is a key to understanding the new growth model of the Chinese economy. Any research on the China's future economic growth omitting the topic of SMEs and their relationship with financial innovation would be incomplete. In this regard, this book would provide such Chinese business researchers with a valuable reference.

In summary, as China increasingly becomes a key player in the world economy, understanding the structure, operation, and future changes of the Chinese economy becomes increasingly critical. As the impact of the recent RMB devaluation[4] and the dip in third quarter GDP growth indicated, the influence of the Chinese economy on the global one cannot be ignored. Given the RMB's joining the SDR of IMF,[5] the Chinese economy's influence could even grow larger. Therefore, we hope this book "Financing without Bank Loans—New Alternatives for Funding SMEs in China" will be a well-timed publication with important value for a wide spectrum of readerships, either as a reference book or as a guideline in understanding, gaining knowledge of, research and teaching, and making business decisions about China and issues related with China.

---

[4]Wall Street Journal: http://www.wsj.com/articles/china-moves-to-devalue-the-yuan-1439258401.

[5]https://www.imf.org/external/np/sec/pr/2015/pr15540.htm.

Acknowledgments

This book is a result of a joint effort among the researchers from the City University of New York, the Small and Medium Enterprises Research Center, and the HSBC School of Business at Peking University.

In terms of the writing of the book, Dr. J. George Wang wrote the Preface, Chaps. 1–4, 9, 12, and 13, while Dr. Juan Yang wrote Chaps. 5–8, 10, and 11. Graduate students of the HSBC School of Business at Peking University also participated in the research projects by collecting some case data and drafting the Chinese versions of some of the alternative methods of SME financing. Among them, Wen Wu studied small loan and guarantee, Li Shasha studied mutual guarantee and asset-backed mortgage, He Yang studied bond issuance and supply chain financing, Chen Jie studied venture capital, Hu Bo studied OTC market, and Li Qiang studied the third party platforms. Dr. J. George Wang and Dr. Juan Yang rewrite all alternative ways of financing in English and finalized the book for its submission.

In addition, Allison Wang of the Stern School of Business at New York University edited and proofread the entire book. Toby Chai, the editor of Springer Publisher, initiated the book writing on Chinese business and economy, and provided much support along with the production of this book. All the efforts and contributions of the above individuals toward the publication of this book are greatly appreciated. Of course, the authors are solely responsible for any errors and omissions.

Contents

Chapter 1
Funding for "The Leftover Eighty Percent"—Micro and Small Loans for SMEs

When Dr. Muhammad Yunus and his organization, the Grameen Bank in Bangladesh, jointly received the Nobel Peace Prize in 2006,[1] Dr. Yunus stunned the world with his trailblazing efforts to issue micro loans to the "poorest of the poor." The countries which the Grameen Bank serviced have millions of underfinanced firms and individuals that have been categorized as the "least creditable" borrowers, ones that need funding desperately but would never have been able to obtain loans from traditional commercial banks. It was one of the first times that the financial industry saw a live, functional example of credit issued by a "financial institution" denominated not in 5 or 6 digits, which for decades had been the only norm, but in single and double digits. Even more surprisingly, in such a group of borrowers whose credit scores were far below even "sub-primers," the default rate on Grameen Bank's loans was less than 2 %, a number on par with the typical default rate of any large commercial banks with strict risk control standards.

Considering these observed results, there is no doubt that Dr. Yunus truly deserved the prestigious honor he received and the implications of this project—microcredit for less creditable borrowers—have the potential to be profound. As is the case in most countries, less creditable borrowers make up the majority in the countries serviced by banks like Grameen Bank, while the funding from commercial banks typically flows only towards those who are highly creditable borrowers; in general, these most highly creditable borrowers tend to be corporations. Even China, which has experienced the fastest historical growth and ranks second in the world in terms of GDP, is not an exception. As Jack Ma of Alibaba once criticized, only 20 % of Chinese borrowers are fully serviced by large state-owned commercial banks, and he insisted that there needed to be intervention from "interrupters" to cover the remaining, under financed 80 %.[2] From this perspective, Grameen Bank became the inaugural interrupter of the bank loans industry. It proved the operational feasibility of lending to less creditable borrowers at loan

[1]http://www.nobelprize.org/nobel_prizes/peace/laureates/2006/yunus-bio.html.
[2]http://money.sohu.com/20130604/n377910523.shtml.

J.G. Wang and J. Yang, *Financing without Bank Loans*,
DOI 10.1007/978-981-10-0901-3_1

units previously considered too small, and completely changed the mainstream "wisdoms" prevalent in traditional commercial banking.

Since the inception of Grameen Bank, micro and small loans have emerged as a fast growing sub-business line for lenders in the financial industry, especially those in China. Given the limited number of fund suppliers, the restricted coverage by large state-owned commercial banks, and the huge quantity of unsatisfied funding demand, micro loans provide underfinanced SMEs and individuals with an alternative funding source. Therefore, it would be intriguing to explore and discuss the development of micro or small loans in China and to analyze, using representative cases, the business models adopted by micro loan firms, the features of micro loans, and the risks inherent to this particular business practice. These topics will be the content of the following sections.

1.1 The Birth and Growth of Micro Loans in China

Micro loans are generally defined as small dollar amounts of debt financing issued to small-sized entrepreneurs, such as sole proprietaries, and impoverished borrowers who lack collateral, steady employment and a verifiable credit history.[3] In China, micro loans are typically issued by formal financial institutions and specialized small loan providers. These specialized small loan providers are either layman or legal persons and social organizations that issue loans without taking deposits,[4] and the value of an issued loan is usually in the range of RMB 1000 to RMB 100,000.[5] In general, micro loans can be classified as either business type and welfare type loans: while the former focuses more on risk control and business continuity and targets higher risk borrowers, the latter concentrates more on the improvement of social welfare in the poverty population by financing the impoverished with micro loans.

In China, the origin of the micro loan can be traced back as far as ancient times; it was a financing mechanism used, for example, in the Zhou Dynasty, in BC 1000. In more modern times—particularly the past few decades—the micro loans issued by individuals have always been considered a supplement to the mainstream financial regime, and an alternative source of funding for the underfinanced. However, because those who require micro loans are typically not covered by the traditional financial system, the very act of issuing micro loans has gained a derogatory reputation in the media as an illegal, underground activity involving

[3]https://en.wikipedia.org/wiki/Microcredit; http://baike.soso.com/v1937549.htm?ch=ch.bk.innerlink#10.

[4]http://www.doc88.com/p-2711294993431.html.

[5]Some small loan firms can extend the small loan to RMB 500,000, such as ZD Credit: http://baike.baidu.com/link?url=j9sprdvFM_nafbOeGvpZckDvRyi5BxyfLFFU0DBAoBooIcIGUX0rvRjqHYoEh__U7jcWKcX8K6xy0GFwCcpyxq.

exorbitantly high interest rates. The first group of micro loans issued “legally” by financial institutions in modern China can be dated to the 1980s, when China received some international assistance programs from the International Agriculture Development Foundation such as the Northern China Grass and Husbandry Development Program in Inner Mongolia in 1981 that provided it with a batch of micro loans. The micro loans involved in these programs, though, were only provided as a part of the poverty assistance program, and did not allow China to create a stand-alone business line for micro loans in its financial industry. The Poverty Assistance Commune set up in 1994 by the Agriculture Development Institute of the Chinese Academy of Social Science in Hebei Province could be considered the first commercialized micro loan provider that offered mutually-guaranteed micro-loans to farmers. According to statistics from China’s central bank, as of June 2014, there were 8394 micro loan firms in the country, with total loan balance of RMB 881.1 billion yuan.[6]

In recent years, however, as the crucial role of SMEs in China’s future sustainable economy becomes increasingly apparent, micro loans primarily issued to support SME growth are receiving stronger backing from the Chinese government. On August 8, 2013, China’s State Council issued its Documentation #87 (2013),[7] which gave the green light for the development of micro loans and encouraged the establishment of credit enhancement facilities to connect SMEs with commercial banks. In addition, the Documentation encouraged financial institutions to increase their risk tolerance level when it came to issuing micro loans. In China’s highly regulated, high-entry barrier financial industry, Documentation #87 marked a clear milestone in the development and growth of China’s micro loan market (Fig. 1.1).

In today’s business environment in China, even though large state-owned commercial banks are also involved in micro loans, the majority of providers of micro loans are now privately-owned micro loan companies. Primarily, there are three types of micro loans: (1) Welfare/benefit type loans, such as the Unemployment Guarantee Loan, the Student Assistance Loan, and the Poverty Assistance Loan issued by large commercial banks; (2) Commercial micro loans issued by Rural Credit Unions—as of June 2013, for example, there were 61 million farmers who received a total of RMB 192.7 billion in loans, covering 27.3 % of China’s total rural population and, in addition, there were another 12 million farmers who received RMB 14.1 billion in loans through mutually guaranteed loans; (3) Commercial micro loans issued by over 100 privately-owned micro loans organizations, which provided about 1 billion in loans.[8]

Since 2010, the micro loan market has experienced fast nationwide growth in China. The total number of microloan providers maintained a 7–11 % growth rate, and there were 7086 of them by June 2013. The total number of employees at these

---

[6]People’s Bank of China: http://www.pbc.gov.cn/publish/diaochatongjisi/3172/2014/20140723134804072473656/20140723134804072473656_.html.

[7]http://finance.ifeng.com/a/20130812/10409006_0.shtml.

[8]Ibid 2.

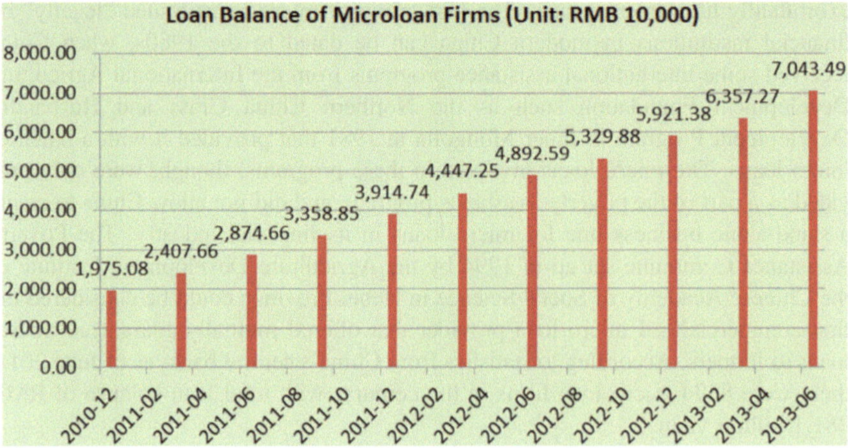

Fig. 1.1 Quarterly loan balance 2010–2013. *Data Source* Wind Information, and Real Estate Financial Research Center, HSBC Business School, Peking University

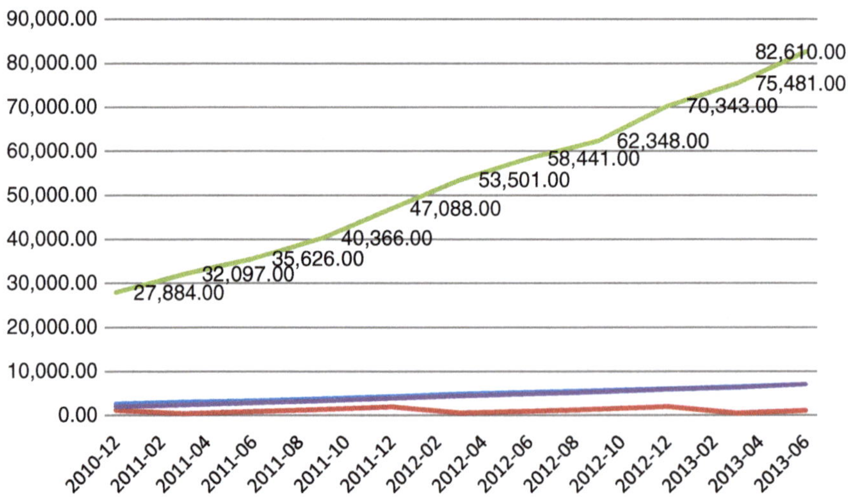

Fig. 1.2 Statistics of micro loan firms. *Data Source* WIND Information

providers also grew at a 7–12 % range, as indicated in Fig. 1.2 below. From a geographical perspective, the strongest demand for microloans came from highly-developed areas with vital SME activities, such as Beijing (12 %), Tianjin (18 %), Shanghai (7 %), Chongqing (10 %), Guangdong (11 %), Zhejiang (8 %), and Jiangsu (11 %).

1.2 What Drives the Cash Flow of Microloan Firms?

As a fixed-income financing tool, the profitability of microloans comes primarily from the interest charged to borrowers. Since micro loan borrowers are typically individuals or organizations that didn't meet the borrowing standards of commercial banks, they tend to have a higher risk of default, and so, to compensate, the interest rates on micro loans are typically higher by far than those on bank loans with similar maturities. In China, an interest rate four times that of the central bank's benchmark rate is the maximum that firms can legally charge on micro loans, with an absolute ceiling at 36 %.[9] In China, since microloan firms are not allowed to take deposits as commercial banks do and the capital from investors, donation funds, and funds obtained from no more than 2 commercial banks but with less than 50 % of the microloan firm's own capital represent the only legal funding sources for micro loans, the interest rates paid to commercial banks or other financial entities represent the financing cost of micro loans. Therefore, it is not the entire interest income but rather the difference between the interest rates charged to borrowers and those paid to the banks, or the "interest spread", that encompass a micro loan firm's profits.

Other factors that can impact a microloan firm's profitability include the default rate, fund velocity, leverage level, registered capital, fund utilization rate, service fees, and management expenses. As is the case for commercial bank loans and other forms of debt financing, default by the borrowing party represents the biggest financial risk. Default debts will not only wipe out the cash flow from interest income but also "eat" the loan principal and cause potentially tremendous losses for microloan firms. Controlling the default rate and lowering it to a tolerable level is the key to success for microloan firms. Fund velocity, however, is also an important factor. The fund velocity indicates the number of times a fund is loaned out over a certain period of time (usually a year), and, all other things being equal, the higher the speed of circulation, the higher the income stream.

Other factors also contribute to profitability. A higher leverage level, for example, will allow microloan firms to surpass the mandated 50 % ceiling of funds received from other financial institutions, making more loanable funds available for borrowers. Similarly, for any given leverage level, the higher the registered capital and the fewer the idle funds within a firm, the higher the profitability of that firm. Service fees can also be a source of cash flow for microloan firms through the charging of a certain percentage of the total loan value in the form of service fees; and, needless to say, reducing operating costs will enhance the profitability of the microloan firms.

As a relatively risker loan market, the required rate of return for microloans is expected to be higher than that for the regular debt market. It is estimated that the average rate of return for the top 100 microloan firms in China is about 17.32 %,

---

[9]China Banking Regulatory Commission, May 8, 2008: http://www.gov.cn/gzdt/2008-05/08/content_965058.htm.

which is higher than the typical loan rate charged by large commercial banks, but much lower than the rates charged by "shadow banks", which are typically in the 40–50 % range.[10]

1.3 The Risks Pertaining to Microloans

As an alternative form of financing to the loans provided by traditional commercial banks, running a micro loan firm in China for less creditable borrowers may incur a certain set of risks and challenges.

1.3.1 The Issue of Business Sustainability

According to existing regulation, microloan firms are classified in China as non-banking financial institutions. As a result, microloan firms can't take deposits from investors or fund suppliers. Their only funding sources would be the shareholders' registered equity capital, donation funds, and the funds from no more than two financial institutions for an amount that is less than 50 % of the registered capital of the firm. The size of these funding sources tends to be limited, and if a firm uses up all the funds they can obtain, future growth will become a tremendous challenge. Compared to state-owned commercial banks or even rural credit unions, which are allowed to legally take deposits, microloan firms are subject to some fundamental disadvantages. This in turn may lead to questions about the going concern status of many micro loan firms and their business sustainability for the foreseeable future.

1.3.2 The Risk of Higher Financing Cost

As non-banking financial institutions, microloan firms are not granted the right to use the inter-bank credit or security markets. As a result, microloan firms are not able to obtain funds from banks at the relatively lower inter-bank offering rates. Instead, they have to borrow from commercial banks and other financial institutions at relatively higher interest rates, which are similar to the rate on regular business loans. This will noticeably increase the financing costs for microloan firms, which, in turn, will increase the financing costs for microloan borrowers. Overall, it will increase the operating risk of microloan firms and likely reduce their returns.

[10]Top 100 Microloan Firm Report, by Financial Consumption Protection Bureau of People's Bank of China: http://money.163.com/13/0108/11/8KMMHISI00254SVR.html.

1.3.3 The Risk of Illegal Fund Collection

Unlike the financial institutions that also serve agricultural and rural areas, which are backed by government capital and policy support, micro loan firms are not provided with any favorable policy treatment from the government in terms of interest rate, reserve ratio, tax rate, fee schedules, or fiscal subsidies. For example, rural credit unions need only pay 3 % of sales tax, but microloan firms need to pay 5.56 %. Adding that to the 25 % income tax and other taxes, the total tax liability for microloan firms is over 30 %. In addition, micro loan firms need to reserve a 1–3 % allowance for bad debt and other management expenditures. As a result, funding source pressure may force some microloan firms to pursue some risky funding sources, such as illegal fund collection, exposing the firms to all the risks that come along with illegal fund collection.[11]

1.3.4 The Risk of Default

In the current financial system, only very few microloan firms are granted the privilege of accessing the Chinese central bank's credit system in order to conduct due diligence on potential borrowers. However, this is problematic, because the borrowers of microloans are typically in the lower segment of the loanable funds market, *particularly* as large commercial banks also start developing microloans, so the quality and credit of the borrowers of microloan firms could be quite low. Micro loan firms, therefore, more than any other institution, would benefit from the due diligence, and because many are unable to do so, the risk of default becomes much higher. Moreover, microloan firms typically have an undiversified business model in which they solely focus on micro loans and do not have other business lines, such as note discount, assets transfer, entrusted loans or insurance, to diversity the risk. In addition, microloan firms don't have licenses for clearing transactions, so they are not able to monitor the actual usage of the loans and conduct post-loan management as commercial banks do. As a result, microloan firms are exposed to a much higher default risk than are commercial banks.

1.3.5 The Risk of Internal Control

Since the size of microloan firms is typically small, 90 % of microloan firms don't have a risk control system and lack the needed funding to set one up. Without a risk control system with a clear segregation of duties and high quality financial professionals, there exists high internal control risk for these microloan firms.

[11]Guo (2013).

1.3.6 The Risk of Company Control

There is a chance that microloan firms may be able to take deposits by becoming a rural bank. According to existing regulations, a microloan firm with 3 years of business continuity, two consecutive fiscal years of profits, less than 2 % default rate, and a 130 % or higher sufficiency rate of debt loss allowance, the government would allow a micro loan firm to legally transform into a rural bank. There is, however, no free lunch. One of the conditions of making this transformation is that microloan firms must complete this process with a bank or other financial institution which has also satisfied the above requirements. As a result, when the microloan firm is legally transformed, the collaborator bank or financial institution, by law, becomes the largest shareholder of the new rural bank through equity transactions, and the current controlling shareholder of the microloan firm will be exposed to the risk of losing control in the established new bank.

1.3.7 The Risk of Business Transfer

If a microloan firm successfully makes the transfer to the status of a rural bank and the collaborating bank has taken over as the primary shareholder, the newly established rural bank would operate much in the way that a typical bank does. Since micro loan borrowers are ones that likely didn't meet most regular banks' credit standards in the first place, and the newly established bank lacks the experience and skills needed to risk control these "sub-prime" clients, it's highly likely that the newly established banks will turn to traditional banking services in order to maintain profitability. If this were to happen, it is true that the original "micro loan firm" will have gained the ability to accept deposits, but the funds received may no longer service micro loan customers.

1.4 Some Front Runners of the Microloan Industry

1.4.1 Ali Microloan—A Growing Shark in the Banking Industry?

Ali Microloan, also called Ali Finance, was established in 2010 as a part of the Ali Micro and Small Financial Service Group. It was widely considered Alibaba's first step into the lucrative financial industry. Ali Microloan's primary product is the micro loans they provide to small-and-micro businesses and start-ups. The loans issued by Ali Finance charge daily interest, require no collaterals, and can be paid back before maturity. Ali Microloan has set up several customer groups based on each of Alibaba's e-trading platforms such as the Ali B2B platform, Taobao, and

T-Mall, subsequently providing Taobao (T-Mall) credit loans, Taobao (T-Mall) order-backed loans, and Ali credit loans. By February 2014, Ali Microloan had over 700,000 customers.[12]

The T-Mall order-backed loan is based on the value of an order in which the seller has dispatched the cargo but the buyer has not yet confirmed receiving the cargo. Ali's evaluation system will assess the order, calculate the maximum loanable amount based on the total value of the order (within certain standards), and, finally, release the loan. The daily interest rate on one of these loans is 0.05 %, which can be converted to an annualized interest rate of 18 %. The ceiling on these loans is $1 million, and the maturity is 30 days.

The credit loan is a loan that does not require collateral or guarantees. After reviewing the credit, risk and loan demand of the borrower, Ali Microloan will grant the borrower credit in the range of RMB 50,000 to RMB 1 million. The daily interest rate on these loans is 0.06 %, and the annualized interest rate is about 21 %. The maximum credit ceiling is RMB 1 million, and the maturity is 6 months. Ali credit loans can be further classified into two types: the "Circular Loan" and the "Fixed Loan," the former of which is a credit line that the customer can borrow and then repay at any time, and the latter of which is a one-time loan issued after approval.[13]

Overall, the loans issued for Taobao and T-Mall customers make up the majority of Ali Microloan's business. For example, in the half year leading up to June 2012, RMB 13 billion in loans were issued, and, cumulatively, RMB 28 billion were issued since 2010 for 130,000 micro and small businesses and start-ups. Compared to a regular loan business, RMB 13 billion is not a big number. However, that number was achieved by the aggregation of over 1.7 million individual loans. At one time, the daily loan issuance volume for Ali Finance was about 10,000, and the daily interest income was over 1 million, a number which stunned the entire industry.

The key to Ali Finance's high volume loan issuance is Ali's big data capacity. Between Alibaba, Taobao, T-Mall, and Zhifubao, Alibaba (the parent company) accumulates a huge amount of transaction data, including the registration information of its customers, platform verification, transaction records, customer behavior, custom import and export volumes and prices, not to mention information provided by sellers such as sales records, bank statements, utility bills, and personal identifications. Ali Finance also designed a psychological testing system to assess the personality and trustworthiness of borrowers, converting the result to a credit score equivalent. In addition, Ali entrusts a third party to conduct offline due diligence for B2B business lines.

Ali Finance possesses a unique data base and achieves high liquidity of funds, which is hard for banks and other financial institutions to compete with. For every

[12]http://baike.baidu.com/link?url=q5rUYRZgI95ElrWXdas0RQHFaBDXcPGSYeD3lz9c4iQag1xhWPcux-059T6Wm7PbrMOaGG9DnwNRa0hyYthFz_.

[13]http://tech.163.com/13/0124/22/8M136H0A000915BF.html.

Ali Finance loan in the amount of RMB 8000 to RMB 10,000, the issuance of loan can be completed within seconds of the submission of a loan application. The efficiency is unparalleled.[14]

Ali Finance also conducts post-loan management. After the loans are issued, Ali Finance can monitor the fund flow through Zhifubao and other payment channels. If the company finds that the fund use was inconsistent with the purpose the borrower stated on his/her application, Ali can freeze the funds through Zhifubao to ensure loan safety. As a result, with an average loan value of RMB 7600, a total credit line within 1 million and a maturity of within 6 months, the average default rate on Ali loans is less than 1 %.

Ali's success was remarkable, and received wide-spread attention from observers in and outside the financial industry. However, to what degree Ali's success can be replicated to outside of the Alibaba ecosystem, a business model which would certainly be beneficial for the micro and small business community, remains a question to be addressed. As mentioned earlier, the key to Ali Finance's success was its big data and its widespread coverage of digital transaction. It can use its data to adequately compensate for its lack of access to the credit score system of China's central bank. However, for other micro loan firms that have neither access to the credit score database nor big data, this particular business model for success may not be replicable. Nevertheless, even if the results are not reproducible on a mass scale, Ali Finance is credited for setting a milestone in the microloan industry in China.

1.4.2 A Front Runner of Microloan Business—ZD Credit

ZD Credit was established in Shenzhen on April 19, 2010, with registered capital of RMB 100 million.[15] It is a firm that specialized in micro loans, and does not have a permit to take deposits. Since its inception, ZD Credit has expanded its presence to 22 cities, including Shanghai, Xian, Chengdu, Chongqing, Wuhan, Changsha, Beijing, Guangzhou, Nanjing, Shenyang, Hangzhou and other cities, with over 60 branch offices. By the end of 2013, ZD Credit had issued a total of RMB 320 million in loans for about 55,000 micro and small firms and individuals nationwide. The primary customers of ZD Credit are small and micro enterprises, and ZD's main products are credit loans without collateral or guarantees, as classified in Table 1.1.

As a non-deposit-taking firm, ZD Credit obtains funds primarily from the commercial banking system, after which it lends out funds at higher interest rates and takes the interest spread as profit. Under the Chinese central bank's current rules, microloan firms can legally charge an interest rate of no more than 4 times the

[14] http://finance.eastmoney.com/news/1354,20130122269707028.html.

[15] http://www.szmfa.org.cn/_d271305991.htm.

Table 1.1 ZD Credit's Major Products

	Consumer loan	Business loan
Product	Fixed loan with 6–36 month maturity and ceiling at RMB 300,000	Fixed loan with 6–24 month maturity and ceiling at RMB 500,000
Customer targeted	Age at 18–60 years old, work at the current job for over 4 months with monthly income over RMB 1500	Age at 18–60 years old, running a micro or small firm for over 6 months
Documents needed for loans	Personal ID, income verification, home address proof, company ID	Personal ID, income verification (bank statements), Address proof (firm and individual), operation permit

central bank's benchmark rate. As a result, ZD Credit devoted a lot of effort to obtaining funding from commercial banks in wide geographic areas.

The most notable feature of ZD Credit probably is its effective risk control. Its key principle in risk control is "smaller amounts, diversified borrowers, and monthly repayments." The average loan value of ZD loans is RMB 50,000. Borrowers come from various industries and different geographical regions, and borrowers have to repay the debt principal on a monthly basis instead of the usual one-time payment at the end of maturity. These designs and mechanisms enabled the firm to recognize early warning signals of default, improving the efficiency of fund use and hedging risks. As a result, the default rate was maintained at about 1 %.

Another important feature of ZD Credit is its strong IT support system. As a microloan firm, ZD Credit provides loans that are low in value and high in transaction number, a case which is characteristic of most micro loan firms. As a result of this traffic, automation of the process is of critical importance for the reduction of operating costs and for quality control. At ZD Credit, an automated system covers all the important parts of the loan process including loan application, loan review, loan approval, loan contracts, loan issuance, post-loan management, payment collection, and overdue debt collections. In addition, the firm's IT system also collects historical data to help ZD Credit evaluate each customer and form the firm's credit rating schedule. Needless to say, the information collected and summarized by ZD Credit's IT system can also help the firm in marketing analysis, financial management, performance evaluation, and payment collections.

1.5 The Future Development of Microloan Industry

As a supplement to traditional commercial banking, the micro loan industry fills an important gap in covering the underfinanced "80 %" of SMEs and individuals. The fast growth of the industry in past years is an evidence of strong market demand for this financial product. At the same time, however, any new financial product developed for the lower-end segments of the market comes with its own set of challenges, especially those pertaining to the development and future growth of the industry.

One challenge is the legal status of microloan firms. Under current regulations, a micro loan firm is classified as a regular legal entity, rather than a financial institute. As a result, microloan firms are not authorized to take deposits, and their funding sources are very limited. Therefore, the sustainability of this new financial service requires a re-classification of the legal status of micro loan firms that moves them into the legal category of a financial institution.

Secondly, even if financial institution status is granted, microloan firms need to have more diversified funding sources. Since the borrowers of microloan firms are typically ones with relatively higher default risk and the depositors are typically the most conservative investors, there's a low likelihood that such conservative investors would be willing to deposit their money into these "transformed" banks, especially if the investors have better options in the market. Unless these "transformed" microloan firms can successfully capture a niche segment, in which the promised returns for investors are higher than what regular commercial banks offer, there remains a question as to whether or not these new firms can get sufficient funding. Because of this, microloan firms may need to explore other funding channels, such as equity and bond issuance as well as funding from the international financial market, in order to obtain more funding sources.

Thirdly, regarding the interest rate level, the reserve ratio, the tax rate, fee schedules, and fiscal subsidies, microloan firms should be granted the same status as rural or agricultural banks. Fundamentally, there exists a certain degree of "market failure" in SME financing. Since SMEs are relatively higher risk borrowers, investors require higher return to compensate for the risk they are undertaking. On the other hand, however, a SME, as a smaller-sized firm, usually has limited financial ability to afford the higher payment. There are needs for external intervention to break this vicious cycle, and government support could be a pivotal solution. Such government support has already proven effective in the US, where small business loans are guaranteed by the US Small Business Administration (SBA).[16]

Fourthly, credit checks will be the key for risk control in the micro loan business. Just as is the case in any other sub-sectors of the financial market, the asymmetric information between borrowers and lenders is one of the root causes of default risk for loans, and a thorough and accurate credit evaluation of potential borrowers is the most effective remedy. Establishing a nationwide credit checking system will, in the long run, allow microloan firms to get access to the credit checks. As it is now, microloan firms that don't have access to credit history databases have to conduct the required due diligence themselves, which will significantly increase the financing cost for micro loan firms, and eventually, for SME borrowers as well.

Finally, it is imperative for micro loan firms to find professionals and develop loan products and lending techniques that complement the characteristics and risk

[16]https://www.sba.gov/loanprograms.

levels of their target group, which are SME borrowers. As a segment with much unsatisfied demand but much higher risk, compared, at least, to regular commercial banking, different financial products and risk control techniques need to be developed. These will be fundamental for the future growth of the industry. The higher possibility of default for micro loans can easily wipe out all the earnings of microloan firms, were those defaults to occur. The sustainability of this industry depends heavily on innovative business models in the micro loan business.

As can be expected, the microloan business, as an integrated component of financial innovations in China, has tremendous potential for future development. Fundamentally, it was generated by unsatisfied market demand for loanable funds by "eighty percent" of potential fund demanders in China. The industry's emergence and fast growth all point to its indisputable value in helping the most vital and innovative Chinese companies in their development, which, in turn, helps to upgrade China's economic structure and improve the sustainability of Chinese economic growth. With the introduction of internet technology and more diverse participants, a more competitive micro loan market with more clearly delineated regulations will eventually fall into place, becoming an important component of the multi-layered financial system of China in the near future.

Reference

Guo, L. 2013. Compliance risk of microloan firms: A Shangdong Case. *Business Manager* 6.

Chapter 2
Can "Guaranty" Be Guaranteed?—SME Loan Guaranties

In 1993, when China's first credit guaranty entity, the China Economic and Technology Investment Guaranty Company, was established with the approval of China's State Council, the Chinese guaranty industry came into existence, and it has now been around for 20 years.[1] As a business that provides credit enhancement for microloans with relatively higher risks, the associated guaranties make the healthy development of microloans and SME financing possible. At present, the guaranty industry in China operates through government funding as its mainstay, commercialized non-governmental guaranty firms as its primary provider, and multiple forms of guaranty. The challenge, however, lies in the sustainability of the business models currently entrenched in the guaranty industry.[2] Several scandals, which occurred in the guaranty industry in recent years, have triggered concerns about the workability of the guaranty business in the long-run,[3] bringing to light inherent risks and causing experts to predict a nearly inevitable reshuffling of the industry.[4] As a result, it would be greatly instructive to explore this important but volatile industry for the business models adopted, the features of the guaranty firms, and the risks inherited in this industry with some representative case studies, in the following sections.

2.1 What Is a Financial Guaranty?

A guaranty in debt financing is generally defined as a promise by a guarantor to repay the principal and interest to the beneficiary of the guaranty on behalf of the guarantee, in the case that the guarantee can't fulfill his or her loan obligations on

[1]Bosi Data: http://www.bosidata.com/jinrongshichang1208/493271FT27.html.
[2]Sun (2010).
[3]http://news.51zjxm.com/tourongzi/20120802/19279.html.
[4]http://www.rzdb.org/db/hyzx/hyyw/30847.html.

J.G. Wang and J. Yang, *Financing without Bank Loans*,
DOI 10.1007/978-981-10-0901-3_2

the debt.[5] The financial products that are covered by guaranty agreement include loans, debt securities, over-drafts, deferred payment, and credit lines from commercial banks. As the most important guaranty products, a guaranty for debt financing bears double characteristics of finance and intermediaries, and, as a third party guarantor, provides a credit guaranty to lenders, typically financial institutions such as commercial banks, companies and individuals; and borrowers, typically comprise companies and individuals. Guaranty for debt financing is generally considered an intermediary credit activity.

Guaranty for debt financing can be generally classified into property right guaranty, guarantor guaranty, and loan guaranty. In the case of a property guaranty, the debtor may take the property right that an individual or institution has on fixed properties—such as land and buildings, tangible assets such as machinery, equipment, finished products, semi-finished products, and raw materials, and intangibles such as rights from contracts, bank accounts, and patents—in the case of default. Guaranty on property right can take two forms: one is collateral, in which the guarantee agrees to transfer the ownership of collateral to the debtors for the purpose of guarantying the loan. However, when the debt obligation is fulfilled, the transferred right will be returned to the borrowers. The second type is a guaranty that doesn't involve in the transfer of a property right, and is purely an agreement among the lenders, borrowers and guarantors.[6]

A guarantor's guaranty is a legal promise by the guarantor to undertake certain responsibilities on behalf of borrowers for the lenders, which can result in a secondary legal promise for a debt agreement. In the case of default, the guarantor assumes the responsibility of the borrowers. There are several forms of guarantor's guaranty. (1) The investor assumes the role of the guarantor, and establishes a professional and project-specific company in order to manage projects and arrange the financing; (2) A related third party is selected as the guarantor; and (3) A professional commercial guarantor is chosen. Because of diversified operations and the fees that are charged, the professional guarantors can guaranty the debt transactions, and diversify their own risks. Typically, these professional guarantors are commercial banks, investment banks, and other specialized financial institutions, and the products they provided are typically bank credits or bank guaranty.

A loan guaranty is a third party promise for borrowers to lenders. In the case of default, the guarantor will be responsible for the unpaid principal and interest. The guaranty agreement becomes effective once borrowers have received the loan, and the agreement becomes invalid when the loan principal and interest are fully paid back by either the borrowers or the guarantors. Loan guarantys are the primary business line of credit guaranty companies, and their major functionalities are to facilitate financing to SMEs, diversify risks, and secure the safety of credit loans.

---

[5]http://baike.baidu.com/link?url=m95gkjzTww9g1Qqbl5P2Fmxbba-wMDpxBB_VqRPSlDMuTWHqUNsMKtEhDJ66e7H1.

[6]Ibid 5.

2.2 A Glance at Financial Guaranty Industry in China

Created as a companion to microloans, the financial guaranty industry grew rapidly as microloan firms mushroomed in China in recent years. Because the borrowers of microloans are typically in the "eighty percent," with relatively lower credit and relatively higher risk, finding a way to enhance the creditability of the borrowers and/or transfer the risk to a third party with stronger risk-bearing-ability becomes the key to sustainable growth in the microloan industry. Financial guaranty provide exactly these two functionalities to satisfy these yet unsatisfied demands in China.

Since 1993, the financial guaranty industry has undergone several stages and experienced fast growth, but not without ups and downs: (1) from 1993 to 2000, only a sparse number of financial guaranty firms existed, and they were basically supported by government funding; (2) from 2001 to 2010, as China's entered into the WTO and the development of private sectors burgeoned, the financial guaranty industry was put on a track of fast growth, thanks to the massive inflow of private equity. In particular, when the 2008 global financial crisis broke out, guaranty became even more crucial in SME financing. As a result, more capital, including foreign investments, were encouraged to enter into this industry, and the resulting growth was explosive; (3) In 2011, when China's central government agencies issued some guidelines regarding the regulating of financial guaranty, the entire industry became more organized, in terms of pre-established conditions, scope of business, rules and regulations, and legal responsibilities.[7]

As of year-end 2010, there were 6030 financial guaranty firms nationwide; among them, 1427 (23.7 %) were state-owned and 4603 (76.3 %) were owned by either private capital or foreign equity. There were 29 firms with a registered capital of over RMB 1 billion, with over 40 % of the firms having registered capital of over RMB 100 million. The total assets in the industry had reached RMB 592.3 billion, with net assets RMB 479.8 billion, and a guaranted balance of RMB 1.153 trillion that was growing at 64.6 % on a year-over-year basis. The rapidly expanding financial guaranty industry was serving over 140,000 SMEs in 2010 alone, with a guarantyd loan balance of RMB 689.4 billion, numbers which increased by 58.3 and 69.9 %, respectively, on a year-over-year basis.[8]

Meanwhile, as government agencies began announcing regulations on the industry, self-disciplined organizations in the industry were also being established. As industry norms began to set in, financial guaranty firms were also starting to operate in a more standardized manner. As a result of this systematic overhaul, the payment ratio in 2010 was at a low of 0.7 %, the loss ratio was down to 0.04 %, the total reserve balance reached RMB 35.3 billion, the guaranty allowance ratio was at 3.1 %, and the guaranty coverage ratio was at 507.28 %.[9]

---

[7]Bosi Data: http://www.bosidata.com/jinrongshichang1208/493271FT27.html.

[8]Ibid 7.

[9]Ibid 7.

As a fast growing industry with the majority of its customers in the lower end of the market, the risk inherent to financial guaranty could not be ignored. In 2013, three financial guaranty firms, Zhong Dan, Hua Ding, and Chuang Fu, were exposed by media as having incurred severe violations of the laws and regulations as a result of their operations, and commercial banks were mandated to terminate their collaborations with financial guaranty firms. The industry visibly slowed in growth: in 2012, the total guarantied balance was RMB 2.17 trillion, growing only 13.5 % over the previous year.

In particular, the payment ratio significantly increased from 0.16 % in 2010, for example, to 0.42 % in 2011, and further to 1.3 % in 2012. The total payment amount reached RMB 25 billion. The most significant payments were primarily from the steel and solar industries; a single payment in each could be as high as RMB 1 billion. As the payment ratio went higher and higher, however, the guaranty coverage ratio didn't increase accordingly. By the year end of 2012, the guaranty coverage ratio reduced to 280.3 %, down by 327 % points over last year, and the guaranty allowance ratio was only up infinitesimally, from 3.1 to 3.2 %.[10]

Overall, because financial guaranty is a risk transfer and credit enhancement tool for less creditable borrowers of microloans, micro loans won't be able to develop or grow independently of the financial guaranty industry; they have to grow in tandem. The ups and downs of financial guaranty in past years simply indicate that the industry is still in its early stage of development. As long as the financing needs of the "eighty percent" are still not satisfied, microloans will definitively be needed to fulfill that demand, and financial guaranty, the "brother" of microloans, will be similarly indispensable.

2.3 The Business Model of Financial Guaranty

Despite being companions to microloan firms, financial guaranty firms are quite different from microloan firms in their methods of operation. While microloan firms depend primarily on their own funding sources to generate cash flow, such as through lending with relatively low leverage, financial guaranty firms, as a risk transformer and SME credit enhancer, generate cash flows through guaranty premiums, consulting fees, and other businesses, such as lending with their own funds.[11] Since financial guaranty firms undertake the contingent liability in the case of default, their leverage level is much higher than that of microloan firms.

The business model of financial guaranty firms can be classified in different ways. One method is to categorize the loans into debt financing-related guaranty and equity investment-related guaranty. Because guaranty firms will undertake the

[10]China Industry Consulting, http://www.china-consulting.cn/news/20121122/s81921.html.

[11]Ruan (2012).

debt repayment responsibilities only when the borrower cannot fulfill his/her obligations to repay the debt in the case of debt financing-related loans, financial guaranty is considered a quasi-form of debt financing. The primary income source, under this model, will be the guaranty premium. Because the guaranty premium is typically about 2–3 % of the total loan value, and guaranty firms need to pay 100 % of the loan in the case of default for the original borrowers, financial guaranty is considered a relatively high risk but low return business.

In contrast, guarantys related with equity investments combine financial guaranty and venture capital investments. By obtaining returns through venture capital investments with convertible debt, there is an increased potential for higher equity investment returns, and is a way for financial guaranty firms to compensate for the relatively higher risk. Through this method, the nature of financial guaranty can be transformed from quasi-debt financing into quasi-equity financing. If the borrowing firm is successful in going public, the guaranty firms will be able to obtain equity shares through convertible securities they received as a "premium" on the guaranty. In the case that the IPO is unsuccessful, the guaranty firms will then receive compensation through liquidation at a priority higher than that of equity shareholders. Compared to "pure" venture capital firm, the risks bore by the guaranty company will be smaller, so the number of convertible securities received by the company will be less than the number received by venture capital investors for the same amount of debt guaranty, or equivalent amount of the venture capital investment. Incidentally, in the case of a successful IPO, the return for guaranty firms will be less than those for a venture capital as well.

As in many other financial areas, where asymmetric information is the root cause of risk in a financial transaction, asymmetric information is also one of the primary risks in financial guaranty. There are two facets to the asymmetry: one is the asymmetric information between the guaranty firm and guarantied SMEs, and another is within the guaranty firms themselves, between the guarantor and its agencies. But, no matter which party among these is dominant in any given transaction, it is always the financial guaranty firms that ultimately bear the default risk of borrowers, seeing as they "guarantied" that they would cover the risk of the loan transaction.[12]

The more fundamental issue regarding the risk of financial guaranty, however, lies in the business model of guaranty itself. Because the premium on a guaranty is typically but a small fraction of the total value of the transaction it guarantied—say, 2–3 %—but the guaranty firm needs to cover 100 % of the loss in the case of default, the guaranty companies have less than abundant incentive to take on these loans. However, creating a stricter risk control system and providing a certain level of scale for these companies may be the key to reducing risk, and make the business more attractive for guarantors. Stricter risk control will help eliminate unqualified borrowers while reducing the numerator of the default ratio, and the larger scale of the business may increase the denominator of the default ratio and provide room for

[12]Gu (2011).

the law of large numbers take effect. Currently as it is, even with re-guaranty and re-insurance, there will be no significant change to the nature of risk transfer in the guaranty business. In 2012, the mean multiplier for guaranty was 1.76—that is, the value of guaranty loans was only 1.76 times that of the registered capital of financial guaranty firms. Given the annualized interest rate on 1-year loan of about 6.56 % and the fact that the guaranty premium of the loan wasn't allowed to exceed 50 % of the bank interest rate, the annualized return (including other income sources) of guaranty firms was only 5.77 %. If further incorporating the operating cost into this equation, along with tax and other expenses, the net return for financial guaranty firms was truly on the bottom of the pile.[13]

One of the recent "innovations" in the guaranty market to address this issue is the "mutual guaranty", a situation in which several firms form a group in order to apply for bank loans jointly. While each firm aids in enhancing the overall credit for other members of the group using their own credit, it also shares the default consequence if any one of the group members suffer bad luck. It's clear that mutual guaranty are a double-edged sword, and, depending what stage of the business cycle each of these firms are in, it can be either beneficial or detrimental.

Another proposal for mitigating the risk issue is the "risk fund pool", which requires borrowers to pay into a "risk mutual fund". Commercial banks will use the fund as collateral when issuing loans to the borrowers. The value of the loan amount is typically in the range of RMB 500,000 to 5 million, and the required risk fund contribution is about 15–20 % of the total loan value. In addition, another risk reserve fund is also required, which is typically 0.5–2 % of the total loan value, for the established mutual assistance group members by region or by industry.[14]

2.4 The Shepard of the Chinese Guaranty Industry—Shenzhen HTI Corp

Shenzhen HTI Corp, established on December 29, 1994 with a registered capital of RMB 1.2 billion, was Shenzhen's first guaranty firm.[15] It provided guaranty, consulting and investment services for high tech companies, especially firms and industries with government policy support. Since its inception, Shenzhen HTI Corp has guaranteed over 1000 companies, and supported many start-ups in their pursuit to become the leading firms in their respective industries.[16] As one of the fourteen initiators of the National Guaranty Alliance in China, Shenzhen HTI has become one of the most well-known and influential firms in the guaranty industry in China.

[13] Financial Guaranty Online: http://www.rzdb.org/db/hyzx/hyyw/30847.html.

[14] http://baike.baidu.com/view/10055028.htm.

[15] http://www.szhti.com.cn/.

[16] http://baike.baidu.com/link?url=f5OywIj1IWUM_1F9hxUDHNZfD6lRTXaOuHiFk1qEOotT0uzkE2mfRHt_KOFBoKh3DSSGYn18ueXljiURlvv5I_.

Shenzhen HTI started as a guarantor of projects with government policy support, and positioned itself as a "bearer and extender" of government industry policies and fiscal policies. HTI determined that, since it worked on government-policy-supported projects, it would be easiest to collaborate with state-owned commercial banks to obtain funding for the firms it plans to guaranty. HTI's primary business line is financial guaranty for high tech start-ups, but it also operates other business lines such as commercial guaranty and venture capital investment. HTI's products and services include guaranty for working capital loans, guaranty for fixed asset loans, guaranty for bank notes and commercial papers, guaranty for letter of credit, guaranty for project bids, and guaranty for law suits.

HTI developed several new business models such as the "exchange premium for profit sharing", the "exchange premium for options", and the "exchange guaranty for investments", and through these business models achieved an aggregate RMB 12 billion of guaranty, providing guaranty services for over 2000 firms and undertaking over 3000 projects in a 19-year time span. Through the services of HTI, another RMB 10 billion yuan of investments were brought in for the guaranty firms and their projects. According to the 3.56 ratio of input and output for high-tech firms in Shenzhen, these guaranties lead directly to RMB 43 billion in high-tech product value, and indirectly supported many other SMEs on the supply chain of these guaranteed firms, with an estimated product value of RMB 60 billion. In addition, HTI invested over RMB 112 million on various high tech start-ups, and enabled them to grow and become leading firms in their respective industries. HTI's annualized total return across all these firms is over 21 %. Here are several examples of such firms.

2.4.1 BYD, the Warren Buffet Favorite

BYD is among the most famous firms that HTI has guaranteed. A high-tech start up, BYD was founded in 1995 and specialized in producing rechargeable batteries.[17] Since 1996, HTI has provided 2 million yuan financial guaranty every year. In a particular instance, HTI issued an over 9 million guaranty in 1998 for a 3-year loan to support BYD's R&D in the MH-Ni battery. In 2000, BYD further received guaranty of RMB 70 million for a 5-year loan to set up its high-tech park, which now spans 40 acres of land. 6 years later, BYD repaid back all its loans in advance, and became one of the largest battery and hybrid car makers in the world. In September 2008, BYD received a USD $230 million equity investment from Warren Buffet at a market valuation of USD $2.3 billion.

[17]http://www.bydauto.com.cn/.

2.4.2 SINOVAC Biotech, Ltd

SINOVAC Biotech (NASDAQ Ticker: SVA) is a bio-tech start up that produces vaccines combating infectious diseases.[18] When the firm first started operating, it had long R&D cycles and inadequate short-term cash flow, and so continuity and survival became a major concern. In 1999, when the company's existing loans reached maturity, SINOVAC applied for a guaranty of RMB 9.7 million and loans of HK $7.2 million from HTI in order to restructure its debts. Through due diligence, HTI carefully assessed the potential of SINOVAC's products, and provided a guaranty for RMB 18 million. With HTI's support, SINOVAC successfully passed through the bottleneck and became the largest vaccine producer in China, now with 60 % market share. The cumulative total of the loans guaranteed by HTI over the years is over RMB 100 million.

2.4.3 Shenzhen Terca Technology, Ltd

Shenzhen Terca, established in October 2000, is a technology firm specializing in electrical brakes for buses.[19] When it first sought out a guaranty from HTI, Terca was only a micro firm in the niche-sized high-end bus market. However, through thorough market research, HTI assessed that, since China has the largest bus market in the world, the demands for high end busing should increase as the Chinese economy grows. As a result, the demands for brake parts of such high end buses should rise as well. Based on this assessment, HTI decided to provide RMB 2 million guaranty for Terca, and increased its guaranty to 8 million in the following years. In 2005, HTI further provided 20 million guaranty for the set-up of Terca's industrial park. Today, Terca is the largest producer in its market in China.

2.4.4 Hans Laser

Hans Laser (Shenzhen Stock Ticker: 002008) is a laser cutting equipment maker, set up in 1996.[20] In 1999, HTI invested RMB 4.38 million in Hans Laser, and held 51 % shares of the firm. Within one year of HTI's investment, Hans Laser achieved annual sales of RMB 60 million. On April 4, 2001, Hans Laser purchased back 46 % of the shares held by HTI, with a premium over RMB 10 million. HTI gained 600 % return for its initial investment within 2 years. In 2004, Hans Laser went public on the SME Board of the Shenzhen Stock Exchange.

[18]www.sinovac.com.

[19]www.terca.cn.

[20]www.hanslaser.com.

2.4.5 *Shenzhen HYT*

Shenzhen HYT is a mobile communication equipment maker, set up in 1995.[21] HYT developed the first walkie-talkie in China. However, HYT didn't have enough funds to commercialize its product. It was HTI that provided the guaranty for HTY's first RMB 500,000 loan. In the following years, HTI separately provided more guarantees up to a total of RMB 20 million worth of loans, including the funds for building HTY's headquarters and factories. At present, HTY is the largest walkie-talkie maker in China with sales over RMB 800 million in over 70 countries. Its customers include the United Nations, the US Post Office, the Italian Police, and the Russian Police.

2.5 The Future of Guaranty Industry in China

The financial guaranty industry in China, after over twenty years of development, is facing several prominent challenges. As the history of the industry indicates, financial guaranty in China were originally designed to be a complement to government policy, and to fill a gap in the financing of high tech start-ups such as Shenzhen HTI. As the Chinese economy moves forward, however, the financing difficulties facing SMEs emerges as a new bottleneck in China's economy, one which threatens the sustainability of China's future economic growth. As we have seen that there has been a "market failure" in financing SMEs in China, financial guaranty were considered "credit enhancers" for SMEs, intended to obviate the need for SMEs to obtain adequate collaterals and credit before securing badly-needed loans. Ideally, this type of financial guaranty should be undertaken by the government through government funding, a practice carried out in countries such as the US, Japan, and South Korea.[22] In practice, however, it moves towards commercialized financial guaranty in China, due to inadequate funding from government budget, and inadequate regulations from related government agencies.

The issue with non-government-led commercialized guaranty lies in the potential lack of sustainability of the business model, given the significant asymmetry for guaranty firms between income and risk. Even with some government policy support, such as capital injection, risk compensation, awards, and the requirement of risk reserves, the results were unimpressive: in 2013, the multiplier of guaranty was only about 2.3, just slightly higher than 2.1 in the previous 3 years, but much lower than the multiplier of 20 in South Korea, of 50 in the US, and of 60 in Japan.[23] In these countries, setting up a nationwide SME guaranty system is considered common practice. In the US and Japan, for example, there is a fixed budget

---

[21]www.hytera.com.cn.

[22]http://www.rzdb.org/db/hyzx/hyyw/30860.html.

[23]Ibid 21.

that is allocated to the SME credit guaranty fund every year, and guaranty payments came from both guaranty funds and guaranty premiums.

Strictly speaking, the framework for a government-led national guaranty system in China has been in place since 1999, when China's Economic and Trade Commission issued its "Guidelines on Setting up Credit Guaranty System for SMEs",[24] at present, there are over 2000 guaranty firms funded by central, provincial and local government. The issue, however, is that the size of this effort, the funds provided and the capital structure had resulted in insufficient funding for these established guaranty firms. One way to improve this system would be to utilize government funds as the primary funding source, and to require that policy banks either provide low interest loans to guaranty firms or issue bonds for finance guaranty payments.

Here, it is important to clarify something about the legal status of the guaranty firms: guaranty firms don't patently appear to operate funds directly; however, they help fund operators, such as commercial banks, select qualified borrowers, and manage and control risk in the same way that commercial banks and other financial institutions do. As a result, guaranty firms should be treated as financial institutions in the context of policy regulation. The credit rating system used by commercial banks and interbank markets should also be open to guaranty firms under certain conditions. Other financing and investment channels with high liquidity, high frequency of issuance and low risk, such as the interbank bond market, central bank notes, and bank funds, should also be open to the guaranty firms.

Furthermore, a floating guaranty premium system should be adopted to help guaranty firms better react to changes in the market place. Tax deductions or exemptions should be considered for guaranty premium income received by guaranty firms. Because the guaranty premium is one of the primary sources for guaranty default payments, establishing a reduced or exempted tax for guaranty firms as a risk reserve fund will help enhance the guaranty firm's ability to reduce risk. In particular, sharing the risk with commercial banks could be a systematical way of reducing systematic risk in the entire industry.

For guaranty firms, having diversification in their business portfolio is crucial to the overall healthy development of the guaranty industry. Instead of depending solely on commercial banks as a funding source, guaranty firms can also consider non-banking guaranty, direct financing guaranty, private bonds, collective trusts, private equity funds, and non-financial guaranty such as project guaranty, legal financing guaranty, commercial guaranty, and other business lines. It can be expected that more comprehensive financial firms, with diversified business lines, will become mainstream in the future. The guaranty business will become only one of many business lines in a comprehensive financial firm's portfolio. The funding sources of guaranty firms should be "guaranteed".

After over thirty years of development, the traditional Chinese economic growth model is facing numerous and very valid questions as to its sustainability. These

[24]http://policy.sme.gov.cn/zhengcefagui/content/content.jsp?contentId=1122064419024.

questions have become serious concerns for decision makers, participants, and stake holders of the Chinese economy. Because SMEs and their innovations have been identified as the key drivers in this new stage of China's development, adequate financing for these businesses, which make up the majority of the business community, and their innovative activities will, no question, become a game changer, determining either the success or failure of the transition of Chinese economy. Given the inherently risky nature of SME financing, auxiliary tools that can serve the function of credit enhancement, such as guaranteed loans, should be indispensable. Consequently, it is reasonable to expect that the financial guaranty industry in China will continue to grow, although it is clear that a stronger legal positioning and a better funding solution for financial guaranty firms need to be first in place. While policy-oriented guaranty firms may take the lead, non-governmental commercialized guaranty firms will fill the gap for the remaining uncovered business areas.

References

Gu, H. 2011. Reshape the risk control of SME financial guaranty. *Theoretical Research* 4 (in Chinese).

Ruan, X. 2012. The mechanism of microloan and financial guaranty and development strategy. *Policy Research* 33 (in Chinese).

Sun, P. 2010. The status of guaranty of SME loans and the policy solutions. *Journal of Shangdong Business School* 24(1) (in Chinese).

Chapter 3
Is Three Better Than One?—Mutually Guaranty Loans

When Robert Shiller, a Yale professor and Nobel laureate in economics, was invited to give a talk about finance on Bloomberg Radio, he identified risk management as the very essence of finance: because the future is full of uncertainty, finance and insurance are developed to manage risk, share risk and hedge risk.[1] It is thus only natural that commercial bank loans need to be "insured" or "guarantied" in one way or another if the risk associated with loans—or, more specifically, with the borrower—is considered high. When a borrower's assets cannot by themselves adequately cover the identified risks, external help needs to be on hand. Financial guaranties, as credit enhancers, are specifically designed and developed to play this "external" role.

However, as discussed in the previous chapter there are many outstanding issues in the relatively underdeveloped guaranty industry in China. Comparatively low guaranty income coupled with the relatively smaller size of guaranty firms and relatively high risk calls the sustainability of the industry into question. In order to address these challenges, some new methods of guaranty were created, and among them is a business model called the Mutual Guaranty Group Loan or Mutual Guaranty Loan. Under this model, the ball is kicked back to the borrower's side of the court. If the guaranty firm, as the third party, cannot fully cover the risk inherited in these single, individual borrowers, then, the fund providers will ask these borrowers to form a group with at least three borrowers to borrow collectively and guaranty for each other. So the question becomes: will these three (borrowers) be better than one (guaranty firm) in mitigating the risk associated with SME financing? Since Mutual Guaranty possess some distinct features differentiating it from the classic guaranty model analyzed in Chap. 2, we have devoted a separate chapter to this particular form of financial guaranty.

[1]http://www.businessinsider.com/robert-shiller-explains-finance-2014-11.

J.G. Wang and J. Yang, *Financing without Bank Loans*,
DOI 10.1007/978-981-10-0901-3_3

3.1 The Definition of Mutual Guaranty Loans

A Mutual Guaranty Loan is defined as a loan transaction in which more than three borrowers form a group to borrow collectively and guaranty the loan for each other. Even though the borrowed loan can actually be used by only one member of the group, in the case of default, all other members have to declare themselves willing to share the repayment of the loan.[2]

Because the borrowers of microloans are typically SMEs with relatively low credit scores and inadequate collateral, forming a group may help increase the borrowers' credibility and reduce risks. Because the groups self-select, the members of the group may have better knowledge about the other members of the group than would a commercial bank or third party; this would reduce a significant amount of uncertainty. Also, because the quality of the other members' credit impacts the borrowing firm, the firm will be predisposed to only select other firms with true loan demands, stronger repayment ability, and sound credit. Therefore, in some sense, by the time a group submits a loan request to banks, the borrowers have already been somewhat pre-filtered. Meanwhile, since the group members know each other in some way or another, they are in a better and more convenient position to monitor the fund use of the eventual borrowers/fund users, and are more able to push the borrower to repay the debt on time at maturity.

Because the majority of the borrowers of Mutual Guaranty Loans are SMEs, the value of each individual loan is typically in the range of RMB 2 million to RMB 10 million. The percentage of all microloans that are currently Mutual Guaranty Loans is still small, only about 5 %, despite the rapid growth of this product in past years. However, the total actual number of SMEs that are involved in these transactions may be much higher than the percentage suggests.[3]

From an industry perspective, Mutual Guaranty Loans appear to be more concentrated in certain industries. About 50 % of all Mutual Guaranty Loans can be found in wholesale trading industries, since firms in these areas typically don't have a large number of fixed assets to use as collateral, and trading partners in the wholesale market can be conveniently selected to join a Mutual Guaranty Loans group. The manufacturing industry with high labor intensity and low capital is another industry with a relatively high number of Mutual Guaranty Loan transactions. Since firms in the industry are typically located in a development zone or an industrial park, it is also relatively easy to find group members who can participate in the group loan.

Geographically speaking, there are more Mutual Guaranty Loan transactions, in terms of absolute value, in the southern and eastern areas of China, where more SMEs are located. However, in the mid-west areas of China, there are more Mutual

[2] http://baike.baidu.com/link?url=qELr9uMhmLM1FFwM_6IspD_hfItI34PEVgH5GWu69W18zuJXN8fKIAKr8FewrNQwpKuZ55_RBf85bjIlQm5D3K.

[3] http://www.cs.com.cn/sylm/zjyl_1/201406/t20140617_4419412.html.

Guaranty Loan transactions as a percentage of total loans obtained, since the challenges in SME financing are more severe in those areas; as a result, a higher percentage of SME loans have to take the form of Mutual Guaranty Loans.

3.2 The Procedure of Mutual Guaranty Loans

As a subsect of loan financing, Mutual Guaranty Loans are subject to a procedure of issuance very similar to that for regular loans issued by commercial banks, including application, review and approval. The major difference for Mutual Guaranty Loans lies in the pre-application process. Before applying for a Mutual Guaranty Loan from banks, the applying firms must form a Mutual Guaranty group and then complete the application for the loan as a group. More specifically, the entire procedure is as such:

(1) Three or more companies come together to form a Mutual Guaranty group. Each firm within the group has to negotiate with the others in order to determine the quota of the respective loan amount that each firm needs. Then, the group will submit their collective loan application to a commercial bank. There is no unique or singular way to form a group—it can be formed by the members of certain credit union, formed freely, independent of any existing organizations, or it can be formed with the guidance of government, industrial organizations, or even banks.
(2) The formed group will submit the loan application to the bank, either at the counter or online.
(3) The bank will conduct due diligence reviews for each individual member of the group, and determine if the requested loan will be granted.
(4) If the application is approved, all the members of the group need sign the legal documents with the commercial bank, and agree to jointly bear the responsibility of repayment of the loans.
(5) All members of the group need to set up an account in the bank in order to deposit the required guaranty reserve.
(6) The bank will issue the loans.

For example, five manufacturing SMEs would like to apply for a loan, and all the firms have stable customers and incoming cash flow. When the market is booming, the firms may experience an increased need to finance their working capital. However, due to inadequate collateral, none of these 5 firms can obtain the loan from bank individually. In this case, these 5 firms can form a Mutual Guaranty group with a pre-determined quota and a guaranty agreement, and then apply for the loan from a bank. If the loan, say, RMB 25 million, is approved after due diligence, and the quota was predetermined to be equally split, then the loan will be divided by 5, and each member will receive 5 million. Each member will also need to pay 20 % of guaranty reserve, with similar shares of borrowed funds.

Table 3.1 Documents needed to apply for mutual guaranty loans

Applicants	Documents needed
SMEs	Operation Permit, Owner ID, Company Charter, Board of Director Resolutions, Proof of Use of Funds, Ownership of Collaterals, and Value Assessment Report
Proprietors and contracted farm operators	Loan Application, Personal ID, Marriage Document, Paycheck Stub, Proprietor's Operation Permit, Sales Records, Proof of Use of Funds (Sales Contract, Shipping Contract, Manufacturing Contract, Bank Statements), Ownership of Collaterals, and Value Assessment Report

The documents needed to apply for Mutual Guaranty Loans, in general, can be summarized by Table 3.1.

3.3 The Business Model of Mutual Guaranty Loans

Mutual Guaranty Loans can help SMEs receive debt financing from banks that each firm cannot obtain individually without forming the Mutual Guaranty group. It also allows more entities to share the risk. Compared to the format of the financial guaranty model, in which a single guaranty firm has to bear all the default responsibility for a borrower with unmatched guaranty premium and default compensation, the risk under this model is spread much more effectively. Mutual Guaranty Loans shift the risk from one guaranty firm to the three or more firms that are part of the group.

However, even though Mutual Guaranty Loans diversify the default risk among more parties, this financing model creates new risks of its own. One could be called "seemingly diversification risk": although the loans are approved for entire group, the actual loans are used, on many occasions, by only one borrower within the group. Because of this, when tracing the root cause of risk, it becomes apparent that the loan is only as secure as the business operations of the one or few borrowing firms that actually *use* the loan, rather than the firms who collaborated to *apply* for the loan.

The second type of risk is the risk of fraud. As mentioned above, the actual user of the approved loan could potentially be only one firm, and it is further possible that the firm using the funds may even not be a member of the group that applied for the funds. In this scenario, the information provided to the bank by the group would be entirely irrelevant to the actual use of the loan, and default risk would increase significantly. In particular, the fund the group received from the banks could be used to re-lend to other borrowers in the illegal "shadow" or underground market in order to earn extremely high but illegal interest in an act of usury. At the same time, when the group repays the debt, it may also involve in the "shadow" market in order to get funds to pay back the banks. Of course, the actual user of the loan may also pay other members of the group for helping his/her firm obtain the loan.

A more severe case of fraud is the potential collusion among all group members to jointly deceive the bank in order to obtain a loan that they never intended to repay in the first place, a risk that is increased for groups formed by related parties. In the case of such moral hazards, Mutual Guaranty Loans will lose all ability to adhere to the loan contract and monitor and restrict the use of loan for each other within the group, all of which greatly increases the default risk.

The third type of risk is a systematic one. Since the members of a Mutual Guaranty group are typically firms in similar lines of business, whether in the same industry, on the same supply chain, or so on, when some market-related or systematic changes occurs either in the general economic conditions or government policies of that industry, all the members of the group will likely be impacted in the same way and in the same economic direction. In the case of such permeating market changes, it would be exponentially more difficult for each of the group members to cover the losses suffered by the others.

Another type of risk comes from the business model of Mutual Guaranty Loans themselves. Although other members of the group can help repay the debt in the case of default, these repayments will subsequently damage the financial status of the paying firms. As a result, the deterioration in the business of the borrowing firms becomes "contagious," leading to the deterioration of the businesses of other firms that helped pay the debt for the defaulting firm(s); a "chain" of risk is actually being set up when the Mutual Guaranty group is established. In particular, when a firm joins more than one Mutual Guaranty group across industries, the negative impact may end up widely spread across many companies in many sectors. The Mutual Guaranty Loan defaults in the steel trading industry in the coastal areas of China in 2014 are some real time examples of this type of risk.[4]

Finally, the risk of over-credit may also exist. Some Mutual Guaranty groups may receive multiple loans from the same financial institution in the form of individual short-term loans, individual operational loans, and SME loans. Sometimes, the group may also receive debt financing from more than one financial institution. In this case, the same assets will likely be used to guaranty multiple liabilities, which may surpass the firms' ability to fulfill their obligations.

3.4 Some Cases of Mutual Guaranty Loans

3.4.1 China Construction Bank (CCB): Mutual Assistance Loans

The China Construction Bank offered loans to various unions, which are groups formed by several small borrowing companies. Every borrower within the union bears the responsibility for the unpaid debt of other union members. The total loan

[4]http://news.xinhuanet.com/fortune/2014-02/19/c_126157093_2.htm.

amount was determined by considering the borrowing firm's risk level, the firm's anticipated usage of the loans, and other factors. The maximum loan value is RMB 15 million, or no more than the 20 % of the borrowing firm's sales revenue last year. The duration of the loans is no more than 1 year, and the contract is renewable.[5]

For CCB loans, the borrowing union is formed voluntarily by all members, with many members being the "legal person" of a SME or a proprietor. Members in a single group are typically on the same supply chain, within the same industry, or in the same geographical area. The total loan amount is simply the sum of the loan given to each individual member of the union, and the maximum amount for the credit line for each individual member is RMB 10 million. The granted credit line can be used repeatedly throughout the contracted period of time—typically one year. The interest rate varies depending upon the borrower's credit and other factors. Both the required usage of the loan and the repayment method are flexible; repayment can take the form of either equal-installment-payment of both principal and interest or periodic interest payments with the payment of the principal due at maturity.

The advantages of the Mutual Guaranty loans offered by the China Construction Bank include: (1) Fast processing and convenient procedures: when the union is formed, each member of the union will be assessed and scored in terms of risk and credit, and the total credit line for each member will be established. As a result, when a member firm needs financing, the loan can be issued promptly. (2) Lower financing costs. Since CCB doesn't need a guaranty from professional guaranty firms, the financing cost for member firms will be tangibly lower, especially compared to the characteristically high (and sometimes exorbitant) interest rate of private lending. (3) Since borrowing firms can get funds as needed and repay whenever they have cash, bank fees associated with the transactions will also be lower. (4) Because each member firm needs to pay repayment reserves as a certain percentage of the loan, the repayment status of certain member firms won't impact the business operations of others.

3.4.2 *China Minsheng Bank*

As the first large non-state-owned bank, China Minsheng Bank also provides Mutual Guaranty loan products. The basic features of China Minsheng Bank's loans are the relatively low threshold and the simplicity of application requirements. Similar to CCB, Minsheng doesn't require any guaranty or collateral from borrowing firms. Minsheng also loosens the requirements on the required time of business continuity for the borrowers to 3 years, on the condition that the union is

[5]http://lingbao.smx.gov.cn/jrtd/lbjrfw/82205.htm; http://www.rongdaitong.cn/jingyingdaikuan/1019110.shtml.

formed by 3 firms of similar size or on the same supply chain. In the execution of the loan contract, each firm in the union bears the responsibility of repayment for all other union members in case of default.[6]

The maximum loan amount is RMB 30 million for the entire group and 3 million for each individual member. The maximum duration of the loan is 1 year, and repayment can take the form of equal-installment principal and interest payments, monthly—(or quarterly) interest-and-end-of-maturity-principal payments, or some other repayment method that was agreed to by the bank. The appropriate usage of loans includes purchases of raw materials, office leasing, daily operating expenses, and other working capital needs.

3.4.3 *Huaxia Bank*

As another major non-state-owned commercial bank, Huaxia Bank also provides Mutual Guaranty Loans for SMEs. The mutual guaranty union can be formed by 3–7 SMEs. Each member of the union negotiates for each individual portion of the total loan internally, with the other members, and agrees to provide repayment responsibility for other members in the case of default. Huaxia Bank primarily targets SMEs with high tech parks, industrial associations, local chambers of commerce, and well-developed wholesale markets. The maximum loan value for each individual firm is RMB 20 million, and the term of the loan is less than 12 months.[7]

3.4.4 *Bank of Communication*

As the "Distant Fifth" of China's Big 5 state-owned commercial banks, the Bank of Communications also provides group loan services through its provincial branches in Jiangsu, Anhui, and Gansu. The products it offers include chatted loans, bank notes, trade credit, and other financing services. A member of a Mutual Guaranty union applying for loans through the Bank of Communications is typically a member of a business organization such as an industrial association or a chamber of commerce, but there is typically no direct business relationship among the group members. In addition, the borrowing firms need to have opened a basic account, such as regular savings account, with sound credit, in the bank, and they must use

---

[6]China Minsheng Bank: http://www.cmbc.com.cn/cs/Satellite?c=Page&cid=1356495600898&currentId=1356495500099&pagename=cmbc/Page/TP_PindaoLayout&rendermode=preview.

[7]Huaxia Bank: http://www.hxb.com.cn/home/cn/SmallBusiness/O2O/lbd/list.shtml.

the Bank of Communication to conduct transactions and clearance. The maximum loan value is RMB 20 million, and the loan term is 3 years or less.[8]

3.4.5 PingAn Bank

PingAn Bank is a formidable player in China's commercial banking industry with many diversified business lines across the Chinese financial market. For borrowing unions of PingAn Bank, there are typically 3–5 members, and the members jointly apply for a loan from the bank. The maximum loan value of each individual firm within the union is RMB 10 million, and the cap for the entire union is RMB 50 million. All borrowing firms are required to pay a risk reserve fee as a percentage of the total loan value, and the term of the loan is 1 year or less. No foreign currency-denominated loan can be provided, and the interest rate cannot be lower than PingAn Bank's basic interest rate.[9]

3.5 The Future Development of Mutual Guaranty Loans in China

Like all tools developed for the financial industry, especially those developed for SMEs, Mutual Guaranty Loans also have major pros and major cons, a duality which is inevitable for new, innovative products. The question, however, is whether the mutual guaranty group loan model, with three or more borrowers, is ultimately, empirically better than the loan model with only one individual borrower, particularly when comparing with other alternative financing methods such as guaranty by external professional guaranty firms.

As indicated by both the literature already produced on the subject and the discussions in the previous sections of this book, the crux of debt finance lies in the controlling of the default risk caused by asymmetric information between borrowers and lenders and the uncertainty of the future market. It is especially true that for small business borrowers, the risk level of asymmetric information is relatively higher, and the collateral and creditability that typically help to mitigate the default risk is usually less sufficient. The "extra" guaranty from other members of a "credit union" may help compensate for this insufficiency in collateral and credit history. From this perspective, mutual guaranty loans can provide an advantage over single-borrower loans for institutions who lend to SMEs.

One valuable advantage of this additional guaranty from a multiple-member group comes from the reduction of asymmetric information, since the other

[8]http://www.rong360.com/gl/2012/12/24/957.html.

[9]http://www.pingan.com/bank/corporation/yingdongli/company/index.jsp.

members of the group may possess information about the borrowers that banks don't have. Mutual guaranty within the group of each of its members help banks further filter loan candidates without having to acquire that information themselves. Even though all members of the group are SMEs, and may not have adequate physical assets to sufficiently cover the potential loss in some cases, the "social capital"[10] possessed by all group members can help better prevent loans from "intentional" default.

While this bundled approach diversifies the risk from one borrower to more than 3 borrowers, the downside of Mutual Guaranty loans is that this "bundle" also spreads the risk and potential losses from one borrower to over 3 borrowers in the case of a default. As a result, Mutual Guaranty loans can help reduce the "intentional" default or "firm-specific" risk, but may amplify the negative impact of downside effects that would originally have impacted only one firm. In particular, in the case of adverse market/industry-wide events, members of the union that come from the same industry will suffer concurrent losses, which in turn will compound the possibility of default by the group as a whole.

As a result, there is a trade-off inherent in the member-selection process: if all members come from the same industry or the same supply chain, their familiarity with one another's company operations and products helps reduce asymmetric information, but, at the same time, there then exists an increased risk of default of the entire group in the case of an adverse market-wide event. On the other hand, if members come from unrelated industries, market risk may be diversified more efficiently, but because of their lack of familiarity with one another, the firms will be less effective in ameliorating asymmetric information. In this case, some third party, such as chamber of commerce or government agencies, may need to be called into help vet the members of the group.

Compared to guaranty loans provided by professional guaranty firms, Mutual Guaranty loans have the benefit of lowered financing costs. Typically, the loans guaranteed by professional guaranty firms charge guaranty fees as a percentage of the total loan value, while there exists no such fee for Mutual Guaranty loans. The downsides of the Mutual Guaranty loan, however, lie in the questionable effectiveness of the guaranty provided for one another by the group members and the true risk diversifications, such as those discussed above. Consider, in comparison, that professional guaranty firms can reduce the risk of default by achieving scale adequate for the Law of Large Numbers to take effect, thus allowing the professional guaranty firm to calculate default risk as a percentage of the overall probability distribution and control it.

All in all, despite certain drawbacks, it is clear that Mutual Guaranty loans deserve a spot in the portfolio of SME financing in China. Because SMEs typically lack the collateral and credit history to satisfy the requirements of commercial bank loans, they need the amplifiers provided by group loans in order to enhance their

[10]Francesco Columba, Leonardo Gambacorta and Paolo Emilio Mistrulli, 2009 http://www.bis.org/publ/work290.pdf.

credit and provide lenders with additional assurance regarding repayment. In particular, for the SME borrowers that can be grouped into specialized markets (such as steel, construction materials), similar customer segments (such as serving hospitals, colleges), collective business organizations (such as industrial associations, chambers of commerce), or government agencies, the success of Mutual Guaranty loans is increasingly likely. It can be expected that, as more experience is accumulated and more empirical practice is executed by borrowers and lenders in the industry, Mutual Guaranty loans will find their proper place in the market, servicing more and more customers in the financial industry in China.

Chapter 4
Targeting Sophisticated Investors—Private Placement Bond

When Shenzhen Coolead Industry Co. issued the first SME private placement bond in China at the Shenzhen Stock Exchange in June 2012,[1] a new outlet for SME financing was opened. As a financing tool targeting more sophisticated institutional fund providers, the private placement bond brought in a large amount of additional funding to the SME community. In a matter of only one year, 177 private placement bonds with a combined value of RMB 21.3 billion were issued. However, just as with any other type of debt financing, default risk is always on the other side of the coin. Since these private placement bonds were typically issued at 2–3 year terms, there were many concerns regarding their timely repayment as they approached maturity; in fact, as of the end of 2014, 11 of the private placement bonds issued were indeed declared to have defaulted, incurring a total default amount of RMB 538 million at a default rate of 2.26 %.[2] Therefore, it would be interesting to explore the private placement bond in China—its basic features, the business models, the inherited risks, and the associated case studies, which will be exactly the contents in the following sections.

4.1 The Basic Features of Private Placement Bonds

As defined by the "Pilot Program Regulations" issued by the Shanghai and Shenzhen Stock Exchanges, a private placement bond (PPB) is a bond with a specified term length and coupon rate that is either issued by or transferred to a small or medium-sized enterprise (an SME, as they are defined by the company

[1]http://bond.hexun.com/2015-03-16/174089308.html.
[2]Ibid 1.

J.G. Wang and J. Yang, *Financing without Bank Loans*,
DOI 10.1007/978-981-10-0901-3_4

Table 4.1 Basic features of private placement bonds

Basic features	Contents
Issuer	Non-listed Micro and SMEs, not including real estate and financial firms
Size	Could be more than 40 % of net assets, but less than total net assets
Term	More than 1 year, but less than 3 years
Interest rate	No more than 3 times of bench mark rate with same terms
Issuance	Non-public, and no more than 200 accounts for issuance, transfer and holding
Use of fund	Flexible
Trading place	Shanghai and Shenzhen Stock Exchange platforms for fixed income products, or OTC through security firms
Investors	Qualified institutional and individual investors
Guaranty	Credit enhancements are encouraged but not required

classification system of China's Ministry of Industry and Information) in a private, non-public way.[3] Similar to junk bonds in the US, PPBs in China have comparatively higher risk and higher yields than the bonds publicly issued by large corporations through the capital market.

There are nine elements involved in the issuance of private placement bonds: the issuer, the issuance scale, the bond term, the coupon rate, the method of issuance, use of funds, the circulation channel, classification of investor type, and guaranty and ranking. These are summarized in Table 4.1. In particular, the Chinese government had expressed desire to support the five following types of firms in their issuances of PPBs when PPBs were first incepted: (1) firms located in well-developed urban and provincial areas such as Beijing, Shanghai, Tianjin, Chongqing and the Zhejiang, Jiangsu, Guangdong, Hubei, and Shandong provinces; (2) high tech, agricultural, and innovation-based firms: (3) firms with sound financial status and net assets over RMB 100 million; (4) SMEs with third party guaranties or collateral; and (5) pre-IPO firms (Fig. 4.1).[4]

Compared to traditional financing products, PPBs have several distinct characteristics in terms of the review process, the term of issuance, the financing scale, financing maturity, use of funds, and financing costs. For the review process, PPBs need only to file with regulation agencies, a process which can be completed within 10 business days, and are not required to obtain approval, a process which typically lasts a month or more. For the terms of issuance, there are no specified thresholds for the issuer's net assets, profitability, liability, or credit scores. For the financing scales, as a non-public issuance, PPBs and their issuers are not subject to the restrictions that constrain public bonds, namely that the debt scale must be less than

[3]http://www.sse.com.cn/lawandrules/regulations/
http://stock.stcn.com/common/finalpage/edNews/2012/20120523/391071801593.shtml.

[4]http://www.doc88.com/p-0854363078217.html.

Fig. 4.1 Key features of PPB

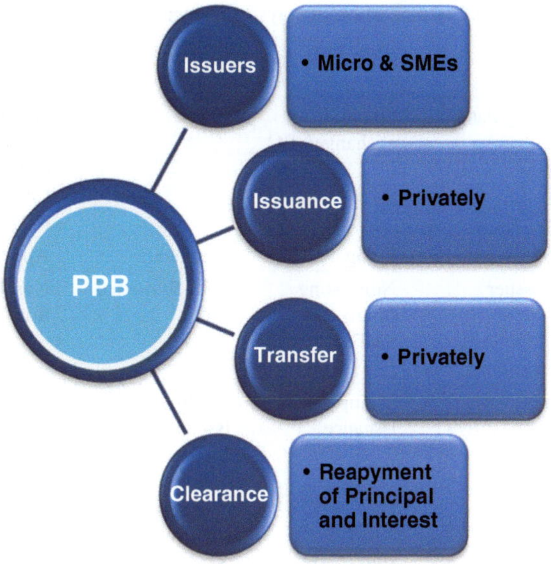

40 % of firm's net assets; the issuer can individually determine the size of bond issuance. Regarding the bond maturity, the typical term for a PPB is 1–3 years, which, compared to typical bank loans used for financing working capital needs, is much more attractive and competitive. For the use of funds, there is no specified requirement for usage after funds are provided. In this way, PPBs are relatively flexible, and the issuers can determine the use of funds based on their own business needs. For the financing cost, PPBs are categorized as a form of direct financing, so the interest rate is higher than that of the corporate bond, but still lower than the rate on bank loans and trust products; in particular, by issuing relatively longer-term PPBs, the issuers can lock in the relatively lower rate. In addition, investors that qualify for PPBs tend to be institutional investors, which can help bolster the reputation of the issuers (Table 4.2).

4.2 The Development of PPB in China

The journey of PPBs in China started in 2012 when China's SEC proposed a pilot plan for a new financing product—the SME private placement bond—in March of that year. Two months later, both the Shenzhen and Shanghai stock exchanges published the "SME PPB Pilot Guidelines", followed by the China Security Association's "Guidelines for Security Firms Undertaking SME PPB." On June 7th, 2012, nine SMEs filed with the Shenzhen Stock Exchange at a coupon rate of between 9.5 and 13.5 %, and a maturity of 1–3 years. One day later, an SME PPB

Table 4.2 Comparison of ways of financing of PPB with other financing tools

	SME PPB	Corporate bond	Enterprise bond	Short and medium term securities
Regulator	Stock exchange/SEC	SEC	National Development & Reform Commission (NDRC)	Inter-bank trader association/people's bank of China
Review	Filing	Approval	Approval	Registration
Issuer	Non-listing Micro and SMEs	Publicly-traded firms	Non-listing firms	Non-financial firms with legal person status (Including Public Trade Firms)
Issuance	Multiple issuance	Multiple issuance within 2 years with the first one within 6 months after registration	Single issuance within 6 months after approval by NDRC	Multiple issuance within 2 years with the first one within 2 months after registration
Review time	Within 10 work days	About 1 month	About 6 months	About 3 months
Net assets	Not required	Net assets owned by parent firm over RMB 1.2 billion	Net assets owned by parent firm over RMB 1.2 billion	Not required
Profitability	Not required	Profitable for 3 consecutive years, the average distributable profit more than 1 year interest payment	Profitable for 3 consecutive years, the average distributable profit more than 1 year interest payment	Not required
Issuance size	No requirement	Less than 40 % of net assets of the firm	Less than 40 % of net assets of the firm	Less than 40 % of net assets of the firm
Term	1–3 years	3–5 years	Over 5 years	3–5 years for medium term, less than 1 year for short term
Use of fund	Flexible	Working capital and existing debt payment	Working capital and project investment	Operating expenses, can't be used for capital investment
Trading place	Exchange's fixed income security platform	Exchange's quotation system	Inter-bank market and stock exchange	Inter-bank market

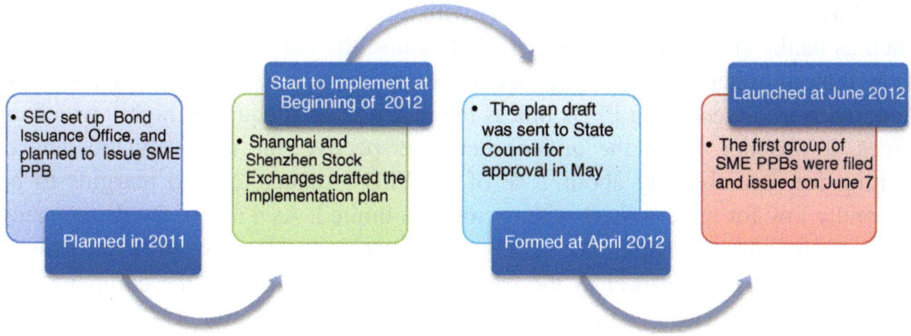

Fig. 4.2 The launching process of private placement bonds

called 12SDM was issued in the Shanghai Stock Exchange.[5] The entire launching process of the PPB in China[6] is summarized as in Fig. 4.2.

As a new financing product for SMEs, the PPB at its initial launch received a warm welcome from the market. The first PPB, with a 9.99 % coupon rate and issued in Shenzhen Stock Exchange, was sold out within one day, and the first PPB with a 9.5 % coupon rate and issued in the Shanghai Stock Exchange was sold out in half a day. Within one month of the first issuance, 27 firms filed for PPB issuance with China's SEC, and 19 of those applications were successful. The total bond value in these transactions was RMB 1.85 billion. The majority of the applicants during this round were high tech firms or agricultural firms backed by government policy support, and they paid a fixed interest rate in the range of 8.1–13.5 %—a much lower percentage than the over 20 % of gross margins. Among this first group of issuers, 7 of them were privately owned companies and 4 were high tech firms. The scale of the issuance differed from RMB 10 to 250 million, and the terms of the bonds varied among one year, one-and-a-half years, two years and three years. During the initial period of issuance, many security firms were actually investing using their own accounts.

However, after the first wave of issuances passed over, the private bonds market quickly cooled down. In the subsequent 4 months, there were a total of only 26 PPBs issued (7 in July, 12 in August, 3 in September, and 4 in October), compared the 26 PPBs issued in June alone. In October and November, zero PPBs was filed with the SEC.

There were several reasons for the slowdown of the PPB market and the gradual diminishing of interest. From a supply-side perspective, loosened monetary policy led to over-liquidity in the market, which drove down the overall bank loan interest rate. As a result, financing SMEs that are able to obtain bank loans lacked the interest to pursue PPBs, which, as non-public issuances without collateral, still required liquidity premiums. From a demand-side perspective, the majority of the

[5]Ibid 3.

[6]http://www.sinotf.com/GB/SME/TradeLaw/2014-10-09/zNMDAwMDE4MTQzNw.html.

PPB buyers were institutional investors with a more conservative investment style, such as banks and insurance companies. Because the default risk of PPB is higher than that of other credit debt products, such institutional investors tend to be deterred from investing in PPBs unless the return were adequately high—which, at times, it was not. From the underwriters' perspective, the relatively low underwriting fee, usually only about 1 % of the PPB issuance, caused margins to be generally low for underwriters when scale was limited. As a result, the discrepancy between the payoff schedule for sellers and buyers led to the downturn and loss of demand in the PPB market in the early second half of 2012. One company, the Shanghai Pudong Hanwei Valve Company, had planned to issue a 90 million PPB with a 3 year term and 9 % coupon rate in July, but ultimately failed due to insufficient interest from buyers.[7]

The revitalization of PPB market was a result of the participation of public equity funds and individual investors. On October 15, 2012, the first public equity fund, Penghua SME Bond Fund, was established and opened publicly to all individual investors,[8] and this created an outlet for individual investors to invest in PPBs. Since then, the PPB has gradually become a key product in the wealth management portfolio of security firms, and the return on some PPB investments, such as on the Guangdong Development Hongli Bond, ended up being even higher than the return on indexes and other bond products. The total funding collected by issuers through private placement bonds reached RMB 4.96 billion in the last quarter of 2012.[9]

The development of PPBs also expanded geographically in China after the intervention of public equity funds. The bonds which started in Beijing, Shanghai, Tianjin and the Guangdong, Jiangsu and Zhejiang provinces in June 2012 is now expanded to 22 provinces and cities including Hubei, Anhui, Inner Mongolia, Guizhou, Fujian, Xinjiang, Guangxi, Jiangxi, Dalian, Yunnan, Ningxia, Heilongjiang, Shaanxi, and Hunan. Cumulatively, the Shanghai and Shenzhen Stock Exchanges have accepted more than 300 issuance filings totaling RMB 41.3 billion. Among them, 210 issuances were completed with 26.99 billion yuan of total funding received.[10]

In addition, regional equity exchange centers started to issue regional PPB products, issuances that are totally independent from national stock exchanges such as Shanghai's or Shenzhen's. The Zhejiang Regional Equity Exchange Center, established on October 18, 2012, was the first to conduct over-the-counter PPB issuance at the regional level. As a regional equity exchange center, the Zhejiang Center serves only SMEs in Zhejiang province, but the financing services it provides covers a wide range of equity financing options such as PIPEs (private

---

[7]http://www.ceh.com.cn/cjpd/2013/04/187013.shtml.

[8]http://finance.qq.com/a/20121015/003073.htm.

[9]http://finance.eastmoney.com/news/1354,20120327198348595.html.

[10]http://www.zjblf.com/view.asp?id=945&bcg_id=663&bcg_id1=660, http://other.caixin.com/2013-07-04/100551254.html.

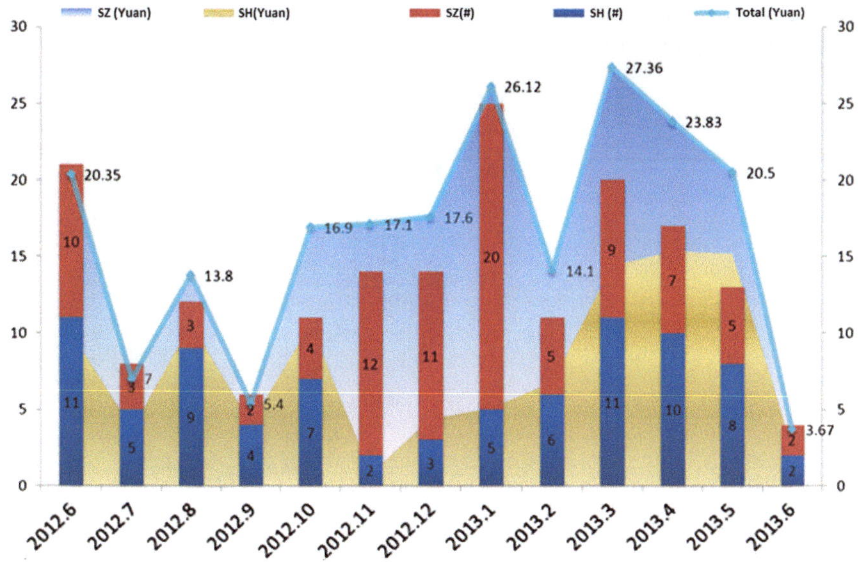

Fig. 4.3 The number of issuance and total value of SME PPB at Shanghai and Shenzhen Stock Exchanges

investment in public equity), PPBs, ABS (asset backed securities), and institutional investments. As of May 2013, the Zhejiang Regional Equity Exchange Center had accepted eight total issuances of PPB filing totaling RMB 850 million in value. Among them, four issuances were completed, with a total financing value of RMB 550 million.[11]

Up to July 25, 2013, there were a total of 84 PPBs traded through the Shanghai Stock Exchange(SH) totaling RMB 10.3 billion in value. There were a total of 93 PPBs were traded in Shenzhen Stock Exchange(SZ) with cumulative value of RMB 11.025 billion. These are summarized in Fig. 4.3.

When it comes to term lengths, the Shanghai Stock Exchange issued 50 PPBs (60 %) with 3-year terms, 32 PPB (39 %) with 2-year terms, and only 1 PPB (1 %) with a 1.5 year term.[12] In the Shenzhen Stock Exchange, 55 PPB (59 %) were issued with 3 year terms, 2 PPB (2 %) were issued with 2.5 year terms, 28 PPB (30 %) were issued with 2 year terms, 2 PPB (2 %) were issued with 1.5 year terms, and 6 PPB (7 %) were issued with a 1 year term.[13]

The range of coupon rates for bonds on the Shanghai Stock Exchange is from 6 % (on the 13 Guangdong Electric bonds) to 14 % (on the 12 Zhejiang Pupai

[11]http://www.zjex.com.cn/.

[12]http://www.sse.com.cn/.

[13]http://www.szse.cn/.

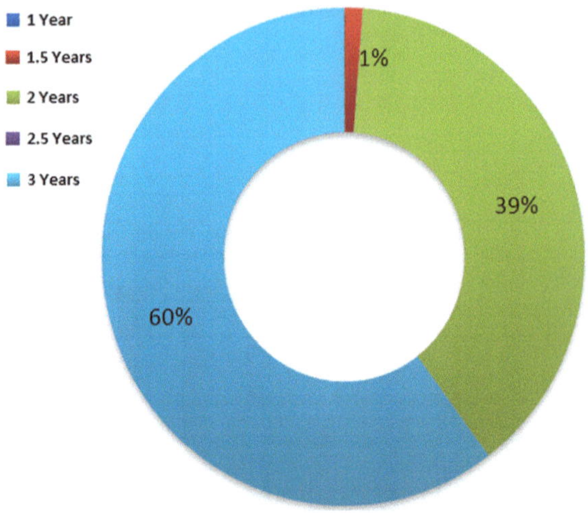

Fig. 4.4 Term structure of SME PPB at Shanghai Stock Exchange

bonds). The average coupon rate is 9.12 %.[14] On Shenzhen Stock Exchange, the range of interest rates is from 7 % (the 12 MinBao bonds) to 11 % (the 12 Taole01 and 12 Guangdong Construction bonds). The average coupon rate was 9.26 %.[15] The majority of firms (75 in total) issued PPBs with a coupon rate in the range of 9–10 %. Legally, the coupon rate is supposed not to surpass 3 times the interbank rate on bonds with the same terms; in reality, however, the coupon rate tends to be relatively high, indicating the higher default risk associated with PPB issuers given that they are typically small in size and weak in repayment ability (Figs. 4.4, 4.5 and 4.6).

In terms of the geographical distribution of the issuers, 42 or about 24 % of firms came from Jiangsu Province. 35 firms, or 20 %, came from Zhejiang Province, followed by Beijing's 21 firms at 12 % (Fig. 4.7).

In the case of ownership, the issuers of the bonds come from a wide spread spectrum, from state-owned, privately owned, collective ownership, joint ventures with foreign capitals, to solely-owned by foreign companies. Among the 84 issuers on the Shanghai Stock Exchange, 49 firms, holding 58 % of shares, are privately-owned firms and 20 firms, holding 24 % of shares, are state-government owned. In Shenzhen Stock Exchange, among 93 issuers, 60 firms are privately owned with 65 % shares, and 19 firms are local government-owned with 20 % shares (Figs. 4.8 and 4.9).

In terms of industrial distribution, 27.12 % (48 firms) came from manufacturing industries, 20.34 % (36 firms) came from consumption related industries, and only 2.26 % (4 firms) came from energy related business lines.

[14]Ibid 11.

[15]Ibid 12.

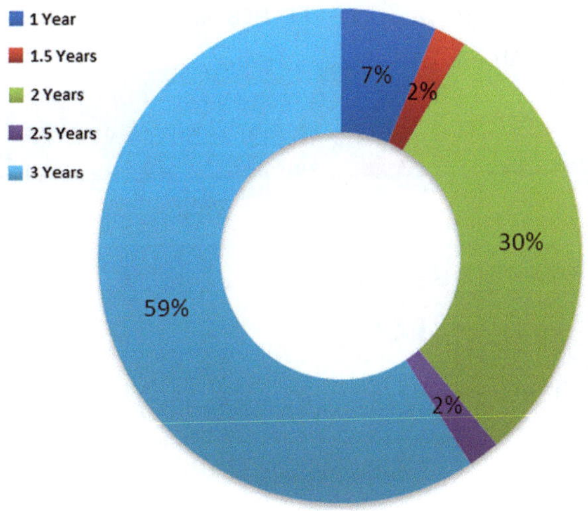

Fig. 4.5 Term structure of SME PPB at Shenzhen Stock Exchange

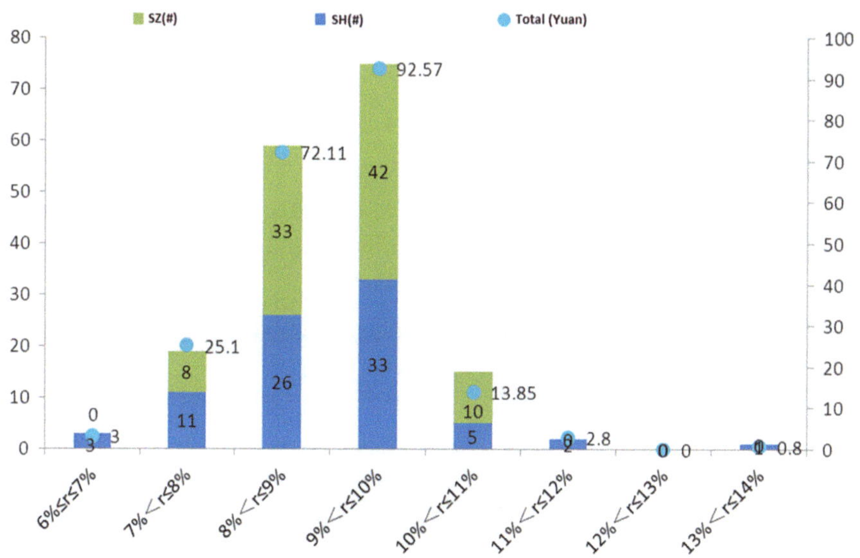

Fig. 4.6 Interest rate structure of SME PPB at Shanghai and Shenzhen Stock Exchanges

In terms of interest structure, 95 firms chose a fixed interest rate—44 from the Shanghai Stock Exchange and 51 from the Shenzhen Stock Exchange. Only one firm at the Shenzhen Stock Exchange chose a variable interest rate (Fig. 4.10).

In terms of bond ratings, on the Shanghai Stock Exchange, one bond was rated AAA, two bonds rated AA+, 14 bonds rated AA−, two bonds rated as A+, and one bond rated as A; the remaining 61 bonds were issued without rating. On the

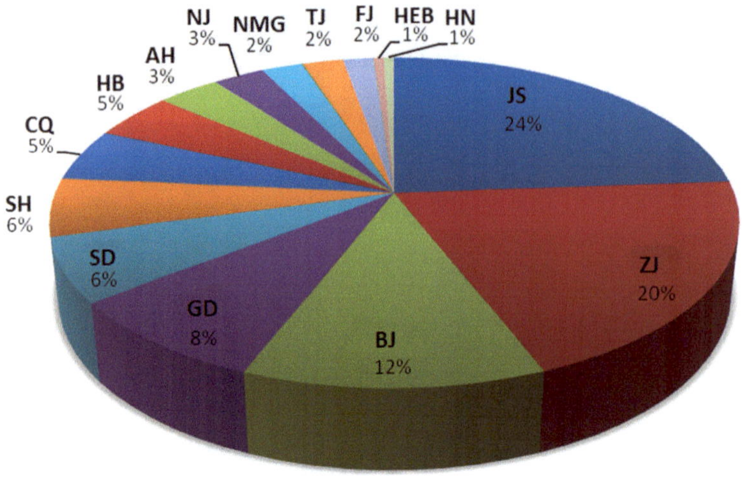

Fig. 4.7 Geographical distribution of SME PPB at Shanghai and Shenzhen Stock Exchanges. *Note BJ* Beijing, *ZJ* Zhejiang, *JS* Jiangsu, *GD* Guangdong, *SD* Shandong, *SH* Shanghai, *CQ* Chongqing, *HB* Hubei, *AH* Anhui, *NJ* Nanjing, *NMG* Inner Mongolia, *TJ* Tianjin, *FJ* Fujian, *HEB* Hebei, *HN* Hunan

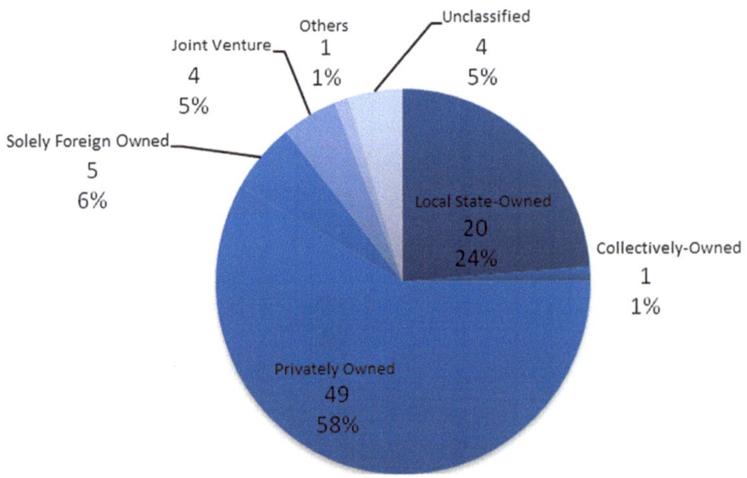

Fig. 4.8 Issuers of SME PPB at Shanghai Stock Exchange

Shenzhen Stock Exchange, there were 2 bonds rated AA, 2 bonds rated AA−, and the remaining 89 bonds were issued without rating.[16] These numbers indicate that only 15.25 % of the issued bonds were rated, with 84.75 % of the bonds issued

[16]Ibid 11.

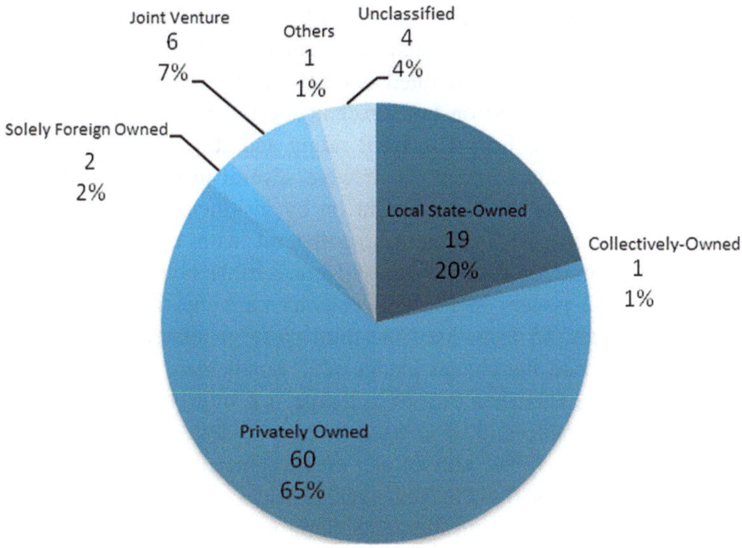

Fig. 4.9 Issuers of SME PPB at Shenzhen Stock Exchange

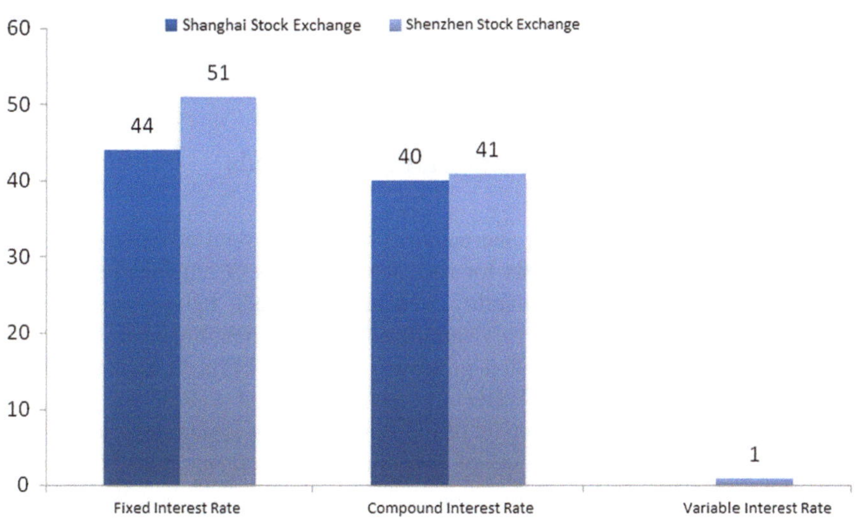

Fig. 4.10 Interest payment of SME PPB at Shanghai and Shenzhen Stock Exchanges

without rating. When rated, however, the rating of the bonds was usually over AA−. The percentage of the rated bonds on the Shanghai Exchange (27.38 %) was significantly higher than that on the Shenzhen Exchange (4.3 %).

Of the issuers (or "issuing firms") on the Shanghai Stock Exchange, 17 were rated. Among them, 3 firms were rated AA−, 2 firms were rated A+, 1 firms was rated A, I firm was rated A−, 1 firm was rated BBB+, and 7 firms were rated BBB. The remaining 67 firms were not rated. In Shenzhen, 1 firm was rated as AA−, 1 firm was rated as A+, 2 firms were rated as BBB+, and the remaining 89 PPBs were not rated.[17] Across the board on both exchanges, the rated firms were all in the investment class, which is firm with BBB rating and above.

In terms of credit enhancement, there were several methods that bond issuers used in order to mitigate the risk brought on by insufficient credit on the part of issuers, such as third-party guarantees, collateral with tangible assets, chattel pledges with securities or receivables, and convertible bonds. On the Shanghai Stock Exchange, 62 issuers took credit enhancement measures; among them, 2 firms used guarantees, 55 firms used the third party guarantees, 4 firms used collateral, and 1 firm used the chattel pledge. 222 bonds were issued without credit enhancement. On the Shenzhen Stock Exchange, 1 firm used a guarantee, 19 firms used third party guarantees, 1 firm used collateral, and one used an intangible pledge; 71 firms issued PPBs without any credit enhancement.[18]

In addition to the national stock exchanges, regional equity exchange centers were also used to issue PPBs. Among them, Zhejiang Equity Exchange Center was the first, issuing its first round of private placement bonds in December 2012. Following the establishment of Zhejiang's equity exchange, the Shenzhen Qianhai Equity Exchange Center, Tianjin Equity Exchange Center, Chongqing Equity Exchange Center, Hunan Equity Exchange Center and Shanghai Equity Trust Exchange Center (OTC) were all also established or undergoing talks to be established.

4.3 The Features of Private Placement Bonds

Compared to similar financing alternatives, there are several advantages to PPB financing. First, the requirements for issuance—in terms of required value of net assets, profitability, extent of liability, and required credit rating—are relatively low. Firms that issue PPBs can vary significantly within these financial parameters. For example, as a part of the first group of issuers of PPBs in Shanghai Stock Exchange, Suzhou Xingning Water Company only had a ROE of 2 %, but Changzhou Fandeng New Materials of the same batch of issuers reported a 37 % ROE; similarly, while the debt ratio of Xingning Water Company was 77.42 %, the debt ratio of Beijing Nine Stars Tech was only 35.07 %.[19] In contrast, other alternative financing methods such as corporate bonds require profitability for three consecutive years and an average distributable profit that is more than one year's worth of interest payments. Even for collective bonds, another alternative financing method, issuers are required to possess assets worth no less than RMB 30 million

[17]Ibid 12.

[18]Ibid 11, 12.

[19]http://stock.hexun.com/2012-06-08/142239210.html.

and no less than RMB 60 million, for regular companies and limited liability firms, respectively. In comparison, PPBs have ostensibly less stringent restrictions for issuance.

Second, PPB issuance is also advantageous in helping reduce financing costs and mitigating the risk caused by misalignment of debt terms. Compared to bank loans, which typically only provide short-term financing of three months, sixth months, or within a year, PBBs have a *minimum* maturity of one year. As a result, the issuer will be able to obtain a relatively stable financing source over a relatively longer period of time. In addition, the coupon rate of PPBs is typically in the range of 6–14 %, which is much lower than the rate on other financing products, such as those conducted through trust channels, which typically have coupon rates in the range of 15–20 %.[20] Lower rates plus longer terms help issuers a more stable financing source and reduce financing costs.

Third, issuing PPBs is remarkably more flexible than issuing many other alternative financing products. While all other comparable debt financing ways such as enterprises bonds issued by non-public firms, corporate bonds issued by public firms, short term notes, intermediate term notes, and SME collective notes and bonds are all subject to the requirement that the scale of the bond issuance is less than 40 % of issuers' net assets, PPBs do not retain that restriction. Bond terms on PPBs can be 1, 1.5, 2, 2.5 and 3 years, or some other specially-selected term length. Many options can be added to the debenture, such as callable, puttable, (coupon rate) adjustable, pre-payoff, warranty, or convertible. The issuer can choose to issue bonds sequentially or all at once, individually or together with other firms. When it comes to credit enhancement options, the issuers of PPBs can choose a guarantee, a third party guarantee, an un-removable guarantee, collateral or a pledge of securities and other non-fixed assets.

Fourth, PPBs allows for flexibility of fund use. Because regulators have not delineated any restrictions on the use for the funds obtained from private bonds, issuers are free to use the funds in whatever areas they would like, including repayment of the existing debt, working capital, capital budgeting, or merger and acquisitions.

Fifth, the issuance of PPBs can help issuers improve their image and reputation in the market. Even though PPBs are non-public issuances, investors that qualify for PPBs are all reputable financial institutions—commercial banks, security firms, fund management firms, trust firms, and insurance companies. Having these reputable investors back private bonds gives good indication of the future growth potential of the bonds, and they are subsequently more likely to be endorsed by investors. This creates a positive cyclical effect which in turn helps the image of issuing firms in the market and with regulators, bringing in more business opportunities for the firms.

[20] http://www.cr.cn/zixun/2015/04/05/1304910.html.

Finally, process wise, a PPB's "filing" process can be completed within 10 business days, while other financing methods that require "approval" from regulators usually take much longer to process.

4.4 A PPB Case Study: Private Bonds Issued by Deqing Shenghua Microloan Firm[21]

Encouraged to do so by the Zhejiang provincial government, Deqing Shenghua Microloan Firm issued a private placement bond through the Zhejiang Equity Exchange Center on July 22, 2013.[22] The initial issuance was RMB 50 million, with a coupon rate of 8.5 % and a term of two years. At maturity, however, the issuer had an option to adjust the coupon rate for renewal, and the investor could choose to sell the bond. The process of the issuance can be summarized in Fig. 4.11.

4.4.1 Innovation in the Risk Control of PPBs

There were several features in the risk control of Deqing Shenghua's PPBs. The first one was the guarantee from its large shareholders. Deqing PPBs were guaranteed by its largest shareholder, Shenghua Group. Shenghua provided PPB holders with a certificate of guarantee that promised the full payment of the bond at maturity in the case of default. The scope of the guarantee included principal, interest, default penalty, damage compensation, and other fees related with compensation.

As a well-diversified conglomerate, Shenghua runs business lines in manufacturing, financial investments, and trade and real estate, and is among China's Manufacturing Top 500, Private Company Top 500, and Zhejiang Provincial Private Company Top 50. In 2011 and 2012, Shenghua achieved annual sales of RMB 14.1 and 16.11 billion with a net income of RMB 464 and 113 million, respectively. Shenghua's operations generated cash flows of RMB 16.09 and 20.07 billion, respectively, in 2011 and 2012, which was adequate to fulfill its responsibility of repayment in the case of default.

The second feature of Deqing's PPB risk control was its bond repayment fund. Deqing set up a specialized account for the repayment of private bonds. Ten business days before an interest payment was due, the full amount of the interest payment would be transferred into the account. Fifteen days before the maturity of the bond, the accumulated repayment is to be no less than 10 % of the unpaid

[21]http://deqing04543.11467.com/.

[22]http://biz.zjol.com.cn/05biz/system/2013/07/22/019483611.shtml.

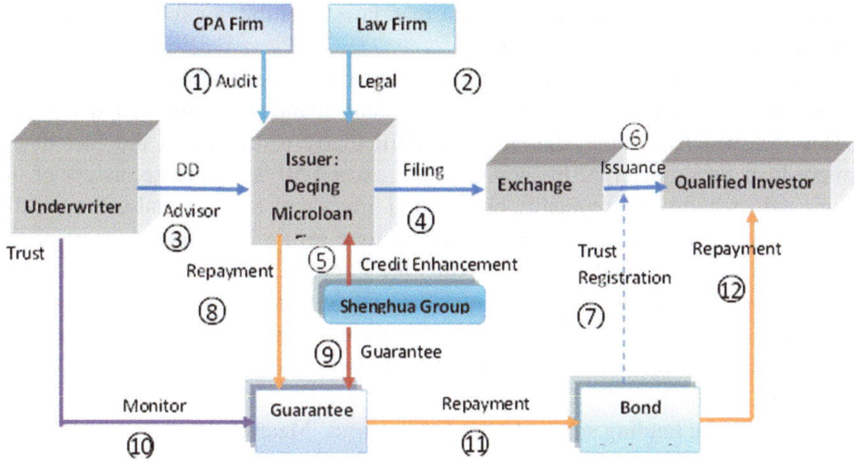

Fig. 4.11 Procedure of PPB issuance of Deqing Shenghua Microloan Firm

balance of bond. When the fund is transferred into this account, the money can only be used to repay the principal and interest of the PPB. The entire account and all its transactions are fully monitored by entrusted entities.

The third feature was the restriction on dividend payouts. If the accumulated interest and principal were not paid fully and on time, the issuer would be restricted from declaring any dividend payouts for its shareholders.

The fourth feature was the emergency compensation plan: the issuer could sell its current assets to fulfill its liabilities. As of the end of 2012, there were RMB 451 million worth of current assets on the balance sheet of the firm. Of these assets, 97.89 % were cash and marketable securities. The issuer could easily collect adequate cash to repay the liability on the due date.

The last feature was the engagement of a third-party trust to monitor and manage post-PPB issuance activities. Deqing tapped Caitong Security Co., Ltd as the trustee of its PPBs, therefore delegating Caitong the responsibility of protecting the interest of Deqing's bond holders. As one of the requirements of the partnership contract, Deqing had the obligation to periodically provide related information to the trustee, and inform the trustee of any possible default in a timely manner.

4.4.2 The Impact of the Deqing PPB Issuance

The primary value of PPBs lies in that they provide yet another legal funding source for micro-loan firms. As discussed in earlier chapters, microloan firms fill an important gap in financing SMEs and the under-financed 80 % of society, but their own sustainability—that is, the sustainability of the micro loan firms themselves—

remains uncertain, especially since current laws prohibit microloan firms from taking deposits from general public.

As a result, the capacity of microloan firms to provide funding is limited to the firms' own registered capital, bank loans, inter-financial institutional debts, and loans received from their shareholders. Particularly restricting is the fact that a micro-loan firm's external financing cannot exceed 50 % of the net assets of the firm, and, as had been frequently observed, a firm's registered capital was typically extinguished within 2–3 months of a micro-loan firm's inception. As part of the effort to resolve the funding source issue, the Zhejiang provincial government has issued guidelines on the further reform of microloan firm, allowing microloan firms that serve SMEs and agricultural firms to increase their external financing percentage from 50 to 100 % and raise their leverage ratio from 1.5 to 2.

Therefore, the launch of Private Placement Bonds opportunely provides capital and enlarges the funding source for microloan firms. Meanwhile, these bonds attract private capital and transfer that capital to underfinanced SMEs via a legitimate legal channel. As a result, the effective utilization of idle funds in society is improved.

4.5 The Future Development of Private Placement Bonds

As a new alternative method of debt financing for under-financed SMEs, Private Placement Bonds represent a new effort in the development of products that better balances the risk of serving SMEs with their need for financing. While regulators relaxed the requirements for the issuers in terms of financial parameters, thus increasing the risk of default for investors, the right to issue Private Placement Bonds was limited to only the most qualified investors; as a result, these guidelines self-select only seasoned investors, ones who have had more experience in the market and are more able to identify and absorb risks.[23] Because PPBs only started circulating in China a few years ago, for less time than it takes for a PPB to reach maturity, we do not have adequate data to assess the risks associated with this new financing product. However, several possible development directions can be reasonably expected for the future.

First, there's a likelihood of collective issuance of private placement bonds in the future. Because an individual issuance of PPB tends to be smaller in scale with lower credit and less sufficient guarantees, the resulting risk is typically high, and the liquidity of the bond is low. Following the example of collective notes issuance in the inter-bank market for SMEs, a collective issuance of PPBs can also be developed. Individual issuers can come together to form a collective PPB, and the issuance can then be conducted through exchanges with unified design, unified naming, unified credit enhancements, and unified registration and issuance. The hope is that more SMEs will be able to enter this market and utilize PPBs in order to

[23] http://www.ieforex.com/zgjj/20150108/464400.html.

lower their financing costs. On the investor side, collective PPBs are advantageous in that they may be able to diversify the default risk, thus encouraging more interest and participation on the part of investors. An example of this occurrence in the market is the 2013 collective private placement bond issued by Guangzhou Guanyu Packaging Material Co., Ltd and Guangzhou Yaolun Automobile Co., Ltd, which sold PPB at a 9.8 % coupon rate and successfully obtained funds of RMB 55 million.[24]

Second, it is possible that the PPB may be made convertible in order to attract more investors who are looking for a higher upside and willing to take higher risks. The current conditions of relatively high risk and relatively low returns that are associated with private placement bonds may be deterring the participation of more aggressive investors. Through convertible PPBs, investors will be able to gain more upside potential if the financed projects or firms succeed using the provided financing and they need only take the risk of debt investors. More importantly, by linking the debt market with the equity market, convertible PPBs can increase the liquidity of private placement bonds, therefore enhancing the bonds' value.

Third, structural products may be developed to compensate for the risk inherent to PPBs. In addition to convertible bonds, the PPB can also be bundled with products from private equity funds, wealth management funds, and trusts with a credit rating. Adherent to the principle of high-risk/high-return, the returns associated with ranked private placement bonds will differ based on the risks the bonds entail. For PPBs with lower risk, only a relatively low return can be obtained; for PPBs with higher risk, a higher return will be provided. By stratifying the bonds into these categories, more diversified investors could be attracted.

Finally, government policy may influence the growth of the PPB market in coming years. Compared to enterprise bonds and corporate bonds, PPBs require a significantly lower level of information disclosure. While this is beneficial for the sake of expediency, it also creates a higher degree of asymmetric information. Since investors determine expected price based on expected value, the adverse selection and moral hazard would drive more qualified SMEs from the market and limit their development. However, if the government can help in credit support for these higher quality firms through a public information disclosure system or platform with more transparent information, PPBs will become much more attractive to these better-quality firms. In addition, preferential policies such as tax benefits for both issuers and investors of PPBs can help accelerate the healthy growth of the private placement bond market.

[24]http://finance.china.com.cn/money/bond/zqzx/20130227/1300705.shtml.

Chapter 5
The New Membership of Loan Club—P2P Online Lending

It was not a surprise to see that some successful internet-based financing business, such as P2P (peer to peer) online lending, were so quickly adopted and developed in China since its inception in Britain in 2005. In 2006, CreditEase was founded in China, and soon, PPDAI and RENRENDAI were launched in 2007, followed by Hongling venture capital in 2009, and subsequently by PingAn Group's LUFAX (also known as Shanghai Lujiazui International Financial Asset Exchange Co. Ltd.) coming into market in 2011.[1] In the past a few years, P2P online lending was developed rapidly in China and successfully "intruded" into the financial industry. The traditional tough threshold for non-state-owned funding providers in commercial lending market has been dissolved by barbaric growth of online financial companies, and P2P online lending has become an increasingly important force in traditional loan market. Why did P2P grow so rapidly in China? What was the innovation of P2P business model in China? Could such high paced growth be sustainable? And what is the risk underlying such great opportunity? Let us unfold all of these issues in the following sections.

5.1 The History of P2P Online Lending in China: Born in Britain, Grow up in China

P2P online lending, abbreviated for peer-to-peer online lending, is the operation of lending funds via internet to unrelated individuals, or "peers", without going through a traditional financial intermediary such as a commercial bank. As the name stated, the P2P online lending takes place at P2P lending companies' websites, where the borrowers can post their loan demand information while the investors can lend the money out. Mr. Tang Ning, the founder of CreditEase, one of the earliest

---

[1]Wang and Xu (2015).

J.G. Wang and J. Yang, *Financing without Bank Loans*,
DOI 10.1007/978-981-10-0901-3_5

P2P companies in China and the first Chinese online lending platform listed in the New York Stock Exchange,[2] once recalled that, when he worked in Wall Street, he happened to meet Dr. Yunus, the pioneer of microcredit and microfinance. He was truly impressed by the 98 % of the repayment rate without collaterals in Grameen Bank, which was founded by Dr. Yunus and aimed to provide credits to poor people or small business. Mr. Tang realized at the moment that the credit of poor people may probably not be worse than that of the rich people, and credit is the critical fortune that can change the fate of poor.[3]

"When the credit rating system in China is not well established", Mr. Tang added, "how to help the thousands of millions of people who were excluded from the traditional financial channels to build their credit history, and get access to funds becomes the key issue that China's P2P online lending companies need to solve in the practice".[4] As the internet and mobile devices make the customer interface and transactions more convenient and easier, online lending can help make funds reach the people who can best use them to create value, and greatly boost the growth of real sectors of the economy.

P2P online lending was originated from U.K., representing an innovative way of private lending among individuals. Zopa, the first company to offer the peer to peer online lending in the world, was founded in February 2005. The founders of Zopa believed that everyone could have a better financial transaction experience without a commercial bank.[5] Zopa provides a useful platform for individuals to borrow and lend to each other, and the lending rate was totally determined by borrowers and lenders themselves. Zopa was only responsible for evaluating the possible risks of borrowers. Zopa's platform represents the most primitive P2P online lending model.

Since the 21st century, the peer to peer interrelationship has become inextricably linked due to the presence of internet, and the ways of communications have also been more and more diversified. The earlier ways for people to communicate on the internet were email or instant messaging, and since then, many e-business platforms, such as C2C, P2P, C2P, O2O,[6] had developed. Most recently, the social network became a hot pick. The interpersonal communication has experienced an evolving process which changed from simple information exchange to diversified functionality, and then, to emotional satisfactions. Just because of such links and demands existing among people, the progress on internet innovations will never stop.

[2]CreditEase's carve-out Yirendai went on IPO at New York Stock Exchange on December 18, 2015, http://www.bloomberg.com/news/articles/2015-04-15/china-peer-to-peer-lender-yirendai-said-to-plan-300-million-ipo, http://www.lendacademy.com/crediteases-online-platform-yirendai-becomes-third-major-p2p-lender-ipo-chinas-first/.

[3]Tang (2013).

[4]Ibid 2.

[5]Zopa, P2P Online Lending Platform in the UK: http://www.zopa.com/.

[6]C2C means Consumer to Consumer online trading. P2P means peer to peer transactions. P2C means Producer to Consumer, and O2O means from Online to Offline which brings online customers to offline service and goods.

The online lending is just one of these most recent developments, a combination of internet and private peer to peer lending. Similar to the traditional debt financing, the online lending could occur between any two individuals that don't know each other but shared the same network. The risk for the possible default or fraud requires a third party to provide special service to either enhance the borrower's credibility or reduce the lender's risk for not being paid back. The online lending platform just came into being to meet this need by setting up the rules of transactions, and defining the rights and responsibilities of debtors and creditors, which can greatly benefit both borrowers and lenders.

As a new way of debt financing, P2P online lending allowed small credit to be provided to a wide group of borrowers, including SMEs, that is in need of funding but unable to obtain funding under the traditional financial regime. Meanwhile, the lenders can make a small amount of investment by lending money to borrowers via a third party online lending platform. While online lending could help SMEs obtain the financing in business fields, it could also help alleviate the issue of unbalanced consumption for low income consumers, due to their uneven income flow over their life time, and the investors with extra money and desire to invest could find the matching credit demander though such an online platform at lowered cost.

Generally speaking, the major customers that the P2P online lending platforms serve are those short-term and microcredit borrowers. The borrowing amount often ranges from RMB several hundreds to 300,000 with the loan term of one year or shorter. The online loans are typically used for either personal liquidity such as paying the rent, decorating the house, purchasing a computer, wedding plan, travel budget or business financing such as running a start-up.[7] Such a loan will help the consumers and business founders to better handle various conditions caused by insufficient fund. The borrowers do not need to provide the collateral to receive the loan, and the third party platform will set up the loan limit and the suggested interest rate by evaluating the business borrowers' operating efficiency, management skill, growth potentials, and of course, the default risk.

With the slow-down of China's economic growth, the high speed expansion of China's commercial banks is hard to continue, either. The worsened liquidity for SMEs in 2007 triggered the rapid development of online lending in China, and the structure of the financial market has experienced a significant transition. Since 2007, P2P online lending in China has undergone three waves of development:

The first wave came in the year of 2007–2008, driven by the tightened monetary policy in China, and thereafter, the private lending via internet started to boom. The earlier group of P2P online lending platforms also appeared during this period of time. Starting from the end of year 2009, P2P online lending began the second wave of development, due to the credit rationing impacted by global financial crisis. Since the January 2010, the central bank of China raised the required reserve ratio for 12 times and the interbank lending rate started to surge.[8] As a result, the private

[7]http://www.iwencai.com/yike/detail/auid/38f1b81ea188a2b3.

[8]http://bank.hexun.com/2011/p2p/.

lending was prospering under the tightened monetary policy, and the online P2P platforms started the third wave of development.

Since then, the business model of P2P has become more diversified, and a growing number of P2P online lending companies expanded their business services to offline as well.[9] The typical P2P online platforms do not participate in the actual loan transactions and do not have their own sale persons or loan officers, and all their lending business are conducted online. Expansion to offline, however, makes the P2P online platforms to possess some characteristics of microfinance companies.

It is not exaggerated to describe the P2P development in China by "Sturm and Drang". According to the "2014 Online Lending Industry in China", the total estimated balance of P2P loans amounted to RMB 103.6 billion in 2014, and it had risen by 3.87 times in one year, and the number of P2P platforms had come to 1575 in 2014.[10]

The key for the rising of P2P online lending lies in such two facts: first, it meets the unsatisfied demand. The typical customers for P2P online lending are often short of adequate pledge or collateral, and their demand for loan is often not so large but highly customized. As a result, they usually cannot get the credit from the traditional channels, and thus, they have to pay higher cost to obtain the loan from "private lending", including the P2P lending. Second, the P2P online lending also provides the relatively higher payback to investors. Due to the long existing interest ceiling for deposit in China, the depositors therefore have the strong desire to seek the higher rate of return for their extra funds. The annualized rate of return for P2P could reach 8–20 % or even higher,[11] which exhibits great attraction to investors. With the stalemate of real estate market and continued sluggish of stock market, the P2P online lending, naturally, became a hot pick for many investors. The higher reward in P2P can be attributed to either the efficiency of internet platform to match the supply and demand of fund and cost advantage, such as no physical local branches, or the risk premium to compensate the higher risk for investors to lend out.

In summary, the popularization of the internet, e-business and electronic payment make the P2P online lending technically feasible, and the long-term financial repression for SMEs and low income consumers in China offers the great demand for P2P growth. Under the financial repression, the financial intermediaries have not efficiently resolved the issue of funding SMEs, while the new model of P2P online lending helps bring the "private" lending to "public", and greatly lower the information asymmetry and cost, which is also a supplement to existing commercial banking system.

---

[9]Ibid 1.

[10]Wang et al. (2014).

[11]2013 CEIBS Lujiazui Institute of International Finance Project Report: "P2P Internet Lending Platform: Angel or Demon?" http://opinion.caixin.com/2013-11-04/100598710.html.

5.2 The Business Models of P2P Online Lending

5.2.1 The Major Models in Western Countries

The P2P online lending market in U.S. and U.K. is relatively mature, and P2P online lending has been widely accepted in these countries. On one hand, the lenders could receive higher return on their investments; and on the other hand, the borrowers could meet their fund demand more quickly and conveniently. In the U.S., the leading P2P online lending companies are Prosper and Lending Club, and in U.K, there is Zopa. Those companies provided C2C financial services, and smooth the fund transactions between borrowers and lenders without the bank involving at all.

Zopa started operation in U.K. since March 2005. On Zopa's website, the loan borrowers list the amount, offered interest rate and term, and the lenders will view those loan requests and pick up the preferred targets. Some of borrowers just ask quite low interest rate and they may not be able to get the loans needed. Even though there is no intermediary agency for such a transaction, the customers generally can still find the best matching product through Zopa's website. For considering the risk to lend to the risky individuals, Zopa also invented an investment supporting system for lenders. Under such a system, the lender's money will be divided into 50 shares, and the funds will actually be lent out to 50 different borrowers while the same borrower cannot get more than one share. Because the probability for all borrowers to default at the same time is low, so the default risk facing lenders is thus reduced. In addition, the lending and borrowing parties will get the legal contract from Zopa, and Zopa checks the repayment record every month, and takes the similar remedial action to commercial bank in the case that some borrowers are not able to pay back on time.[12]

Prosper in the US is another successful P2P online platform. The creditors and debtors release the information to Prosper, and Prosper acts as the intermediary between the two parties and receive the service fees for its services. Prosper has grown well since its inception in February 2006. Prosper achieved the borrower's credit history from the third-party credit agency, Experian, and categorize the borrower's credit into AA, A, B, C, D, E, and HR 7 levels. The borrowers with the highest level will get the lowest interest rate. Conceptually, the borrowers can get the loan with lower interest rate compared to what they can borrow from the traditional bank, while the lenders can invest their extra money with higher interest rate than the deposit rate from banks. Thereafter, both parties win. What Prosper needs to do is to ensure the safe and fair transactions.[13]

Generally speaking, the investors can gain higher reward via Prosper or Zopa. The current interest rate in Prosper is 6.73 % and up.[14] The higher lending interest

[12]Ibid 5.

[13]www.prosper.com.

[14]Ibid 13.

rate often reflects higher intrinsic risk. Prosper and Zopa rely on service fee to make profit, and both lending and borrowing parties need to pay certain transaction fees for using their platforms.

5.2.2 The Business Model and Operating Procedures in China

In a broad sense, there are three ways to form an e-finance in China. The first one is the so called online banking that the traditional financial institutions provide their financial services online. The second one is the online financial services that are provided by the well-established internet companies when they entered into the financial industry, such as Alibaba's Yu'er Bao[15] and China's large online retailer Jingdong's supply chain finance.[16] The third type is the online financial services provided by these grass-root growing platforms, such as P2P online lending.[17]

Since P2P emerged in China in 2006, its impact has rapidly spread all over China. The online platforms not only grew up fleetly in the first tier cities such as Beijing, Shanghai, and Shenzhen, but also undergone fast development in some second and third tier cities. As of the end of year 2014, the total loan balance of P2P online lending amounted to RMB 103.6 billion with the total investors above 110,000.[18] However, comparing with the business model for Lending Club, which is to provide the pure intermediary credit service online, the China's P2P platforms have more diversified business modes in the past few years. In addition to the pure intermediary role, the platforms also act as pledger and debt collector simultaneously, which was largely due to the less developed credit system in China.

The first P2P online platform in China was PPDAI.COM, founded in August 2007, and followed by RenRenDai, Hongling Venture Capital, and EDAI365. The business model of PPDAI was very similar to Prosper, where the borrowers will post their requested borrowing rate based on the guided rate on different credit scores released by PPDAI, and the lenders will evaluate the possible risk of borrowers based on their credit ratings and profiles, and then, decide if their funds (or part of funds) should be lent out. PPDAI will ultimately assess the fraud risk, and could terminate transactions to protect the benefits of investors if the identified risk is higher than the threshold.

Even though there are many lending platforms in China and their business models vary from each other, their basic operation procedures share many similarities. In general, they could be categorized as lenders' flow and borrowers' flow.

---

[15]https://financeprod.alipay.com/account/finance/index.htm.

[16]http://jr.jd.com/.

[17]Since 2014, more and more P2P online lending platforms with the background of commercial banks, state-owned companies, or listed firms started to enter into this industry. Ibid 1.

[18]Ibid 7.

The lender's flow is relatively simpler. The lenders just need to register online with the platform and complete the verification of their identifications. Then, the lenders could search for the posted loan request lists, and make the investment decisions. Some P2P websites even introduced the priority-auto-bidding tool for lenders, such as RenRenDai's "optimized wealth management plan" that could help the investors to automatically place a bid. Since all the fund transactions go through the third party payment platform, all lenders will need to pay specific service fee when they recharge their investment accounts with P2P platforms. The above mentioned companies, except for Hongling Venture Capital that charges VIP fee and 10 % of total earnings as management fee, in general, do not charge any other fees to lenders.[19]

In contrast, the borrower's flow is more complicated. Because the borrowing process is completed online, it is quite different for different platforms and other private financial institutions. However, the basic operating process contains the similar steps: (1) the borrowers register online with the platform; (2) when borrowers need funding, they are asked to provide their identification and personal financial documents, such as the pay stub, the property titles, and the vehicle titles, and also list the loan requirements including the amount, term, and interest rate, on the website; (3) the P2P platform will evaluate the borrower's credit and post their assessment on the website; (4) the lenders, after the assessment, will bid for total or partial amount of posted loan requests; (5) during the listing period, if more bids reach the same listed loan target, the one with the lowest interest rate will win; if no bid reach the goal, the borrowing plan fails; (6) the website will automatically generate the electronic loan contract, and the borrower is required to pay off the loan with agreed interest rate on time.

Currently, the average annualized interest rate for the P2P online lending ranges from 13 to 20 %. Such interest payment goes to lender. While borrowers also need to pay service fee, management fee, and certification fee, it makes the overall annualized rate for the borrowers go up to about 30 %.[20] The deep margin between the borrower's and lender's interest rate minus the operating cost constitutes the profit of P2P platforms.

In essence, P2P lending is a way of inclusive financing, and a necessary complement to traditional commercial banking. With P2P online lending, every involving party can get benefit from it, and that is also why the P2P platforms can make decent profit with effective risk management. On the borrower side, the micro and small business and low income consumers can obtain the badly-needed loans promptly, even with a higher cost. On the lender side, the smaller investors can receive higher returns on P2P investment compared to other financial products available to them. At the same time, the P2P platforms can receive the service fees

---

[19]Ibid 7.

[20]China Finance Online (NASDAQ:JRJC), http://bank.jrj.com.cn/2013/01/31135015030224.shtml. As China's online lending industry is further regulated, the average interest rate is expected to come down further.

and generate the net profit by operating the platform with reduced cost on human resource, fixed asset, advertisement, and other cost components.

5.3 The Risks in Online Lending

The online lending industry emerges with the development of the internet, and is currently still in the early stage of its development in China without adequate laws and regulations designed specifically for online lending industry and clear industrial standards. At present, the high quality and low quality platforms co-exist, which highlights some significant risks in the industry as follows.

The first one is the credit check risk. The credit check is at the core of the essential technologies of an online lending platform, and the key of credit check lies in the control of loan size, which is the maximum amount of funds that can be lent to borrowers after a comprehensive examination of the borrowers have been taken. As for a credit loan, the P2P online lending platforms usually adopted the way of credit rating. Based on a comprehensive evaluation against a borrower according to several parameters, including borrower's basic information, financial status, income and expenditure, business operations, previous credit records and other information, the platform will set up a credit line based on the credit rating. The key component of credit rating is to quantify the default risk based on the borrower's ability and willingness of repayment through the analysis of the borrowers' credit information. However, as the nationwide credit rating system in China is still under-developed, it is usually difficult for online lending platforms to find out the borrower's debt status outside the commercial banking system. In addition, it is also difficult for platforms to conduct post-loan management to monitor the actual use of loans. As a result, it would be extremely hard for P2P online lending platforms to rate proper credit scores to the borrowers, and it would be even harder for online lending platforms to appropriately set up the loan limit, increasing the risk of default.

The second one is the risks of intermediate account. Intermediate account is a custody account opened by a third-party institution to deposit transaction funds for both sides of lending in order to reduce transaction risks. The purpose of the opening up of an intermediate account in a P2P online lending platform is to make it more convenient to verify transactions and transfer funds. At present, P2P online lending platforms in China commonly open an intermediate account in commercial banks or third-party payment platforms to facilitate fund transfer and settlement. However, the general attitude of the entrusted third party is that they allow the opening of the account in their institutions, but unwilling to take the responsibility of supervision of the account. As a result, it leaves the balance and the liquidity of intermediate account in a no supervision status. As commercial banks are usually unable to adequately assess the impacts the online lending risks on the banking system, they typically refuse to provide third-party supervision for online lending platforms. As a result, even though the funds are kept in a third-party account, the right of disposal of funds is still in the hands of the online lending platforms.

Hopefully, the issue of new guidelines by China's central bank will help mitigate this issue.

The third one is the risks of guarantee payment. Since Hongline Venture Capital pioneered in the guarantee payment in the online lending industry, this model has been followed by many other platforms. After a few years of development, the model with guarantee payment to lenders has become the mainstream of the industry. In the process of online lending, guarantee companies will provide guarantee services to specified loans. In the case of default, the guarantee company will provide funds to cover the loss of the lenders. For a guarantee company in online lending industry and online lending itself, the guarantee risks always exist. The fund chain of a guarantee company is actually very fragile. Different from large guarantee companies backed by commercial banks and government, all small guarantee companies have to face and deal with this challenge. In China, the guarantee fee is generally from 3 to 5 % of the guaranteed value. Once the default occurs, however, the guarantee company needs to pay 100 % of the total loss, which causes the guarantee company to take high risks on the basis of a low income. Even with the issuance of new guidelines by China's central bank, which prohibit the guarantee by the platform, the guarantee risk borne by professional guarantee companies still exist.

The fourth one is the liquidity risk, which refers to risk that a loan transaction cannot be completed during the specified period of time due to insufficient transaction volume in the market or lack of counterpart who is willing to trade. When a borrower has ability for repayment, but cannot get access to sufficient funds, or cannot acquire sufficient funds at a reasonable cost in a timely manner, to support his/her asset expansion or pay maturing debts, the liquidity risk arises. The online lending platforms outside China, typically, only provide intermediary information services, without participating in lending activities directly. So there is no liquidity risk for them. However, most online platforms in China adopted the advance payment model. So the liquidity there means the ability that a platform can cope with a lender's repayment requirement after it promises lenders to pay advance payment for the overdue loans.

The primary cause for liquidity crisis is the fund mismatch, including quantity mismatch and term mismatch. The quantity mismatch divides a large loan request into several small loans, and the term mismatch divides a long-term loan into several short-term loans. As most lenders prefer small-amount and short-term loans, fund mismatch becomes a commonly used way to attract lenders. Most of the newly established online platforms divided a long-term loan into several loans with one-month term. When the time is due, the follow-up funds are needed to pay maturing debt. If there is no follow-up fund available, the platforms will have to pay advance payment, and the lenders will be at risk of insufficient advance payment.

The fifth one is the transparency risk. The transparency of P2P online lending platforms highly depends upon the information disclosure from two sources: information disclosure from P2P online platforms and that from related guarantee companies. As for the information disclosure from platform, it includes borrower`s credit status, the platform's operation status, and the historical overdue records.

With actual data about operation status and records of previous defaults, the lenders can better evaluate the platform and the risk of the projects posted by the platform, and then can better ensure the safety of their own funds. As for the information disclosure from the platform's guaranty companies, it requires these companies to disclose the status of their guarantee business and their historical guarantee records. The reputation and guarantee terms of the guarantee company are directly associated with the fund safety of the lenders. In order to grow their business, some platforms sometimes claim "100 % principal guarantee". But in reality, it is nearly impossible to achieve what they promised. As a result, the information disclosure of the guarantee companies directly impact the healthy development of P2P online lending industry and protection of the interests of lenders.

The sixth one is the technical risk, which refers to the safety of internet. The online lending platform depends heavily on the use of internet. As a result, the technical risk of internet, such as hackers' attack on a platform and blackmail of protection fees, is the first and foremost risk of online lending.

The seventh one is the legal risk. As a platform of information exchange between lenders and borrowers, online lending platforms play the role as intermediary as defined in Contract Law and Regulations in China. So, in concept, the platform should be just an information intermediary not directly involved in loan transactions. But in practice, there are a number of platforms that have deviated from the pure intermediary role. As a result, such platforms face some additional legal risks such as risk of public issuance of securities by platforms, the risk of illegal fund raising or fund collecting, the risk of fraudulent fund-raising, risks of illegal intermediary activities, and the risk of violating the confidentiality obligations, among others.

The next one is the leverage risk of lenders. Online lending, as a new industry, has no standardized norm on the determination of the interest rate. For attracting customers and establishing their brands, many online lending platforms usually offered high interest rate for the lenders at the very early stage of their development. As a result, many lenders could be attracted by these high returns. However, the lenders involved in online lending, typically, are the middle to low-income individuals with relatively less funds to invest, so the total return is relatively low as well. Therefore, some lenders may choose to invest in the high-interest online lending by borrowing funds with low interest rate from their relatives and friends or by using their own credit cards, incurring leverage risk.

The last one is the ethical risk. The online lending industry is, currently, still in a state where there is no entry barrier and no detailed regulations. Some platforms were nominally set up for borrowing and lending, but in fact, they embezzle the lenders' funds or even run away after then. And such illegal use of investment funds by online lending platforms that is giving rise to a loss to lenders is called "ethical risk". These are old stories that the platforms involved in fraud. In June 2012, the "Taojindai" cheated lenders for more than 1 million Yuna, and its operator was soon arrested by the local police. In November 2013, "Lewangdai" in Laiwu of Shandong Province failed to meet lenders' withdrawing and caused a loss of 30 million Yuan to lenders. Its operator was arrested under the charge of "illegally taking public funds" by the Procurator in Laiwu. In addition, the operator of "Pengchengdai", an online lending platform in Shenzhen, ran away overseas with 80 million Yuan that were invested by his relatives, friends, colleagues and other lenders, and, at present, he is still nowhere to be found. The most recent one is the online lending firm eZubao that took $7.6 billion in Ponzi scheme.[21]

In addition, it becomes normal for many platforms to keep lender's funds for their own use, which is called "self-financing". Because of the lack of restrictions, the self-financing platform is likely to invest lenders' funds into those projects with high potential return, but high risk as well, or even to use it to repay the personal debts of the platform operators. It has been observed that many collapsed platforms took self-financing.

5.4 Some Representative P2P Online Lending Cases in China

P2P online lending in China has three primary models. The first type is the online P2P platform without guarantee of the principal repayment in the case of default. PPDAI, for example, will not share the loss with the investors in the case of default, and act as the pure information intermediary as required by China's central bank.

The second type is to provide guarantee for the investors, as represented by Hongling Venture Capital, which promised to pay back the principal by the platform to the investors in the case of the default. Hongling, in fact, inaugurated a new era in P2P online lending history in China by introducing the platform guarantee. However, such a model is no longer workable since China's regulation agencies banned the platform guarantee in 2015. On July 18 2015, China's central bank issued "Guidelines on Internet Banking Development" and clearly stated that the P2P online lending platform could not commit to insure the lender's principal, and its role is limitd to be only a pure information intermediary.[22]

The third type only provides transaction information online, and primarily provides services offline. CreditEase is a typical representative of such model. Some later comers, such as Zendai E-loan (onlinecredit.cn)[23] and PingAn Group's LUFAX, also adopted this model or a similar one. They both operated strong offline supporting system, and only act as the online platform for information exchange (Table 5.1).

More specifically, the three types of platforms vary in concrete business models, operation process, risk management, and growth potentials. The detailed comparison is laid out as follows.

---

[21] http://www.nytimes.com/2016/02/02/business/dealbook/ezubao-china-fraud.html?_r=0.

[22] People's Bank of China: http://www.gov.cn/xinwen/2015-07/18/content_2899360.htm.

[23] Zendai's e-loan is founded by Shanghai Zendai Group in 2012, aimed to provide online microfinance to needed customers, http://www.zendai.com.cn/.

Table 5.1 The comparison of three typical P2P companies

Name	Launch time	Registered capital (RMB)	Loan volume (per month)	Bad debt ratio (%)	Profit	Difference
PPDAI	August 2007	1 M	10 M	0.97	Low level	Purely online firm with 400 K users and 10 K loan on average Each loan is limited to <200 K
Hongling	Early 2009	10 M	30 M	1.4–1.6	5 M	Focus on offline evaluation and initiated the principal guarantee
CreditEase	2006	5 M	Over 100 M	<2	Make it even	Diversified product: offline service, financial management, P2P loans

The Data Source: The Lending Disintermediation Experiment, New Century Weekly, 2011, Issue 33

A. PPDAI

PPDAI, headquartered in Shanghai, was founded in August 2007, and it was the first online lending platform in China.[24] PPDAI provided the microcredit without pledge, and adopted the online bidding system to carry out the lending process. Through PPDAI's website, the borrowers need to first post the loan request information, describing clearly the reason(s) to borrow, the amount of loan, offered interest rate, and loan term. Then the lenders will place a bid, and the bid with the lowest interest rate will win. During the listing period of time, if the total bidding amount reaches the borrower's request, this round of listing succeeds. The online service will generate the electronic loan contract automatically, and borrower is legally required to pay back the part of principal and interest monthly. If the total bidding does not reach the listed borrowing goal, such a listing is considered failure. In general, the agreed interest rate is determined by borrower and lender (the demand and supply of credit) simultaneously.

[24]http://www.ppdai.com/.

The cash inflow stream of PPDAI comes from service fee, which consists of transaction fee to close a deal, and the service fee when the parties recharge the account or take the money out via the third party payment platform.

There are two distinguished features for PPDAI's risk management. First, PPDAI requires the borrowers to repay the loan monthly, thus the amount needed to pay every month is relatively small with less pressure on borrower side, and the lender can get money back periodically to reduce the total default risk. Second, PPDAI introduces the social factor into the credit evaluation process. The borrower's ID card, local residence (Hukou) certificate,[25] marriage certificate, and degree diploma all can be used to help increase the credit rating of borrowers. However, the original documents are not required, and thus the authenticity cannot be guaranteed. PPDAI believes that the social network and friends group are also the important parts of credit system. Having more known and common friends within PPDAI, and more borrowing and lending activities, the higher credit rating the person can have. Moreover, PPDAI publishes the black lists for bad-credit borrowers periodically.

If credit rating system in China is well developed, purely online model without repayment guarantee is certainly going to be the main stream for P2P online lending. With the under developed credit rating system, however, what would be the best P2P online lending model will take in the future remains as a question to be answered. Even in the well-developed market such as U.S.A and U.K. where Prosper and Zopa gained great success, the entire P2P lending size is still relatively small.

More specifically, some issues may need to be addressed for PPDAI in its future development: First, no guarantee mechanism has been provided by PPDAI, which certainly reduce the policy risk for the platform. However, if a borrower defaults, PPDAI will not bear any risk or share the default cost, and all risk will go to lenders, which will significantly increase the risk for investors. Thus, while there are many borrowing lists posted on PPDAI's website, the successful lists are quite few. Second, the borrowing process is complicated, which is not easy to follow for customers. In addition, high service fee may also hinder the popularization of the platform.

B. Hongling Venture Capital

Hongling Venture Capital aims to build an efficient and convenient credit channel between start-ups and personal investors. The borrowers need to satisfy certain requirements, such as age above 18, with ID card, and verifiable job, before they can enroll with the platform. After uploading their personal files online, the borrowers will get a credit rating, and then, can list their loan request on the platform's website, and wait for lenders to bid.

[25]A Hukou is a household registration record that officially identifies a person as a resident of a local area and includes identification information such as name, parents, spouse, date of birth, and address.

The interest rate on loan is generally determined by platform, and often exceeds 15 % annually. The revenue of Hongling primarily comes from four parts: (a) the on-site audit fee. The borrower with borrowing amount over RMB 100 K will need on-site audit. 1 % of the loan value over 100 K will go to Hongling as audit fee. (b) The management fee to borrowers, which equals 0.5 % of principal, and is collected monthly based on loan term. (c) The management fee to lenders, which is charged when a lender receives the payment, and is equivalent to 10 % of received interest. (d) Guarantee fee that is charged to borrowers, and determined by the credit rating of borrower. It is collected after the loan is secured.[26]

Hongling was developed based on PPDAI model, and they share many similarities in business model and operation process. The differences are primarily reflected in: (a) Hongling charges 10 % of loan amount as security deposit. (b) Hongling launched VIP service to which Hongling promised to pay back the principal in the case of default. The major revenue sources of Hongling are the 2 % transaction fee of total loan value for borrowers, and VIP membership fee RMB 180 yuan per year for lenders. Such a revenue generating model is somewhat vulnerable. If the bad debt ratio increases to over 2 % plus VIP membership fee, the company would get into real trouble. (c) While it was expected to see a large growth of transaction volume after the principal guarantee was introduced, it was not the case. It could imply that Hongling tried intentionally to control the transaction volume to reduce the risk. The larger is the transaction, the higher is the risk Hongling bears.

The current Hongling's risk management mechanism is composed of four lines of defense. The first line is the certification of customer's identity, and at the same time, all transaction funds are under commercial bank's monitoring, which are safer and trustable. The second line is that Hongling will send out message, call or people to collect the payment if it is not paid on time. The third one is Hongling's website that is authorized to record those default borrowers' files, and report the black list for those having bad credit history. These data could also be used by banks, telecommunication carriers, underwriting brokers, human resource centers, and other organizations. The last line is the loan deposit as mentioned above. However, with the new guidelines issued by China's regulators, which prohibit the guarantee by platform, Hongling's model is facing tremendous challenges.

C. CreditEase

CreditEase Group, founded in 2006, is a national leader in P2P online lending market in China. Currently, it has more than 14000 employers, and accumulated loan value around RMB 12 billion. In comparison, the earlier-established PPDAI only has about RMB 400 million accumulated loan values. CreditEase recently received two rounds of venture capital funding totally for RMB 100 million from KPCB China, IDG Capital, and Morgan Stanley. Its subsidiary Yirendai launched

[26]http://www.my089.com/.

its IPO on the New York Stock Exchange (NYSE) on December 18, 2015, and its American Depository Shares (ADS) were priced at $10 per share with total 7.5 million shares, raising capital USD75 million.[27]

The secret for such a rapid growth in CreditEase lies in its innovation on debt securitization. After the CreditEase lends the money out, they will restructure the debt and convert it to a fixed income derivative, and then sell it to investment funds and individual investors. This debt securitization is targeted at a large-scaled and untouched financial market—the one with investors holding RMB 100–500 K extra funds. Under the traditional investment regime, 100–500 K is an awkward range. It is too risky for the investor to invest all of their money in the stock market, while the interest rate from banks' debt financing products is too low to attract these investors. Meanwhile, the threshold for higher-returned trust products is usually too high for these investors, which generally requires the investable fund over RMB 1 million.

At CreditEase, the average loan issued by CreditEase is about RMB 100 K. In contrast, the traditional P2P online lending loan is averaged at RMB 10 K, and the general customers are those online lending experimenters. CreditEase's debt securitization allowed the firm to sell the standardized fixed income products in smaller values to more smaller-sized investors. As a result, CreditEase was able to attract adequate investors to finance the loan requests posted on its website, and achieve high speed growth. From 2007, CreditEase has grown over 200 % in total revenue every year.[28]

There are several issues for CreditEase model, however. Comes first is the high service charge. During an interview with "Global Entrepreneur" in 2012, Mr. Tang Ning, CEO of CreditEase, indicated that the average service charge to borrowers from CreditEasy accounted for only about 10 % of total loan value.[29] However, since 2013, there were quite a few loan contracts with CreditEase were exposed in media. The nominal loan interest rate plus various service fees, in these contracts, amounted to around 30 % or even 40 % of total principal. In comparison, the traditional P2P lending just charges the customers the service fee around 2–4 %.[30]

This brought the question whether the rising interest margin was due to the expansion of offline service and the resulting increase in the cost and drained liquidity. The focus on offline business of CreditEase model determines its major costs laying in maintaining and managing the offline service team and the corresponding back up expenses. As a result, if the individual productivity has not been improved significantly, the total transaction costs would be hard to decline. In some sense, CreditEase is similar to an independent wealth management company, but it creates and sells its own financial products.

---

[27]http://www.crowdfundinsider.com/2015/12/79017-yirendais-shares-debut-on-nyse/.

[28]http://finance.ifeng.com/news/corporate/20121207/7400950.shtml.

[29]http://businessleaders.com.cn/11/27859_1.html.

[30]Ibid 1.

In addition, the transparency issue also exists in the repackaged debts. Currently, CreditEase released a few standardized financial products including the "CreditEase Bao" with the expected annual interest rate above 10 %, and the various other short term personal financial products with the maturity varying from 1 month to 1 year. These financial products mismatched with various loans with different amounts and terms.

While the bad debt ratio released by other P2P lending companies is typically around 1–1.5 %,[31] CreditEase has not announced its bad debt ratio yet. In the U.S., Prosper has the default rate for the best quality customers (AA group) around 1.55 %, the default rate for the riskiest N/A customers reach 29.44 %, and the overall write-off is about 13.61 %. Thus, the actual profit margin is quite low, considering the gross return being around 10–15 %.[32] In comparison, the reported average loss rate of China's P2P online lending companies is truly "remarkable". The other possible reason for this significant difference could come from the fact that there is no agreed-upon threshold for default loan. Some companies use nonpayment for 60 days to define default, while others adopt 90 days as standard, and someone else may implement some other conditions to estimate default rate.

CreditEase mainly implement five steps of control to mitigate risk: (a) the authentication of borrowers' information. CreditEase strictly audit and evaluate borrowers' profile including their credit history, the ability to pay, the loan purpose, and other factors. (b) CreditEase advocates the small amount lending in each contract, and investing in diversified borrowers. (c) CreditEase sets up the independent risk deposit account, and charges the borrowers the different deposit based on their credit ratings. If borrowers cannot repay the debt on time or default, the risk deposit account will be used to help compensate the lenders. (d) CreditEase mails the statement to investors every month, and let them know where the funds went and what the return and repayment status are. (e) CreditEase made a strategic cooperation with China Citic Bank on fund deposit and settlement, which means that the bank will supervise the whole processes of CreditEase's own fund flows as well as those financed on its platform for MSMEs. As a result, CreditEase has become the first in the industry to reach an agreement with a bank on fund deposit and settlement, a move that is likely to prevent illegal fund collection activities.

Concurrently, CreditEase established the risk reserve fund at 2 % of total loan value. CreditEase will take the responsibility of repayment within the limit of reserve fund, which legally separate the platform credit from the total loan loss of CreditEase. However, after CreditEase repackages the debt and sells it again, the risk insulation seems mission impossible for CreditEase. For the borrowers, since they need to pay 30 % or even 40 % of interest to get a loan, the default possibilities greatly increase as a result.

---

[31]Ibid 7.

[32]http://en.wikipedia.org/wiki/Prosper_Marketplace, http://www.prosper.com/invest/download.aspx.

5.5 The Prospect of P2P in China: A Long and Winding Road

In summary, P2P online lending in China is truly creating a totally new business line. While the P2P online lending industry is far from mature, the future development of P2P may exhibit several distinct trends as discussed below.

Comes first is the diversification of debt products. Due to the fast development of P2P business, the forms of debt products issued through P2P platforms also changed significantly. It evolved from the initial credit debts to guaranteed debts, and now various debt products such as financial leasing, notes, factoring, private placement debt, and trust also come into play. Nowadays P2P is no longer pure peer to peer lending and gradually becomes the comprehensive transaction platform for various online financial products. This happens not only because of the demand by diversification of debt products, but also the need to make the entire pie bigger for the entire industry.

The second is the strengthened financial property of P2P platform. In earlier years, the internet property of P2P platform dominated. The platform that can get quicker development is often the one providing better online experience and advertisement. The intensive competition and accumulated risk, however, make the risk control of platform more critical, and the diversification of debt products also requested the strengthened financial property of P2P platforms. Relative to the growth of other internet related industries, the pace of the growth of P2P online lending slowed down in 2014 and 2015, simply caused by the increased inherent risk.

The third one is the service to the investors that may embrace a big development. The professional institutions with large networks and outstanding research capacity and risk control ability will grow quickly in the near future. The time for the investors to randomly select a platform to invest has likely gone. For the most ordinary lenders, however, they do not have much time, and are neither equipped with sufficient expertise to figure out the risk of each platform. Therefore, the professional service provided by professional institutions could help investors to filter out those higher risk platforms and improve the safety of investor's fund. As a result, it will help to raise the transaction level of entire P2P industry. In the year of 2015, some sub-industry research entities and investment funds for P2P online lending industry had appeared, and the institutional investors and professional consulting companies would definitely play an important role in P2P online lending market in the future.

The fourth one is the continuous increase of new market entrants. A bulk of platforms with various backgrounds is expected to go online soon. These new entrants are likely backed by commercial banks, state-owned companies or publicly traded firms, and their entry could significantly raise the threshold of the industry and intensify the existing competitions. As a result, it could be more difficult for smaller sized players to enter, survive, and succeed in this market. On the other hand, however, these new dominant platforms are usually able to provide lowered interest rate, and thus, the financial costs borne by borrowers could get reduced. Consequently, it could help the convergence of pricing in the P2P online lending market, and improve the legitimacy of the entire industry.

The fifth one would be the exit of many less qualified P2P platforms. So far, there are four types of platforms that were closed shops in the past years: fraudulent and cheating, liquidity difficulty, poor operations, and legal investigations. The major cause of the large amount of P2P platforms going bust was fraudulent and cheating. In the future, influenced by the sluggish growth of macro economy and credit crunch, the late payment and even default are expected to be more often observed, and some small and medium sized platforms will more easily fell into liquidity strain, which may cause "runaway" with customer's funds. In 2016, the industry-wised competition could be even fiercer, and the costs to gain new customers would continuously rise. The price war could present as well. All these changes would demand the higher risk control and operation ability of platforms, and those platforms that lack of core competence would be more difficult to survive. In particular, with the stricter regulation coming out, the number of the platforms with fraudulent and cheating issues are expected to become much less, and the ratio of platform failure due to less competitiveness would increase.

Finally, the national cloud credit rating system will be established. Lack of such system seriously hindered the healthy development of P2P online lending industry in the past, as evidenced by much higher percentage of loans with collaterals and much lower percentage of pure credit loans. As a result, all the platforms would be difficult to grow their business on a sustainable basis, regardless their background to be either the venture capital or commercial banks, and the development of cloud credit rating system will effectively break this bottle neck. A healthier development of P2P online lending industry can be reasonably expected for the years to come.

References

Tang N. 2013. *The value of credit*. 21st Century Business Herald, 5 Aug 2013.
Wang and Xu. eds. 2015. *Financing the underfinanced—online lending in China*. Springer.
Wang Jiazhuo et al. eds. 2014. *2013 Online lending industry in China*. Tsinghua University Press.

Chapter 6
Turn Movables to Liquidity—The Chattel Mortgage Loans

In China, loans with collaterals account for over 80 % of total loan transactions, and are also the most active part with rapid growth.[1] Among these loans, chattel mortgage is a new type with chattel, or movable goods such as receivable or inventories, as collaterals. The lender could seize the chattel in the event of default, and sell it to recover the losses from the loans. Chattel mortgage is specifically designed for the small and medium sized enterprises (SMEs) with low transaction volumes and fast circulations. Since it involves in many participants of financial market, such as commercial banks, small loan companies, logistics and warehousing companies, and SMEs, chattel mortgage has received increased attention in the past years. In this chapter, we will discuss this newly emerged financing approach in China with some representative cases of chattel mortgage to illustrate the operation model, inherited risk, risk control strategy, and development prospect of chattel mortgage.

6.1 What Is Chattel Mortgage

Chattel mortgage is generally defined as a loan arrangement in which chattel, an item of movable property rather than fixed property, is used as security for the loan. Comparing with a traditional mortgage where the loan is secured by the real property itself, the lender of a chattel mortgage holds a lien against the movable property or chattel until the loan has been paid back, at which point, the borrower resumes full control of the chattel.[2] The chattel used as the collaterals is, usually, certified by financial institutions. With chattel mortgage loans, the borrower will need to move its legally-owned chattel such as inventories to the depository

---

[1]Liu (2010).
[2]http://www.investopedia.com/terms/c/chattelmortgage.asp.

J.G. Wang and J. Yang, *Financing without Bank Loans*,
DOI 10.1007/978-981-10-0901-3_6

warehouse that is designated by financial institutions without transferring the ownership, and then, can obtain the funds it needs to finance its business operations.

Chattel is a concept relative to fixtures, referring to movable properties that won't affect their values after transfer. The example of chattel could include inventories, shipments, and accounts receivables, among others. In contrast to fixtures, chattel has greater liquidity and could be transferred easily.

Chattel mortgage supports the various financing options, such as bank acceptance, bank letter, and commercial acceptance, in addition to bank loans, and thus, companies could choose the most preferred way to access the credit. Also, chattel mortgage could adopt the way of "batch pledge" as well, because the financing companies can retrieve the deposited goods by paying the margin when they have sales order, or they can also replace the previous deposited goods by some new collateral that have equivalent value and meet the requirement of financial institutions.

From the perspective of operations, chattel mortgage can be taken in a way that the borrowers obtain the loan by depositing his legally owned chattel to banks or bank entrusted warehousing companies, logistics companies, or other agencies. When the default occurs, the bank is authorized to sell or auction the deposited chattel for prioritized payback. In the practice, it is more common for third party agencies to keep the chattel.

Most of SMEs are growing companies that own various chattels such as raw materials, semi-finished or finished products, and these chattel items sometimes stay in these companies for a long period of time. So if the SMEs are allowed to use these items as collaterals to get a loan, it will greatly improve the SMEs' ability to access finance.

In general, there are three basic ways for commercial banks in China to issue chattel mortgage to SMEs. Comes first is the Inventory Financing that is to use inventories as security for a loan. It could take several forms: (1) Warehousing Financing: the borrower moves its inventory, as security, to the warehouse that is designated by commercial bank, and the inventories will be monitored by a third party agency. (2) Trust Receipt Financing: the entrust receipt is, indeed, a confirmation that the borrowers or importers transfer their ownership of the imported goods to the bank, and use it as a security to obtain the bank loan to pay the related bills on behalf of the bank. (3) Pledging Invoice Inventory Financing: even though a company's inventory could be in and out from time to time, the company can still use it as collateral to obtain the loan from bank by getting the invoice pledged by a third party.

The second way is Accounts Receivable (AR) Chattel Mortgage. The duration of accounts receivable typically won't exceed 90 days, and AR chattel mortgage can take several specific forms: (1) General AR Chattel: bank and company can sign a summarized account receivable pledge agreement, and company uses its total accounts receivable and/or future account receivable as chattel to apply for the loan. (2) Specific AR Chattel: here specific accounts receivable refers to one time payoff accounts receivable and the accounts receivable installment payment under a long term contract. (3) Credit Line Base Loan. When borrower has a lot of accounts receivables in a continuous way, the bank can provide a long term credit limit to borrower. Within this limit, the borrower can get the loan renewed periodically by providing the bank the new account receivable bills.

The third one is Intellectual Property Chattel: borrower can use the technology, creative ideas, and other intellectual properties as chattel to obtain the loan. It also takes several forms: (1) using the intellectual property itself as chattel; (2) using the revenue or license fee from intellectual property as chattel; (3) using intellectual property as chattel to obtain the credit enhancement or credit guarantee by third party.

6.2 The Development of Chattel Mortgage in and outside China

Since 1950s, the warehousing financing already became popular outside China, and the chattel mortgage has well grown since then. The commercial banks have developed various chattel mortgage products to satisfy the financing needs of borrowers. For example, the inventory chattel mortgage alone could be conducted in several ways, such as blanket inventories, public warehousing financing, field warehousing financing, and trust receipt financing, among others. The accounts receivable is considered as the most valuable chattel, and almost 70 % of chattel mortgages in U.S. are accounts receivables.[3]

In China, the chattel mortgage with inventory and accounts receivable has grown steadily. However, comparing with the traditional guaranteed loans and real estate mortgage, its size is still relatively small, and it was primarily developed in the eastern coast area. Guangdong Development Bank was considered the first bank that developed the chattel mortgage in the late 1990s, and, then, it was followed by many other commercial banks. However, as a totally new financing product, the growth of chattel mortgage faced many unsettled issues and challenges. For example, the commercial banks in Shanghai started to launch the chattel mortgage with warehouse receipt pledge for SMEs since the year of 2003, and quite a few successive events of fraudulent chattel mortgage occurred since then. Among these fraudulences, some borrowing companies used the faked warehousing receipts to cheat the bank for getting the loan by either colluding the warehouses that was charged to monitor the chattel, or taking the chattel out of the warehouse without the permission of banks by faking the warehouse voucher. Under the pressure of risk control, the chattel mortgage business was stopped for a while.

In the following years, the commercial banks strengthened the risk management on chattel mortgage and renovated the business process. For example, some banks created a specific department to evaluate the chattel mortgage applications, and monitor the chattel items 24 hours every day. They also supervised all the inbound

[3]Ibid 1.

and outbound chattel goods that are deposited in the warehouse. With the great improvements of the operation process, the chattel mortgage gets rekindled, and, of course, the SMEs were greatly benefitted from these improvements. As a result, more and more banks re-started or continued to launch the better-designed chattel mortgage products to SMEs with improved risk control, and chattel mortgage obtained a larger market share in debt financing market, with higher percentage in the total guaranteed loans.[4]

There are various chattel mortgage products that were developed in the market with minor differences. The general procedure would be as follows:

(1) Credit application: the borrowing companies submit the application to commercial banks for chattel mortgage, and specify the purpose, amount, term, payback source of loan, as well as the conditions of chattel products.
(2) The evaluation process: the banks will review the application documents, and examine the chattel goods. In general, the customer manager will provide a comprehensive investigation report, and risk manager will generate a risk analysis report. The banks will make a decision for the borrower's loan application after confirming the investigation results.
(3) Sign the contract: all bank, borrower, warehouse keeper, and producer (if needed) should sign the related contracts and agreements.
(4) Purchase the insurance (optional): pledger could buy property insurance for the pledged items (if needed).
(5) Transfer the chattel: the company would move the chattel items into warehouse that was designated by bank during the pre-specified time.
(6) Release the loan: after confirming all the requirements for a loan are satisfied, bank should release the loan, and transfer the fund to the borrower's bank account.
(7) Loan management: bank offers the loan management services such as daily reconciliation of balance statement, regular or random on-site inventory audit.
(8) Repay the loan: the borrower will pay off the loan, including principal and interests, and take back the chattel items.

6.3 The Benefits and Risks of Chattel Mortgage

As discussed earlier, the chattel mortgage brings great benefits to SMEs' financing. Comes first is to provide an alternative financing channel for SMEs. Various forms of chattel such as raw material, semi-finished product, and finished product all could be used as chattel, which allowed SMEs to be easier to obtain loan from banks.

---

[4]Ibid 1.

Second, compared to real estate mortgage, chattel mortgage provided better liquidity for the chattel. During the pledge period, the original chattels could be replaced by new ones with equivalent values. As a result, it better satisfies the needs of SMEs in inventory turnover and liquidity operations.

However, the chattel mortgage could also impose some negative influence on the borrowing companies. When borrowers choose the chattel mortgage for loan, they no longer possess the chattel goods. As a result, there is a possibility of impacting the normal operation of the firm, which, in turn, may impair firm's repayment ability.

In addition, there are several issues in the practice of chattel mortgage. The first one is the possible credit rationing by commercial banks. The high risks and lack of control ability of SMEs with short or no credit history often lead commercial banks to restrict their loans to SMEs, when they cannot ensure the repayment ability of SMEs. Asymmetric information between banks and SMEs made it harder for both parties to establish a mutual trust. As a result, the SMEs may not always be able to obtain funding through chattel mortgage.

The second one is the post-loan management. Chattel mortgage requires high level of post-loan monitoring and management for the chattel goods. In China, financial institutions often rely on third party agencies to perform this functionality. However, there are quite few such professional warehouses and logistics companies that can effectively and efficiently do the job, and most of them are located in the large and medium sized cities. As a result, the shortage of professional warehouses and logistics companies became a key obstacle for the development of chattel mortgage in China in the past years. As a substitute, the commercial banks had to send the audit staffs more frequently to make unscheduled examinations on the chattel goods storage in the warehouses, which may largely increase the cost for commercial banks.

The third one is the valuation of chattel goods. Most of chattels have relatively high liquidity and greater variations in their market prices. Therefore, it is not easy to fairly and accurately assess the value of the chattel goods. Currently, however, there is a lack of authentic appraisal companies in the market, while banks always make their loan decisions based on the valuation of chattels. As a result, how to appropriately appraise the value of chattel goods appears as a big issue for commercial banks to expand their chattel mortgage business.

The fourth one is the complicated procedure of chattel mortgage loan. Due to high risk of chattel mortgage, banks typically impose strict requirements on category, quality, and expiration date of chattel goods, and the review and decision process may take several months. The long review process, however, could be a disaster for SMEs which often have strong and timely demands for liquidity. SMEs may lose the important business opportunities for not being able to receive the funds in a timely manner, and had to turn to private lending market, instead, for financing.

The fifth one is the lack of regulations for the chattel mortgage. In China, the relevant laws and regulations about chattel mortgage are almost in blank, and both borrowers and banks often found that they have no laws and regulations to follow, which significantly increased the risk of chattel mortgage.

6.4 Some Notable Cases of Chattel Mortgage in China

6.4.1 The Chattel Mortgage Warehousing Model: Zhejiang Yongjin Shareholding Co

The difficulty of expanding the chattel mortgage business, in many occasions, comes from the fact that the lending commercial banks can barely take the needed close watch on the daily price change of chattel goods, nor monitor them in the warehouse for 24 hours a day, and 7 days a week. As a result, the risk for banks to issue a chattel mortgage is significantly increased. In this regard, the emergence of professional warehousing companies, like Zhejiang Yongjin Shareholding Co.,[5] totally changed the game, and helped chattel mortgage business to be developed more rapidly. Under this new model, almost all goods can be used as chattel, and it could be a breakthrough for solving the difficulty facing SMEs in their financing needs. The warehousing financing model may help reduce the financing cost of SME borrowers in private lending market, since SMEs are often forced to seek private lending due to the traditional financing channels unavailable.

As discussed earlier, the warehousing financing refers to the professional warehousing services that are specifically provided to financial institutions which lend out chattel mortgages. It is a combination of finance and logistics industries, and comes from such an actual need: the small and start-up companies that need funding are often hardly to get the sufficient credits or adequate fixed assets to back up the loans they requested, because they do not have needed business scale, good credit history or required fixed assets. What they have in hand that could be used as collaterals are only the raw materials, semi-finished products or final products as well as some commercial documents such as receivables. Chattel mortgage provided such an opportunity for SMEs to utilize what they have to back up the loans that are badly needed. On the other hand, commercial banks often had their own warehouses and hired staff to watch the collaterals when they issue the loans with collaterals in the past, which was totally inefficient. Therefore, warehousing financing model helped resolve the post-loan-collateral-management issue, and motivated banks to grow chattel mortgage business.

In June 2008, a financial manager from a steel company in Hangzhou came to Hangzhou Hengfeng Bank, a local commercial bank, requesting a loan of RMB 10 million. The bank hesitated to issue the loan, because the borrowing company

[5]http://www.zjjinchu.com/.

did not have adequate fixed assets as collateral, neither have any credit guarantees. What the company only had was some chattel goods—cold rolled steel plates worth of RMB 16.66 million at that time. However, given the volatile price change of steel plates in the market, the bank would have to assign a professional to watch the daily market price, and move the collaterals into their own warehouse with designated stuff around to secure the chattel mortgage. The unpredictable risk and high risk control cost made the bank reluctant to engage in the chattel mortgage.

When the steel company was almost losing the hope to get the loan, a turning point came in with the Zhejiang Yongjin's involvement in the deal. On June 26, 2008, Hengfeng Bank, the steel company, and Zhejiang Yongjin cosigned a three-party agreement on chattel warehousing supervision with floating chattel value. Following the agreement, the steel company first transferred the responsibility of supervision of steel plate with the value of RMB 16.67 million to Zhejiang Yongjin, and Hengfeng Bank released the loan for RMB 10 million, which was 60 % of the original value of chattel goods, to the steel company upon the completion of supervision transfer. Right after the loan hit on steel company's bank account, Zhejiang Yongjin immediately sent out their own monitor to start the 24 hours on-site supervision for the steel plates that were stored in the original warehouse of steel company. At the same time, Zhejiang Yongjin set up the original value of RMB 16.67 million as the benchmark, and their professionals kept a close eye on the market price change to ensure that the actual value of chattel goods won't fall below the benchmark. According to agreement, whenever the chattel price fell by 6 % or more, Zhejiang Yongjin must remind the bank to adjust value of chattel, and inform the borrowing company for replenishment promptly to prevent the actual value of chattel to fall below the safety line. Every month, Zhejiang Yongjin provided a monthly statement to bank, reporting any value change of chattel due to the market price fluctuation, and allowing bank to take any necessary actions.

There were dramatic price changes from June 2008 to June 2009. In October 2008, for example, the international price of steel dropped by 55 %.[6] As a result, the steel company had to replenish the chattels several times even within a month whenever bank adjusted the value of chattel goods. The inspection report revealed that the bank adjusted the value of chattel five times during a year. Under such a strict supervision and replenishment mechanism, this chattel mortgage worked out very well. On June 26, 2009, the steel company paid off the entire loan on time, and the bank notified Zhejiang Yongjin to release the chattel. Needless to say, Zhejiang Yongjin received the service fee for providing the professional warehousing and monitoring service throughout the loan process, and all the involving parties got a happy end.

The positive externality of this chattel mortgage case is clear. Zhejiang Yongjin not only provided new way for SMEs financing, but also provided a critical service for banks to make their chattel mortgage business operational. On one hand, the warehousing financing helps turn the illiquid chattel into liquid funds. On the other

[6]WIND Data.

hand, the difficulty in monitoring chattel goods by banks could be easily resolved by the introduction of such a third party warehouse. With the warehouse taking charge of the chattel goods monitor and price change alert, the banks could significantly expand their chattel mortgage business, and many movables that, previously, could be hardly pledged now could be utilized as chattel.

6.4.2 The Hedged Chattel Mortgage Model: Xingye Bank

In November 2013, Xingye Bank worked with CITIC New Edge Futures Co. and issued the first loan on a hedged chattel mortgage in commodity market.[7] By hedging the chattel commodity, the loan-issuing bank secures the value of chattel goods. The process of the hedged chattel mortgage was as follows: The commodity producers or traders deposit their chattel in Xingye Bank, and open a short position for the chattel as hedge in a futures company that was designated by Xingye Bank. Then, Xingye Bank will issue a short-term loan to the commodity producer or trader using the commodity as collateral. Under this model, the futures companies also participated in the process of warehouse-receipt pledge by connecting both commodity producers and banks.

One of the issues with regular warehouse-receipt pledge comes from the possible fraud of borrowing firms by using the same warehouse-receipts repeatedly to multiple loan applications. The outbreak of bad debt in steel and copper chattel mortgage financing in China since 2011 had made banks more cautious to warehouse receipts.[8] Currently, banks often choose to cooperate with large professional logistics and warehousing companies to avoid such a risk. However, the introduction of hedged chattel commodities in the futures market further reduced the risk of high price volatility for the pledged commodities for lending commercial banks.

The hedged chattel mortgage launched by Xingye Bank has some distinct features such as high pledge rates, high efficiency process, flexible repayment schedule, high toleration, convenient replacement, and different location options, among which high pledge rate is the most attractive one to borrowing companies. In traditional chattel mortgage, the pledge rate is often below 70 %, and varies depending on the chattel categories. In the new hedged chattel model, however, Xingye Bank integrated the customers' future position, spot position, and security deposit into their risk assessment, and offered a pledge rate as high as 90 %, which is much attributed to the hedging function of futures market. In the operational process, Xingye Bank implemented a timely and effective valuation control on the chattel's future position through a specifically designed technology program, and successfully locked in the value of chattel goods by using the futures contract to

[7]http://finance.sina.com.cn/stock/s/20131226/080017756638.shtml.

[8]http://finance.ifeng.com/a/20140715/12726656_0.shtml.

hedge the risk in spot price. Under this model, the largest tolerable price reduction for chattel goods could reach 30 %.[9]

The high efficiency is another important feature of this new model. Xingye Bank promised three executions in the same day: the same day loan release as far as chattel ready, the same day chattel release as far as loan is paid off, and the same day replacement as far as new chattel is in place. Compared to the previous chattel mortgage process, the new model greatly reduced the complexity of procedures. So far, there are really few banks in China that can achieve such an efficiency of three executions in the same day simultaneously, except for the Standard Charter and BNP Paribas in China, which can make the release of a loan and a chattel the same day when conducting foreign-currency-denominated financing.

In order to reduce the borrower's cost of financing, Xingye Bank also established a relatively flexible repayment mechanism. On one side, Xingye Bank did not require the extra security deposit or replenishment of chattel inventories when the spot price of chattel goods went down. On the other side, Xingye Bank did not set the minimum period of time that borrower must keep the loan before paying off the loan. Those features are very attractive for borrowers to help them lower their financing cost, while other banks often have stricter requirements on the engaged borrowing companies in this regard.

High toleration, as mentioned earlier, is also an important characteristic of hedged chattel. The foundation of the higher tolerance comes from the introduction of hedge by building a short position in the futures market for the chattel goods. This hedging function will help reduce the risk due to the falling price in spot market for the chattel goods. As a result, it increased the level of bank's tolerance to risk.

In addition, allowance of the replacement is another shining spot of hedged chattel. The standard warehouse receipt does not allow the substitution of collaterals as a default rule, specifically, for the amount, size, and brand of chattels. However, Xingye Bank presented a new chattel mortgage model which allowed the customers to replace the original chattels with items with the same market value within the designated chattel categories by banks, which significantly improved the convenience for SMEs using chattel mortgage financing.

The hedged chattel mortgage model filled a blank in collateral financing market, and revealed great potential in the future. Previously, commodity financing in China, especially for nonferrous metal, most Chinese banks adopted the traditional chattel mortgage model or standard warehousing-receipt financing, such as providing credits to copper and nickel chattels, or issuing loans based on standard warehousing receipts for specified chattel categories that was settled in Shanghai Futures Exchange. Limited to low pledge rate, low operation efficiency, high financing cost, and competition from "on-site financing" in future exchange, banks were usually reluctant to grow the traditional chattel mortgage. With the hedged chattel mortgage, however, banks now can further expand chattel mortgage into

[9]The introduction of hedged chattel and warehouse receipts financing, by Xingye Bank and CITIC New Edge Futures Co., December 21, 2012.

other business areas, different industries, various products, and multiple types of partnerships, which can better help SMEs solve their financing difficulties, improve the efficiency of fund use, reduce the financing cost, and increase the core competency of the entire supply chain.

6.4.3 New Solution for Asymmetric Information: Shanghai Banking Industrial Chattel Mortgage Information Platform

On March 25, 2014, Shanghai Banking Chattel Mortgage Information Platform website was formally launched, as a response to the steel chattel mortgage financing crisis that happened since 2012.[10] The platform started with steel chattel mortgage financing, and planned to extend its service to many other commodities. The purpose of setting up of this website was to resolve the asymmetric information among the participating parties of chattel mortgage, and the platform is expected to help reduce the credit risk through the entire supply chain risk management for the chattel mortgage. The platform was expected to be adopted in the commodity spot market in the Shanghai Pilot Free Trade Zone.

The platform, so far, supports registrations for multiple channels, categories and products, including black metal (such as steel), nonferrous metal (such as copper, and aluminum), and chemical products. The operational process is that the platform integrated the software operating system, cloud computing, and real time monitoring into the general operating procedures of chattel mortgage, including warehousing monitoring, warehouse receipt management, information distribution, to provide a reliable, controllable and convenient monitoring system, with technology and human double-monitoring, for financial institutions, commodity producers, as well as traders. It significantly increased the transparency about the status of chattel goods, and reduced risk. For instance, all steels running on the platform could be tracked through the static warehousing monitoring and dynamic transportation monitoring system, which is similar to give a unique ID for each chattel, and the genuineness of chattel goods on the platform could be guaranteed. As a result, the issues such as fraudulent warehousing receipt and repeated pledge could be alleviated significantly through this logistics and warehousing management system and big data sharing. Currently, the platform performed the functionalities such as information sharing and distribution, warehousing receipt registration and financing, and collateral monitoring, among others, and it is expected to be further expanded to warehousing receipt transaction in the near future.

Up to June 2015, the platform had 6 partnership warehouses with 1.02 million tons inventories running, and the total inventories tracked in this system were 4.3 million tons. The partnership banks in this system include 14 national commercial

[10] http://www.shdongchan.com/.

banks, such as China Construction Bank, Industrial and Commercial Bank of China, Bank of China, Agricultural Bank of China, Shanghai Pudong Development Bank and others.[11]

6.5 The Prosperous Future of Chattel Mortgage in China

The total amount of SMEs in China has exceeded 46 million at present, and their total inventory value national wide was estimated to reach RMB 5–7 trillion. So, if only 10 % of this inventory value were pledged for loans, a credit market that can be generated is going to be worth of RMB 500–700 billion.[12] So far, the chattel mortgage is still in its experimental stage in China with immense development opportunities. Currently, the environment for the growth of chattel mortgage is considered very favorable:

First, from the policy perspective, the healthy development of SMEs has become a priority on Chinese government's agenda. In 2009, the State Council issued "Opinions on Further Promotion of Development of Small and Medium Enterprises", and called for "innovations on financial products and services, improvement on the assets mortgage system and collaterals, and ease the financing conditions of SMEs without sufficient collaterals through the pledge of movable assets, accounts receivables, warehouse receipts, equities, and intellectual properties."[13] Chattel mortgage is well encouraged and supported by Chinese government to be used as an important means to financing SMEs.

Second, from legal perspective, the laws about pledge of property have been improving since 1995 when Law of Guarantee was enacted for chattel mortgage. In 2007, Property Law was passed by legislation, which further improved the legal environment for pledging system. As a result, the chattel mortgage financing was provided with solid legal and institutional foundation for its further development.

Third, from the SME's perspective, SMEs have bountiful chattel resources while they usually lack adequate fixed assets for loans. About 2/3 of SMEs' assets takes the form of account receivables and inventories, which could be used as pledge under the chattel mortgage financing model. The amount of SMEs in China is enormous, and the chattel mortgage should have great potential for its future development.

Fourth, from the perspective of related industries, the rapid growth of logistics industries in China in the recent years provided great technical support for chattel mortgage. Right now, they can offer many specialized services such as ownership certification, price evaluation, logistics operation, and inventory management, among others. These professional companies took over the complicated chattel

[11]Shanghai Banking Chattel Mortgage Information Platform: http://www.shdongchan.com/.

[12]Zhang and Wang (2010).

[13]http://www.gov.cn/zwgk/2009-09/22/content_1423510.htm.

goods management process, and cleared the way for commercial banks to develop chattel mortgages. In addition, the widespread electronic and informational technology well equipped the banks to develop the remote service and real time monitoring system, which also helped the growth of chattel mortgage services.

In summary, the chattel mortgage model, including the warehousing financing, hedged chattel, and chattel mortgage information platform, as discussed above, will encourage companies, especially SMEs, to more frequently employ it to financing their needs. It will not only help companies turn illiquid movables into liquid funds and optimize their resource allocation, but also ensure companies only use the loan for working capital needs, not for investing in stock and real estate market. More and more banks are expected to launch chattel mortgage services, and an increasing number of SMEs will be able to obtain the badly needed funds by using chattel mortgage. As a result, the chattel mortgage business is expected to have a very prosperous future with further improved business models.

References

Liu P. 2010. The classical Chattel Mortgage innovation cases. CITIC Press (in Chinese).

Zhang, W. and Wang, B. 2010. The difficulty and breakthrough of Chattel Mortgage. *Finance Development and Study*, issue 10 (in Chinese).

Chapter 7
Enjoy "Free Rides" with the "Core Firms"—Supply Chain Financing

Supply chain finance is a concept and a financing arrangement that involves all enterprise members along a supply chain. The core value of a supply chain is found in its ability to make loans available to small and medium-sized enterprises (SMEs), which occurs through supply chain financial services. This chapter discusses the origin and history of supply chain finance, and, also, the basic business models, development prospects, and associated risk prevention strategies. The innovation model and the risk control of supply chain finance will be discussed in detail through a case study of a contemporary supply chain finance network platform.

7.1 Definition and Development of Supply Chain Finance

A supply chain refers to a continuous process of purchase, transport, processing and manufacturing of raw materials and parts into finished products, and distribution and delivery of finished products to end users or consumers.[1] All of these activities occurred in what has been described as an interlocking chain, and therefore, the entire process has been named the supply chain. The concept of supply chain has been increasing in popularity since the 1990s, as Martin Christopher, one of the most famous supply chain authors, has stated that supply chains compete, not companies.[2] As a result, real competition actually only exists amongst supply chains rather than individual firms.

There is always a core company and many smaller firms in a given supply chain. The core company is typically a large, powerful business entity like Apple, Samsung, Hyundai, or Toyota. The core companies usually have little financing needs due to their ample cash inflows. However, the creditability these core companies possess would allow them to easily obtain external funding when it is needed.

[1]http://www.ceocio.com.cn/finance/invest/2014-01-20/141012.shtml.
[2]http://www.martin-christopher.info/publications/logistics-and-supply-chain-management.

J.G. Wang and J. Yang, *Financing without Bank Loans*,
DOI 10.1007/978-981-10-0901-3_7

On the other hand, the smaller suppliers along the supply chain may have financing needs but have difficulties to secure the needed funding due to the size of their firms, which typically mean the insufficient collaterals and lower-than-required credit scores. However, the vendors need external funding to finance their working capital needs when they sold their products with credit and the corresponding account receivables. At another end of the supply chain, wholesaler and retailers need to delay their payments for the similar reasons, and may face the similar difficulties in obtaining finance as a SME. As a result, it generates the needs for a more innovative way to help the smaller firms on the supply chain to get financed, and supply chain finance was developed timely to help fill the gap.

Supply chain finance involves in all participants of a supply chain and financial institutions, including commercial banks or other financial institutes, the core corporations, the third party logistics firms, and upstream vendors and downstream distributors of the supply chain. Using the credit of the core corporation of the supply chain, the SMEs on the supply chain would be able to obtain the funding that they won't be able to obtain by themselves. On the other hand, well-funded SMEs in the supply chain will, in turn, help smooth the operation of the core company itself. At an age that the competition occurred among the supply chains, instead individual companies, supply chain financing will significantly enhance the competitiveness of the entire supply chain.

Meanwhile, supply chain finance is a totally different financing model compared to traditional commercial bank loans that grant credit to the ultimate fund users, these single business entities. Under supply chain finance, however, financial institutions focus on the core company of the supply chain, instead. The core company will help finance and manage the fund distributions among upstream and downstream SMEs. In this way, the higher risks associated with single SMEs has been transferred into more controllable risks for the entire supply chain from lender's perspective. With years of business transactions with SMEs on the supply chain, and cargos of the SMEs in the possession, the core company possesses much more information about the loan demanders than commercial banks or other financial institutions. As a result, with the credit of and information possessed by the core company, the lending commercial banks can significantly reduce the degree of information asymmetry, and the corresponding default risk. Simply put, supply chain financing could lead to a win-win happy end for all participants of supply chain financing.

With the rapid popularization and application of internet technologies, network-based platforms are becoming an important tool for many SMEs to be utilized. As the internet, cloud computing, and big data developed, many new online models of supply chain finance have also emerged. Commercial banks now have computerized the traditional offline supply chain financial services, and various e-business platforms have also launched online supply chain financial services with B2B platforms. These network-based platforms have now become a new member of the supply chain finance, which will be discussed in more details later in this chapter.

7.2 The Basic Model of Supply Chain Finance in China

The types of players in China's supply chain finance market include financial institutions, financial factoring companies, supply chain service companies, financial leasing companies, logistics companies, small loan companies, e-business platforms, and software information platforms, in addition to the borrowing firms. The entire customer base tends to be diversified from large companies to SMEs, and even micro companies with small scale companies are playing more and more important roles. Although supply chain finance has been developing in China for more than a decade, it failed to attract public's attention until recently. The basic business models of the supply chain finance can be divided into two categories: a traditional offline "1 + N" supply chain financing model, which is focusing on one core company, and an emerging decentralized financing "N + N" model through the ecological system associated with network-based platforms.

7.2.1 The Offline 1 + N Model

The Offline 1 + N Model refers to a specific model that focuses on "1" core company that integrates "N" suppliers, manufacturers, distributors, retailers, and end users of a supply chain, and financing services are provided to "N" peripheral companies along the supply chain. That's why it is so named. The core company has well-established business relationships with these "N" members across the supply chain, actively manages the supply chain, and cooperates with banks in credit extension. The model makes use of the credit of the core company, and financial institutions will issue loans to suppliers and distributors through the core company in the supply chain. This is the most typical and traditional financing model in supply chain finance, and it is generally applied to industries with relatively well-managed supply chains, such as auto and steel industries.

This 1 + N supply chain finance model does not intend to solve the financing issue of core firm itself. Instead, it provides financial facilitations to micro, small and medium-sized companies (MSMEs) along the supply chain. Such a mechanism works on the condition that the MSMEs must be the critical business partners of the core company, and many their products are in the possession of the core firm, such as in the core-firm-designated warehouse. Currently, 1 + N is the most commonly adopted model in China's supply chain finance, and is also a safer one in terms of risk management.

In the recent years, a "simple, rude, and effective" model has developed from the initial 1 + N model, which is the model that the core company provides financing service to its smaller-sized partners directly using its own resources.[3] Under this

[3]Li, H., "The Innovation of Supply Chain Finance" http://www.chinawuliu.com.cn/xsyj/201408/29/293201.shtml.

varied version of the original model, the core company typically has strong manufacturing abilities or a great deal of control over the distribution channels. More specifically, a powerful core company can often obtain a more favored payment schedule from its upstream suppliers and collection schedule from downstream retailers, which may result in a financing gap for these upstream and downstream companies. Under the varied version of the “1 + N model”, the core company can set up its own small loan companies or/and factoring companies to directly finance these suppliers and distributors.

As the primary model of supply chain finance, the “1 + N model” exhibits large financing values, wide applications, and relatively controllable risk. Since 2014, however, various financial institutions and e-businesses have started to establish online supply chain finance platforms, which constitute the second type of model of supply chain finance, as discussed in the following section.

7.2.2 The Online N + N Model: A Decentralized Network-Based Platform Ecological System

The year 2013 was widely considered the year one of China’s internet finance era. The development of internet, big data, and e-business has substantially shaken the traditional banking industry. The supply chain finance, as one of the ways of debt financing, was not an exception. With internet-enabled technologies, online platforms can provide information interaction and facilitation, and act as an intermediary between buyers and sellers, which can help facilitate the process of supply chain finance. This online model probably represents the most vigorous innovation in supply chain finance, and thus, has enormous potential in the internet era.

For some successful cases, the large e-business platforms often supersede or cooperate with financial institutions to issue loans, and extend credit to members across the supply chain. With the help of available big data for businesses, financing was usually characterized by low financing costs, controllable risk, and higher level of security. Typical examples may include Ant Financial of Alibaba, JD Finance, and the business loan collaboratively issued by CreditEase and Amazon.[4] By exploiting big data collected from its online trading platform, Alibaba can obtain the information for several different types of borrowers. The information is used as the evaluation foundation for loan decisions and lines of credit. The average loan value provided by Ali Finance is much smaller than what is typically provided by banks, but commercial credit that is accumulated from online trading platform can actually be recognized at this finance platform, and could be transferred to real finance credit. Jingdong, on the other hand, has a different story. Based on its advantages in logistics, Jingdong established its own warehouse and has a large number of suppliers with fixed settlement periods, which lays a solid

[4]http://www.ch-tj.com/site/researchdetail/42.

foundation for providing supply chain finance. Suning, a large electronic product provider, was inspired by the bank's factoring business, and launched supply chain finance for its own upstream suppliers. The operation of this model was largely dependent upon the credit that was established by suppliers, and their relatively fixed settlement periods.

All these different online platform models shared something in common. Under these models, the e-business or cloud platforms become the hub for gathering information and capital flows. The role of the "1" (the core company) in the traditional 1 + N model is weakened. E-business platforms, logistics, and supply chain ecosystems become the key words associated with supply chain e-finance. E-business records the orders, bills, receipts, financing, and warehousing activities of SMEs on the cloud service platforms, and introduces logistics or third party information companies to jointly construct a service platform to provide supporting services. Business flow and logistics are undoubtedly the keys to the future development of supply chain finance, and this new model of supply chain finance overturned the old one. The new model focuses on the trading process among the companies, meanwhile, it also works at expanding the large-core-company-centered "1 + N" model to the "N + N" model, which centers on the transactions among SMEs.

As the supply chain finance develops exponentially, it also impelled more participants to enter into this growing field. On the one hand, various commercial banks now have built their own supply chain e-business service platforms successively, and partnered with logistics, shipping, and third party information platforms. On the other hand, e-businesses like Ali and Jingdong also join the game by utilizing the massive trading data that they obtained from their trading platforms, and build supply chain finance channels to help complete the transactions between parties that don't know each other. As a result, their business models are primarily B2C or C2C oriented.

It should be noted that, however, no matter what model is adopted (1 + N or N + N), supply chain finance always features in real trading transactions behind the financing activities, and intends to fill a funding gap for the SMEs in the supply chain for their respective receivables and payables. Therefore, these two models shared in common in their development prospects and risk controls, which will be discussed in more details in the following sections.

7.3 Risk Control

As an innovative financial service model developed specifically for SMEs, supply chain finance has changed the traditional way of financing where banks extend credit only to single business entities. Supply chain finance, such as in "1 + N" model, centers on the core company in a supply chain, and provide suppliers, manufacturers, distributors, retailers, and end users along with the supply chain with comprehensive financing services. However, this new way of financing involves in more complicated relationships among the participants. As all participants are linked in one way or another, a problem occurred on any spot of the supply chain could potentially impact all other participants. It means that the normal operation of the entire supply chain could be affected. As a result, the risk associated with supply chain finance could be very different from the risk associated with traditional financing that only focus on individual firms.

The traditional lending institutes, typically, will assess the qualifications, operating performance, financial conditions, and possible guarantees that are associated with a borrowing company before making lending decisions. In particular, the credit ratings and loan repayment capabilities of the borrowing company will be carefully examined. However, in the supply chain financing, the risks associated with companies across the entire supply chain have fundamentally been changed. Under the supply chain finance model, commercial banks no longer focus on financial indicators, industry scale, fixed asset values, and guarantees for an individual company. Instead, commercial banks emphasize the actual transactions and business relationships behind the transactions of the companies on the supply chain. In particular, they focus on the strength and credit levels of the core company in the supply chain. In other words, the credit standing of the entire supply chain will be evaluated. As the large companies typically possess higher credit rating and have stronger ability of repayment, supply chain financing helps reduce the default risk, and provides a cushion between the commercial banks and the ultimate fund users. Meanwhile, the role played by the large sized core company also provides guarantees or credit enhancement for the SMEs on the upstream and downstream of the supply chain.

However, while the default risks caused by upstream and downstream SMEs are reduced because of higher credit of the core company and repayment sources coming from real business transactions, the transferability of default risk from one firm to another firm on the same supply chain will be much higher. In the case of default by one firm, not only does this impact the default firm, it may also trigger the overall operation risk of the entire supply chain. In addition, the supply chain financing model may also involve in counterparty credit risk, authenticity risk of the trading transactions, risk of the validity of collateral assets, and risks from logistics monitoring companies.

The very nature of finance is essentially about the risk and risk management. For supply chain finance, it offers a new way and possibility to resolve the financing issues of individual SMEs. These financial issues would typically include, first, information asymmetry, because many SMEs in China do not fully disclose all their information, or may even maintain several accounting books; second, the cost of processing the loan applications from SMEs is often too high for financial institutions; third, there lacks adequate collaterals, such as fixed assets, of the borrowing SMEs, among others. Supply chain finance, however, can help mitigate all these issues. As the supply chain loans are actually backed by transactions of the borrowing firms, not by the fixed assets of the firms, the traditional requirement of fixed assets are being relaxed. On the other hand, as the core company is one of the parties in the transactions, and may have long term business relationship with borrowing firms, so the degree of information asymmetry is being reduced. Finally, as the responsibility of due diligence is actually shifted from bank to core company, the economics of scale for financial institutions are improved. As a result, supply chain finance helps reduce the risk for funding SMEs.

Apparently, in supply chain finance, especially for "1 + N" model, the core value of the supply chain lies with the core company, which plays a critical role in integrating the logistic flow, information flow, and capital flow over the entire supply chain. Depending upon the core company's strength, credit and its overall management ability for the entire supply chain, financial institutions provide funding to the upstream and downstream SMEs. As a result, the chances of obtaining finance for these upstream and downstream SMEs are truly determined by the status of the core company. Once the operation or credit of the core company went wrong, it will almost certainly impact all upstream and downstream companies along the supply chain, and supply chain finance as well. Therefore, the "1 + N" supply chain finance model actually shifted the risk from "N" to "1".

The issue, however, is whether the core companies indeed have the ability to guarantee the finance for the whole supply chain. The contingent liabilities accumulated through binding credit may exceed the bearing limit of the core company, resulting in overall repayment crisis among all SMEs along the supply chain. In particular, if there is a moral hazard issue occurred for core companies, the negative impact could be tremendous. For example, in case of adverse changes happened to the core company, and the core company chose to withhold the information to its trading partners in a disguised way, then, the loans can be obtained in a conspired way without the real transactions as claimed. As a result, it may give rise to malicious credit risks.

7.4 A Case Study on Supply Chain Finance: YINHU.COM

Supply chain finance attracted investors' attentions from many industries in China. In addition to traditional financial players such as commercial banks and small loan companies, some P2P platforms has also started to enter into the industry of supply chain finance. The internet finance platform "Yinhu.com" is an example in this regard. Yinhu is a subsidiary of Panda Fireworks (PF), which is a leading company in fireworks industry, and the only fireworks company listed on China's A-share stock market. Yinhu was officially launched in July 2014, and was engaged in financing for the upstream and downstream suppliers of PF.[5] As discussed in the previous sections, the risks for the fund providers will be significantly reduced if the ultimate fund demanders can receive the credit enhancement of the core and listed company. Meanwhile, the credit can be issued through a P2P platform.

[5] https://www.yinhu.com/main.bl.

7.4.1 *An Innovative Business Model*

Yinhu.com has adopted a business model that combines online and offline services, which searches borrowers offline and attracts lenders online. The motivation for combining online with offline comes from lack of credit rating system in China, so that the platforms cannot assess the risk of potential borrowers online. As a result, the platforms have to conduct offline due diligence through site investigation or face-to-face interview to control the risk. Meanwhile, the business scope cannot possibly be expanded rapidly through only offline service. Using internet, funds can be raised more quickly, and the source of funds would not be restricted by geographic regions.

Offline services from Yinhu.com were primarily provided to the various supply chain companies of Yinhu's parent company PF. The funds come from PF, but loans were issued through Yinhu's platform, which was very popular among these SME suppliers. For example, a manufacturing company, located in Yichun, Jiangxi province, applied for a loan on Yinhu.com. The company noted in the financing statement that it belonged to the same supply chain of PF, and it would like to borrow money for short term working capital needs. Moreover, the loan was guaranteed by Wanzai YinHeWan Investment Co., Ltd. in Jiangxi Province, which is the major shareholder of PF. The guarantee was provided by a pledge of equity stock shares. Such loan project with the guarantee of major shareholder of listed company is among the most popular ones on Yinhu.com. Since the listed core company knows the borrowing company better because of its own businesses transactions with the firm, investors would generally perceive less risk associated with such loan projects.

At present, most loans on Yinhu.com involve in supply chain companies associated with PF, including fireworks manufacturing and marketing companies. As of the end of December 2014, the loans issued to supply chain companies accounted for 70 % of the total transaction volumes on the platform. Meanwhile, in July 2014, when the platform was just launched, the loans issued to supply chain companies took over 90 % of the total transaction volume.[6] As a listed firm on the A-share market, the stock price of PF has increased significantly. Much of the increase comes from Yinhu.com, which was able to offer a new P2P-oriented-supply-chain-finance to the borrowers, and collect huge bonuses from the capital market. On the one hand, this model helped resolve the financing issues of SMEs on the supply chain. On the other hand, it mitigated the risk using the knowledge and information possessed by the core firm.

[6]"Exclusive Evaluation of P2P Yinhu.com Subordinating to A Listed Company: 70% Supply Chain Loan", Sina Finance, http://finance.sina.com.cn/money/bank/p2p/20141116/222220832204.shtml.

7.4.2 Risk Control

Supply chain finance generally targets the short term accounts receivables from the upstream and downstream suppliers of one or more core companies, and the resources of the core companies are typically the key for P2P platforms conducting supply chain finance. As a result, risks are generally found within the core companies, and screening core companies must always be the first priority in terms of risk control.

Generally speaking, core companies tend to be larger in scale, and possess stronger competitiveness and powerful positions within certain markets, dominating the upstream and downstream companies. Whether or not a company is judged to be a core company typically depends on its operation scale, industry position, and some other factors. In supply chain finance, the accounts receivables of upstream and downstream companies are typically used as collateral on loans.

The core company of the supply chain that is conducted transactions through Yinhu.com is its parent company Panda Fireworks. As a result, it is easier for the platform to obtain the detailed transaction information, and investigate the authenticity of transactions, because most borrowers are these upstream and downstream companies of Panda Fireworks. On the other hand, investors would perceive controllable overall risks, because of the credit enhancement was provided by the core company.

In addition, there are three highlights in risk control at Yinhu. First, "ChinaPnR", a financial payment company,[7] acts as the third party funds custodian. The account of investors' funds paid to Yinhu will be held in an escrow account managed by this leading third party payment company, ChinaPnR. This ensures that no money will flow through the bank accounts of Yinhu, and avoid the risks associated with funds misappropriation. Second, an unlimited liability guarantee is provided by the major shareholder of Panda Fireworks vis-à-vis the loan programs launched on Yinhu.com. So far, this is the only listed company that provides an unlimited liability guarantee for its P2P online lending platform. At present, the market value of Panda Fireworks is about 3.4 billion yuan with the major shareholder accounting for 42 %.[8] In other words, the value of the guarantee for Yinhu.com is around 1.2 billion yuan. The major shareholder of Panda Fireworks may provide guarantee for an amount of 12 billion yuan for Yinhu.com when calculated by the leverage ratio of 1:10. In other words, based on the current market value of Panda Fireworks, the investment is in a safe net and free of default risk. This will remain true so long as the transaction volume on Yinhu.com is below 12 billion yuan. Third, both the principal and interest guarantee is also provided by state-owned guarantee companies that cooperate with Yinhu.com. This will indemnify the investors in case of any risky issues. In particular, considering the risk for a private guarantee company

[7]ChinaPnR is a financial payment company focused on payment services such as online, POS, and mobile payment.

[8]Sina Finance: Panda Fireworks (600599).

to go out of business, Yinhu.com chooses to cooperate with only state-owned guarantee company and small loan company to safeguard the lenders' money.

7.4.3 Yinhu's Development Prospects

As of the end of 2014, the transaction volume on Yinhu.com had accumulated to 280 million yuan for over 4 months. Among them, the borrowing from Panda Fireworks' supply chain companies accounted for 70 %.[9] Providing financial services through a supply chain may become a viable way for listed companies to enter into the field of investment and financing intermediary services.

By targeting supply chain finance, Yinhu.com is now rapidly expanding its business by using the existing supply chain resources of Panda Fireworks. However, the Yinhu.com may not be fully satisfied by the current supply chain financing demands, due to the smaller financing size and higher concentration ratio only on the fireworks industry. In the near future, Yinhu.com may consider entering into the new field of factoring, housing mortgages, and auto loan businesses.

7.5 Future Development of Supply Chain Finance in China

Financing has always been one of the major factors that impact the growth of SMEs. Supply chain finance, as it is able to finance a large number of SMEs in the upstream and downstream of a supply chain that is associated with core enterprises, is widely considered a viable way of financing SMEs. As Mathis and Cavinato (2010) have pointed out that SMEs may make use of the information advantage associated with large enterprises along the supply chain,[10] so the smaller firms in a supply chain can take this advantage to overcome their credit deficiencies and information asymmetry issues, and obtain their badly needed financing.

Supply chain finance allows the credit suppliers to assess the credit risk of SMEs from a new perspective. Using the supply chain finance, financial institutions such as commercial banks can change their evaluation objectives from a particular SME to the particular transactions of the SME and the entire supply chain, which enables the fund suppliers to avoid over-assessing the risks that can actually be mitigated through its transactions with core companies. As a result, more SMEs will be funded by services provided by financial institutions.

As more diversified financial innovations being developed, more structured financial arrangement among the financial institutions, core companies and the

[9]Ibid 5.

[10]Mathis and Cavinato (2010).

upstream and downstream SMEs could be made as well. Examples may include risk security cushion pools, and industrial funds led by leading companies. All these "derived" financial innovations could help foster the long-term healthy development of an ecosystem for all enterprises across the supply chain.

Apparently, the supply chain finance will involve in big data, factoring, and investment banks in the future development. At the same time, internet technology and internet finance will play an increasingly important role as well. Financing through internet technology will likely be an irresistible trend. However, it needs to be realized that the process that will integrate supply chain finance and online technologies could be complex. The transition for supply chain financing from offline to online via a secure and convenient system may pose some challenges.

Among the various players in online and offline supply chain finance, new and traditional enterprises may have different starting points with different advantages and disadvantages. Online platforms, such as Alibaba and Jingdong, have gathered large numbers of trading companies around their e-trading platforms, and collected various types of transaction data. Their unique positions would allow them to be easier for selecting higher quality borrowers, and selling the less risky assets to vast numbers of investors. Therefore, it is highly likely that these big companies may dominate the supply chain financing industry in the future.

Reference

Mathis, F.J., and J. Cavinato. 2010. Financing the global supply chain: Growing need for management action. *Thunderbird International Business Review* 52(6):467–474.

Chapter 8
An Alternative Link Connecting Industry with Finance—Financial Leasing

As a highly popular industry rising quietly and quickly, financial leasing has been paid an increasing attention in the capital market, and more and more diversified business models have been developed. Different from traditional financial services, the financial leasing company aims to combine financing and acquiring the right of using real assets. This unique way of financing reflects both the growing trend of China's financial leasing market and the general direction of China's financial industry. Meanwhile, it is also an inexorable trend for small and medium-sized enterprises (SMEs), the mainstay that could determine the future development of Chinese economy, to understand and undertake the financialization of some seemingly-nonfinancial-activities. As a result, the financial leasing company could play a huge part in relieving the financing difficulties of SMEs, and therefore, greatly benefits the society. This chapter will give a detailed discussion on: (1) financial leasing's function in relieving the financing difficulties of China's SMEs through its unique business model, and (2) the risk control and development prospect of financial leasing. In addition, this chapter will also explain the reasons why financial leasing is a more effective financing tool through a case study of CMC Magnetics in the photovoltaic industry.

8.1 The Definition and Development of Financial Leasing

If the past decade be the golden age of real estate in China, then the coming decade should be meant for the financial services industry. As a newly emerged financial service, financing leasing tactfully combines financing and leasable real assets, gaining increased popularity in an age that SMEs are suffering funding shortage.

Financial leasing is an arrangement where the lessor, based on the requirements of the lessee for leased items and suppliers, purchases leased items from either the lessee or suppliers and then has them rent out (back) to the lessee. The lessee pays rentals in installments to the lessor. During the leasing contract period, the lessor

J.G. Wang and J. Yang, *Financing without Bank Loans*,
DOI 10.1007/978-981-10-0901-3_8

has ownership over the leased items, while the lessee has the right to use them. When the lease has expired, the lessor transfers the ownership to the lessee at a nominal cost. Therefore, financial leasing is similar to the financial service provided by commercial banks' mortgage: to meet with the financing demand of money-borrowing companies (or lessee), the financial leasing company (lessor) pays for money-borrowing companies (or lessee) or their designated recipients, thereby achieving the financing goal of money-borrowing companies.

Financial leasing is a new financial service in China. With the combination of financing and leasable real asset, the financial leasing providers have the option to recall and dispose of leased items when something goes wrong. Consequently, borrowing companies' credit and guarantee are less required in financing, which better suits the need of financing of SMEs.

The current capital market in China is still underdeveloped, which is especially true for SME financing. It is therefore extremely pressing to expand the financing channels for SMEs. Financial leasing features a relatively simple procedure for financing SMEs: an extendable time of using capital, an actual right to use leased items which is the ultimate goal of financing, and a flexible payment method. Since financial leasing can receive preferential tax treatment, shorten project operation cycle, and prevent interest rate risk and possible exchange rate risk, it is more and more becoming a preferable choice for SME financing.

The modern financial leasing model originated from the United States in the 1950s, and undertook a rapid expansion across the globe due to its distinct advantages. Financial leasing is now the second major financing method, only next to the bank loans, in developed countries in Europe and North America. Its global transaction scale has exceeded USD $700 billion.[1] In China, financial leasing has been developed for just about 30 years since China's reform and opening-up in early 1980s. Until now, financial leasing has been growing into a mainstream financing method in aviation, health care, printing, industrial equipment, shipping, education, construction, and some other industries, and has facilitated the steady and rapid development of the respective industries. By the end of June, 2012, there were some 400 registered financial leasing companies with most being foreign-funded, and the outstanding bond fund amounts to RMB 1.28 trillion.[2] By the end of 2013, there were more than 1000 financial leasing companies, explosively increasing by 466, with about 420 foreign-funded, compared to the beginning of the year.[3] As a fast growing financing service, the financial leasing in China is undoubtedly a sunrise industry which is full of opportunities and developmental potential.

[1]http://paper.people.com.cn/gjjrb/html/2011-03/16/content_769847.htm.

[2]*China Financial Leasing Industry Report, 2012,* the blue book of Chinese lease issued by the Ministry of Commerce of the People's Republic of China Department of Circulation Industry Development.

[3]*China Financial Leasing Industry Report, 2013,* issued by China Leasing Alliance.

8.2 How Financial Leasing Model Works?

In China, financial leasing companies can be basically classified as: (1) subsidiary financial leasing companies that are set up by commercial banks under the supervision of China Banking Regulatory Commission (CBRC), such as China Construction Bank,[4] Bank of Communications,[5] China Merchants Bank[6] and China Minsheng Banking Corp. Ltd.[7]; (2) financial leasing companies whose equity shares are held by large equipment manufacturers, such as Caterpillar Inc.[8] and Zoomlion Heavy Industry Science & Technology Co. Ltd.[9]; and (3) independent financial leasing companies which belong to neither commercial banks nor manufacturers, such as CIT Finance & Leasing Corporation,[10] and International Far Eastern Leasing Co. Ltd.[11]

Regarding the registered capitals of the financial leasing firms, the bank-set-up firms are born with advantages in capital source. Due to cross-selling opportunities from other businesses of the commercial banks, they enjoyed greater business sources than independent financial leasing companies. With the access of customer credit reporting system, and airplanes, ships, and other high-value-leased-items, they have a stronger risk management capability. However, on the down side, these firms may have little competitive edge in the exit mechanism of leased assets, especially in industries such as engineering machinery.

In contrast, the capital source of manufacturers-owned financial leasing firms relies primarily on the good balance sheet of manufacturers, and funding source

---

[4]China Construction Bank (simplified CCB) is one of the four biggest banks in China. In 2015 CCB was the 2nd largest bank in the world by market capitalization. http://www.forbes.com/sites/liyanchen/2015/05/06/2015-global-2000-the-worlds-largest-banks/.

[5]Bank of Communications is one of the largest banks in China, http://www.forbes.com/sites/liyanchen/2015/05/06/2015-global-2000-the-worlds-largest-banks/.

[6]China Merchants Bank is the first share-holding commercial bank wholly owned by corporate legal entities in China. "A Guide to the Top 100 Companies in China", Wenxian Zhuang and Ilana Alon, 2010.

[7]China Minsheng Bank is the first bank in China to be owned mostly by non-government enterprises. https://asia.boschsecurity.com/ap_product/05_news_and_extras_2/02_general_2/2014/q3_2014/solution_1/bosch-security-systems-china-minsheng-bank-integrated.

[8]Caterpillar Inc. is the manufacturer of construction and mining equipment, diesel and natural gas engines, industrial gas turbines, and a wide offering of related services. http://www.caterpillar.com/.

[9]Zoomline is mainly engaged in developing and manufacturing major high-tech equipment in the areas of agricultural, building, energy, environmental, and transport engineering, and it is a continuously innovating global enterprise. http://en.zoomlion.com/.

[10]CIT provides lending, leasing and other financial and advisory services to the small business and middle market sectors, http://www.tisunion.com/portal/company-i-2714.dhtml.

[11]International Far Eastern Leasing Co. Ltd. provides financial leasing solutions to businesses. It also offers financial management, business operation, asset management, and management consulting services. http://www.bloomberg.com/research/stocks/private/snapshot.asp?privcapId=232672369.

from bank credit, and the business advantages of manufacturers. Accompanied by their selling operation, manufacturers-owned financial leasing firms enjoy a strong advantage in the source of leasing assets—as long as they maintain good cooperation and effective communication with equipment sales system. Familiar with the industry of the leased items and clients, manufacturers-owned financial leasing firms do have a stronger advantage in risk control. In addition, there is no doubt that they have extra strength in exit mechanism, because of their relationships with manufacturers in reproduction and sales of second-hand equipment, which is incomparable for other financial leasing companies.

For the independent financial leasing companies, on the other hand, they have little advantage over all capital source, business source and exit mechanism. Due to their independence, however, they may have more freedom in choosing clients with better credentials, which, generally speaking, will equip them with stronger risk control capacity.

Considering the way of the operations, financial leasing can be classified as:

(1) Direct financial leasing, which is a business model where the financing leasing providers purchase leased items, such as equipment, directly from suppliers designated by money-borrowing firms, and have it leased out to the borrowing firms with rental charges. The financial leasing providers, with their ownership of the leased equipment during the leasing period of time and the rental payment, grants money-borrowing enterprises with the right of possession, use, and benefit of the leased items during the leasing contract term. When the leasing term expires, the financial leasing provider transfers the ownership to the money-borrowing enterprises at a nominal cost.
(2) Leaseback, which means that money-borrowing firms sell their ownership of equipment or other fixed assets (leasable items) to the financial leasing providers, and then, sign a leasing contract with the financial leasing company for these leasable items, and regain the ownership after the lease expires. When the lease term matures, the financial leasing company will transfer the ownership of the leased items back to the borrowing firm at a pre-negotiated price. Leaseback is a self-financing model which is similar to the bank loan with collaterals, except for that the "borrowing" firms receive the real assets such as equipment directly, instead of receiving money first, then using money received to purchase the real assets.
(3) Leveraged lease, also known as balanced lease, rent-reducing lease, or on-equity trading financial leasing, is a unique business model of financial leasing that is widely used worldwide at present.[12] The leveraged lease, as the name stated, need to be completed with financial leverage. There are at least three parties involved in the leveraged lease: the fund lender, the lessor and the lessee of the leased items. The lessor pays 20–40 % of the acquisition cost of leased items, and the rest being provided in the form of loan by banks or other financial institutions as a lender. The legal ownership of leased equipment,

[12]http://wiki.mbalib.com/wiki/%E6%9D%A0%E6%9D%86%E7%A7%9F%E8%B5%81.

however, belongs to the lessor. In many developed countries, therefore, the lessor can enjoy a tax reduction that is calculated according to the acquisition cost of equipment under the tax law there.[13] Under this model, the lessor maintains the ownership of the leased items, lease contract and right to collect rent for banks or financial groups as a guarantee to get the loan. The lessee pays rentals for the leased items to banks or financial groups, and, after the deduction of reimbursement loan and interest in an agreed percentage, pays the rest to the lessor.

Financial leasing possesses stronger financing capacity. First, it contains leverage. According to the "Regulations on Financial Leasing Companies", the required capital sufficiency ratio of financial leasing companies is 8 %, which allows domestic financial leasing companies to have risky assets 10 times higher than their net assets. Meanwhile, the "Regulations on Foreign-capital Leasing Companies", in general, requires that foreign financial leasing companies can't have their risky assets more than 10 times higher than their net assets, which enables financial leasing companies to finance externally with financing leverage at least a 9:1 ratio. Second, financial leasing can provide finance based on the net value of leased items after depreciation, which is about 3 times higher than having it mortgaged (at a discount of 30–40 %) to banks for credit financing.

The primary profit source of financial leasing comes from interest margin × leverage + revenue of intermediate businesses (Table 8.1).

As a new way of funding, financial leasing, compared with bank credit and trade credit, has some distinct features. First, the lessee has the right to choose the most needed equipment, propose for equipment replacement, determine the amount of investment, and bears no responsibility on the depreciation of equipment. Second, the lessor provides the fund which is guaranteed by the ownership of equipment, thereby bringing the non-performing loan ratio to a low level. Third, the average term of financial leasing is consistent with physical life cycle of the equipment, which ensures timely replacement of leased items.

In addition, compared with direct purchase, the financial leasing has a significant influence over lessee's financial statement, a financial strength which is conducive to the tax and earnings of the lessee. On the whole, financial leasing is more suitable for the equipment financing of small and medium-sized enterprises. In overseas market, financial leasing are usually promoted through tax shield, accelerated depreciation, tax credit, among others.

For SMEs in China, financial leasing can provide the following advantages:

(1) Less down payment and financial pressure. Generally speaking, financial leasing requires borrowing companies to pay a small amount of cash deposit or a small proportion of down payment, which greatly reduces the amount of down payment of the borrowing companies, and therefore relieves the SMEs' financial pressure.

[13]Ibid 12.

Table 8.1 The primary profit source of financial leasing

Source of revenue	Descriptions	Comments
Net interest margin	Banking-type companies: 4 % and above; manufacturer-type and independent companies: 2 % and above	Banking-type companies have financing channels with lower cost
Leverage	Traditional source of leverage: bond, loan, inter-bank borrowing, and changes in equity financing. New source of leverage: trust, asset securitization, investment funds of leasing, insurance fund, and factoring	Leverage is limited by regulations set up by regulatory agencies: the upper limit of banking-type companies is 12.5:1, and the upper limit of manufacturer-type and independent companies is 10:1. Currently, the average leverage of banking-type companies has reached its upper limit, while specialized leasing companies generally have their leverage below 5:1. In general, bank loan accounts for 75 % of the total financing. The Measures for the Administration of Finance Leasing Companies stipulates that financial leasing companies shouldn't accept the deposit of bank shareholders; in alternative financing, only factoring and trust are frequently used. PingAn Leasing was started in May 2013, which for the first time introduced insurance fund into the financial leasing industry
Revenue of intermediate businesses	Revenue from salvage value	Revenue from salvage value: generally from leasing business
	Fees and commissions: 1–1.5 % of the contract amount	Other revenue of intermediate businesses mainly from manufacturer-type and independent companies
	Financial consulting fees: 0.25–5 % of the project value	

(2) A lower threshold. With equipment as the leased assets, financial leasing providers could undertake a less strict due diligence than commercial banks or other financial institutions. As a result, it would be easier for the borrowing firms to obtain their finance in a simpler manner.

(3) A longer term. Financial leasing generally takes 3–5 years or even longer time to maturity, which can be viewed as a long-term financing. In addition, financial leasing features off-balance-sheet financing, which doesn't affect borrowing companies' liquidity ratio and debt ratio. If the borrowing firms

choose operating lease, then the purchased equipment doesn't belong to fixed assets, and the rentals of each term belong to expenses instead of liabilities. Compared with other financing ways, financial leasing brings debt ratio to a lower level.

(4) Preferential tax treatment, such as accelerated depreciation. With the minimum depreciation period no less than 3 years, accelerated depreciation can be chosen by companies to save tax payment.

On the other hand, the disadvantages for SMEs choosing financial leasing also exist, which may include:

(1) A narrower usage of financing. Financial leasing is limited to financing of equipment, and SMEs who need to purchase equipment but without sufficient funds. If the need of financing includes other usages as well, then financial leasing may not be an adequate tool to accomplish the task.
(2) A higher cost of financing than that of bank loans. The cost of funds for financial leasing is generally higher than that of bank loans, which is largely due to installments and longer term of financial leasing.
(3) Fixed lease leads to a longer payment period, which could be somewhat stressful for some firms. Monthly payments are, typically, a common choice which exerts repayment pressure upon borrowing companies for the entire term of financial leasing that usually lasts for several years.

Being flexible in forms of financing and with a low threshold, financial leasing is highly suitable for SMEs to obtain their badly needed financing. However, not all SMEs may be able to choose financial leasing, because fixed assets such as equipment are required to be part of "financing". If the ultimate purpose of funding is not the purchase of the fixed assets, SMEs in financing need may not be qualified to use this tool. In other words, it would be less useful for SMEs in a non-manufacturing or processing industries.

8.3 Profit and Risk Under Financial Leasing Model

Financial leasing is an alternative way of providing financial service which in essence features the combination of risk and profit. Higher profit typically represents higher risk. Financial leasing's investment return is closely linked to its associated risks, and understanding of which can help better understand the keys to financial leasing.

Financial leasing is based on leasing-assets, which, in short, means that the leasing companies (lessor) "loan" real assets instead of the funds as loaned out by banks. As a business combining financial industry and real sectors, the leasing contains both creditor's rights and use rights of real assets. The diversification of bank lending is the foundation of financial leasing. Compared with bank credit, leasing companies invest more resources to deal with the leasing of equipment to the companies that need to be financed. Considering the fact that bank loan is the funding source of most financial leasing companies, and the rentals of leasing companies should be above bank lending rate to make a profit, one may wonder why financial leasing is better than bank loan for the lessee with sound credit records. Would financial leasing increase the cost of enterprises? And where is the profit of financial leasing mainly coming from?

In concept, financial leasing companies generally can obtain a high yield which is sometimes even called "usury". In reality, however, the fee schedule for financial leasing is, indeed, not so high. For a leasing project, the revenue of financial leasing basically includes service charge, fee that is based on nominal cost of the leased items, and interest differentials of rentals and cash deposit paid by lessee as a security payment. Currently, the service charge of financial leasing is about 2–3 % of the value of the leased items, including the part that pays to intermediate agencies; the fee based on nominal cost is about 1 % of the value of the leased items, which can be waived if the fund is paid back on time; the interest rate of rentals is pretty much same as that of bank loans, and interest differentials of rentals and cash deposit are extremely limited. In theory, therefore, the yield of financial leasing should not be high. High yield of financial leasing in reality actually comes from the lower percentage of funds actually employed in a leasing project, and the high debt ratio of financial leasing companies, not completely, if any, from rentals.

First, the rate of funds actually used in a leasing project. Yield of leasing is a ratio, with the revenue as the numerator and the value of funds used as the denominator. Either increase in numerator or decrease in denominator can increase the numerical value of the ratio. Currently, since the fee of leasing project is higher than bank loan, decrease in "denominator", the fund used, is the only way to raise yield, and, at the same time, to remain competitive. Therefore, the only way to raise yield for financing leasing companies is reducing the rate of capital employed.

In practice, the funds of financial leasing companies employed in leasing project is a small amount, which is made even smaller by the participation of various kinds of external capitals and intangible assets, comparing with the total value of the leased items. In addition, there are three "non-equivalences" in financial leasing, which may be worth of some attentions:

(a) "Input capital of leasing project" is nonequivalent to "actual capital" being used. "Input capital of leasing project" represents the value of leased assets, while the "actual capital" means the actual capital provided by financial leasing companies after the cash deposit is deducted from the input capital of leasing project. Since 30 % of the input capital of leasing project is generally deducted as cash deposit, the actual capital provided by lessor is generally below 70 % of the total value of the leased items. Service charge, nominal cost, and other fees, however, are charged by the total value of leasing project.
(b) "Leasing amount" is nonequivalent to "annual fund used". Since capital has time value, the total value of fund used can't be simply calculated by nominal

amount alone, instead, should be determined by "annual fund used", that is, the nominal amount with time value. A lease is different from a loan without installment, which, in general, loaned out the input capital and get repaid back once and for all, and is synchronous with the time needed. The rentals of leasing project, however, are paid in installments during the lease term, and the actual annual fund use decrease with the payments of rentals with installment. Therefore, the nominal "leasing amount" doesn't equal to the actual "annual fund used" in a leasing project.

(c) The "Annual fund used" is nonequivalent to the "use of risky capital" as represented by cash deposit paid by borrowing firms. During the lease term, the remaining value of annual funds used continues to reduce with the repayment of rental in installments. However, the sum of cash deposit remains the same. Therefore, in the earlier stages of project, rate of capital used could be, say, 70 %, but, as time progresses, the actual capital used by finance leasing companies should be much lower than 70 % with the repayment of rentals, and the proportion of cash deposit in the remaining sum of rentals keeps growing. After the lease term has expired, financial leasing companies may already collect back all the input capital, while still hold the whole cash deposit. Service fees and nominal cost of the leased items are still charged at a pre-specified proportion of the total amount of the project. Therefore, the lower ratio of the risk capital, the higher the yield will be. In particular, financial leasing companies can further reduce the use of risk capital through various other financing ways such as trust lease, project financing, letter of credit, installments, and credit sale of equipment.

Second, debt ratio of financial leasing companies. Debt ratio of companies, for many industries, is generally in the range of 40–60 %. If the percentage is higher than the industrial average, the business will be considered with higher risk. Obviously, if the risk is under control, higher debt ratio could lead to higher yield. As financial leasing companies can usually operate at ten times leverage, it would not be a surprise if financial leasing companies can achieve higher yield.

It is a common knowledge in the financial leasing industry that the revenue from ten projects may not be able to offset the loss from one project, because the leasing companies may earn interests but lose principals. In recent years, due to poor risk control or prevention, which caused a lot of non-performing assets, many financial leasing companies have experienced loss, suspended their business, and even closed-down their shops. Failure in risk control, loss from non-leasing operations, and write-off of non-performing assets are the immediate causes of the severe loss and close-down of financial leasing companies.

In the long run, financial leasing companies will profit less from interest margin and management fees. More cash flow could come from specialized services, effective capital operations, professional technical services, trade credit from batched purchase, and disposal of used equipment.

8.4 Why Financial Leasing Is a Good Choice—A Case Study of CMC Magnetics

8.4.1 Industrial Background of CMC Magnetics

In China's A-share market, a listed PV (photovoltaic) company named CMC Magnetics[14] received much concern from media and general public back a few years ago. In August 2013, CCTV News reported that the cost of solar electricity per kWh of CMC Magnetics would soon be lower than 0.4 yuan, which, like a bomb, caused a heated discussion in the photovoltaic industry. The criticism from its rivals claimed that "it is totally magniloquent, just a laboratory technology, little possibility in commercialization."[15]

Why did the report cause such a heated disputes? What does the cost of solar electricity per kWh below 0.4 yuan mean? Since the cost of thermal power generation is already near 0.4 yuan, and production cost with the coal differs in different coal mines nationwide, so, if the cost of solar electricity per kWh below 0.4 yuan can be applied to mass production, it will directly rival traditional energies even without government subsidies. In addition, the cost of electricity per kWh below 0.4 yuan also means that traditional energies will be totally inferior to the highly effective and clean solar energy.

How was the low cost achieved by CMC Magnetics? Once a semiconductor producer, CMC Magnetics has a long tradition in technology innovations. Its industrialization rate of N-type monocrystalline silicon piece reached at 22–24 %, while the industrialization rate of N-type monocrystalline silicon piece in the PV industry in China is less than 20 %. From business perspective, an increase of 1 % of battery efficiency equals to a decrease of 6 % of the cost of photovoltaic cell components. What's more surprising is that CMC Magnetics' CFZ monocrystalline silicon piece using Czochralski process and zone-melting has its industrialization rate at 24–26 %.

The highly efficient monocrystalline silicon piece abovementioned was combined with C7 LCPV technology from SunPower[16] to build the world's largest photovoltaic power station—7.5 GW PV project. It uses C7 technology to reduce the use of expensive materials and therefore greatly reduces site area and cost of PV

---

[14]CMC Magnetics Corporation is a Taiwanese company that manufactures optical discs. Established in 1978, its factories are located in Taiwan, mainland China (Memorex, HP, Philips, TDK, Maxell) and Hong Kong (Memorex, Philips). http://www.tjsemi.com/.

[15]http://finance.qq.com/a/20130830/001043_all.htm.

[16]SunPower is the largest manufacturer of solar cell modules in the United States. Founded in 1985 and headquartered in San Jose, California, it got listed on NASDAQ in 2005. It now has more than 5000 employees, and its sales amount exceeded 2.2 billion USD in 2010, ranking the third in the global photovoltaic industry.

power generation. Complimentary with each other, CMC Magnetics' CFZ monocrystalline silicon piece and C7 system combine to bring the cost of electricity per kWh under 0.4 yuan.

In April 2014, after obtaining the permit to develop 7.5 GW photovoltaic power station in Inner Mongolia in 2013, CMC Magnetics signed a strategic cooperation agreement with Abba Tibetan & Qinghai Autonomous Prefecture Government on "Efficient Photovoltaic Power Generation Project", and won the contract of construction and operation of the project. By then, the power generation scale of CMC Magnetics reached 10.5 GW.

8.4.2 Why Financial Leasing Was Chosen?

Someone once questioned the ability of CMC Magnetics to collect adequate funding to finance such a big project. The doubt was cleared on June 7, 2014, when CMC Magnetics announced that it was developing financial leasing and factoring business lines. It therefore decided to invest 500 million yuan to its wholly-owned subsidiary CMC MAGNETICS (HK) LTD to support its financial leasing and factoring business in Tianjin. Through financial leasing, CMC fully utilized its bank credit, and its equity assets of photovoltaic power station, production line of silicon wafer, among others, were invigorated.

Meanwhile, CMC Magnetics' overseas sales revenue in 2013 increased by 6 times on a year over year basis. In their forecast, overseas sales revenue would account for a greater proportion in the foreseeable future. As a result, factoring business can be developed, and will help reduce the cost of cell procurement, transaction risks, and the cost of photovoltaic power station.

It is particularly worth mentioning that Tianjin Zhonghuan Financing Lease Co., Ltd., founded in the Tianjin East Port Free Trade Zone by CMC MAGNETICS (HK) LTD, can be viewed as a foreign-funded leasing company. As mentioned earlier, foreign-funded financial leasing companies can't have their risky assets more than 10 times over their total net assets, according to the requirements set up by China's Ministry of Commerce. That is, Tianjin Zhonghuan Financing Lease Co., Ltd. can have a 10:1 leverage with its capital scale of 5 billion yuan at most. Through financial leasing, however, CMC Magnetics can actually obtain 5 billion yuan using only 500 million yuan. It is undoubtedly an efficient while inexpensive way of financing.

Compared with the domestic cost of debt financing from commercial banks in China being generally 6–7 % or even higher, overseas cost of funds is only about 4 %.[17] If assuming that CMC Magnetics used 100 yuan of domestic funds to

[17]http://finance.china.com.cn/money/bank/yhyw/20140522/2419158.shtml.

purchase cells from SunPower, it would pay 6–7 yuan for interest. If Tianjin Zhonghuan Financing Lease Co., Ltd. used 100 yuan of overseas funds to purchase cells from SunPower and then had it leased out to CMC Magnetics, then CMC Magnetics would only pay slightly more than 4 yuan for rentals and interest. In this way, it would greatly save the financing cost of CMC Magnetics. It also means that all what financed companies need to do is to pay agreed-upon rentals and interest in installments, and they can decide if ownership needs to be transferred after the lease expires.

8.4.3 The Implications

With the mushroom growth of SMEs in China, limited funding sources for SMEs are increasingly restricting their further development. As a result, diversified ways of financing emerged at the right time. Compared with equity financing and traditional debt financing, financial leasing represents a simpler and convenient way of financing with its unique advantages for SMEs. Financial leasing can accelerate depreciation, legally reduce the income tax, improve the financial ratios, optimize financial structure, and facilitate the transactions of assets.

The case of CMC Magnetics clearly indicates the new opportunities for SME financing in financial leasing industry, especially overseas financial leasing. The targeted clients can further include overseas brunches of large Chinese companies, red-chip firms listed overseas, and overseas branches of China's SMEs whose core businesses are focused on China.

Recently, several government agencies in China enforced in succession a series of new foreign exchange policies pertaining to financial leasing, such as Circular of the State Administration of Foreign Exchange on Further Improving and Adjusting the Policy of Foreign Exchange Management of Capital Projects,[18] which simplified and adjusted the way of management of several foreign capital related issues including foreign claim, buying and selling domestic non-performing assets by extraterritorial investor, foreign leasing, outflow of profit of domestic enterprises, and personal property transferring, among others. The first article of the document is to simplify the management of financial leasing companies' foreign exchange of capital projects. These newly adjusted foreign exchange policies provided new opportunities for financial leasing industry.

[18]http://www.safe.gov.cn/resources/wcmpages/wps/wcm/connect/safe_web_store/safe_web/zcfg/zbxmwhgl/zbxmzh/node_zcfg_zbxm_zbzh/9d1e970042ac65eca47aecbb69c3a378/.

8.5 Financial Leasing in China: A Market of Three Trillions

Financial leasing in China had a rather late start in financial service industry. Before 2007, the whole financial leasing business was very small in scale and social influence as well. In the past few years, however, financial leasing has made enormous progress, which was primarily caused by more favorable policies, improvement in market environment, and rapid growth of fixed assets investment in China. From 2007 to 2012, the financial leasing market in China has expanded 30 times, and has become the second largest financial leasing market worldwide, next only to the United States. According to *China Financial Leasing Industry Blue Book, 2013*,[19] China's financial leasing balance in 2013 is RMB 2.1 trillion, increasing by RMB 550 billion (35.5 %), compared with the number at the end of 2012. Currently, it is the only industry contained in China' Shanghai Pilot Free Trade Zone,[20] which provides reduction or exemption of tax for the companies stationed.[21]

Another reason for the fast growth of financial leasing in China comes to the fact that more and more companies accept financial leasing as a way to obtain the right of use of equipment, instead of owning it first. As a result, growing demands for leasing equipment in the markets of heavy machinery, aviation, navigation, medical treatment, and some other sectors, have been observed. The number of financial leasing companies rises from 286 at the end of 2011 to 1000 at the end of 2013.[22]

However, China's financial leasing industry is currently facing the following challenges: (a) Insufficient knowledge of financial leasing. Many companies have never heard about financial leasing, or misunderstand financial leasing as a common leasing business, which may lead to less users of financial leasing in China. (b) Financial leasing deals primarily with large-scaled equipment such as airplanes and ships, while financial leasing for other equipment is relatively rare. (c) Capital of financial leasing companies primarily come from limited and monotonous sources, such as state-owned large commercial banks, and the leasing firms typically have less bargaining power to obtain funds or obtain funds with favorable conditions. Since a good sum of money is needed prior to finance a leasing project, the size of the capital of financial leasing companies determines the scale of its

---

[19]Ibid 3.

[20]China (Shanghai) Pilot Free Trade Zone is the first free trade zone in China, featuring specific supervisory policies and favorable tax treatment.

[21]Specific preferential tax treatment includes: (1) subsidiaries of financial leasing companies that are registered within the free trade zone will entitle to the export rebates; (2) upon approval, domestic financial leasing companies or their subsidiaries that are registered within the free trade zone and purchase airplanes with carrying capacity over 25 tons and usage limited to airlines overseas can enjoy a 5 % added-value tax deduction, which is absolutely a privilege compared with the standard 17 % rate of added-value tax.

[22]Ibid 3.

financial leasing business. Although financial leasing companies can operate at a 10:1 leverage, it doesn't necessarily mean that they can actually borrow that amount of money from banks. Insufficient financing channels largely restricts the development of financial leasing companies. (d) Different types of financial leasing companies have different development environments in China. In 2005, China's Ministry of Commerce issued the Regulations on Foreign-Capital Leasing Industry. CBRC also issued the Regulations on Financial Leasing Companies. However, domestic financial leasing firms in China still lack well developed system to support after years of operations, which may significantly limits the healthy development of domestic financial leasing companies. Recently, the draft of the regulations on domestic leasing has been issued,[23] and can be considered a most recent attempt to further improve the system.

In short, despite the rapid development of financial leasing in China, the industry still lacks well developed business model and supporting capital market. It is still far away from well-developed countries in terms of transaction scale and financial leasing penetration.[24] The World Leasing Yearbooks of 2011 and 2012 showed that the financial leasing penetration of developed countries is about 15–30 %. The United States, for example, had its financial leasing value over USD $500 billion, and fixed investments USD $2.29 trillion in 2011, so its financial leasing penetration was over 22 %. In contrast, China's financial leasing contract balance in 2012 was RMB 1.55 trillion, and financial leasing penetration only 4.14 %.[25] It indicates that China's financial leasing industry may have a great development potential in the future.

In October 2013, Guotai Junan Securities, one of the largest financial security firms in China, issued a report entitled "*China's Financial Leasing Industry—Not a Bank But Better Than Trust*",[26] pointing out that China is currently experiencing a development stage that features the combination of financial leasing and operating lease. Benefiting from structural transformation of the economy, consumption upgrade, and the construction of the free trade zones, car leasing, aircraft leasing, medical equipment leasing, among others, are expected to boom. In addition, China's financial leasing contract balance is expected to rise from RMB 1.55 trillion in 2013 to RMB 3 trillion in 2015, with its compound annual growth rate (CAGR) about 27 %, and financial leasing penetration will be rising from 4 % in 2013 to over 6 % in 2015.

---

[23]http://www.mofcom.gov.cn/article/b/g/201308/20130800261630.shtml.

[24]There are currently two common measurements for financial leasing penetration internationally: (1) The ratio for the lease (over 1 year) transaction amount of a country or region accounts over its total amount of investment in equipment (which is used in this book); (2) The ratio for the lease transaction amount of a country or region accounts over its GDP.

[25]http://www.rongzizulin.org/a/news/2013/1029/3511.html.

[26]Full report is accessible at: http://pg.jrj.com.cn/acc/Res/CN_RES/INDUS/2013/10/14/2631c37c-4ee6-4d5e-bef0-be25c1dcbbde.pdf.

China's financial leasing industry cannot be developed independently. Industrial transformation and upgrade should be critically supported by the transformation and upgrade of all related industries. Therefore, to transform from traditional manufacturers to industrial service providers, the service should be the core, which also can't be achieved without financial innovation and network technologies. Financial leasing should charge its rentals according to the service time and different financial products, which would be more reasonable for clients. In addition, for facilitating industry upgrade and enhancing the competitiveness of financial leasing companies, the leasing business should be run in a more professional way and need more innovations in leased-assets and leasing models. Instead of being limited to the only role of "supplement" of bank credit, leasing companies could also focus on professional financing of large-scale equipment, purchase of equipment, operating consulting service, salvage value management, and allocation and management of equipment in operating leasing. Only then can leasing companies maintain their unique competitiveness and continuously gain market shares in such a mixed market.

With the change of the growth pattern and structure of Chinese economy, there will be huge equipment financing needs, especially for SMEs, in industrial equipment, construction, printing, navigation, health care, education, aviation, and many other areas. All these changes will bring a great opportunity and a huge market potential for financial leasing industry. Therefore it can be expected that China's financial leasing industry will keep growing rapidly, acting as one of the best links connecting financial industry and real sectors, and greatly facilitate the development of China's economy for a long time in the future.

Chapter 9
Getting "Patient Capital" for Firms in "Infancy and Childhood"—Venture Capital Financing

When George Doriot founded the first institutional private equity investment firm, the American Research and Development Corporation, as one of the world's first two venture capital (VC) firms in 1946, he helped create an entirely new method of financing technology start-ups.[1] Because VCs are a "patient" capital, willing and able to accompany tech innovators through their entire growth process thanks to a higher level of tolerance for the intrinsic risks of start-ups, venture capital better serves the needs of SMEs that are in their "infant and childhood" stages of development. VCs better accommodate the characteristics inherent to these early-stage SMEs who have a higher risk of failure and no immediate cash inflows. As of the end of 2014, the funds managed by venture capitals has been estimated to have reached $195 billion,[2] and VCs became the third largest source of financing behind only commercial banking and initial public offerings.[3] In China, as technological innovation increasingly replaces relatively inexpensive labor as the key driver of the economic growth, venture capital has begun to play an increasingly important role in financing of tech start-ups. In the following sections, we would like to explore the development of venture capital—a special type of private equity investment—in China, analyze its distinct features, and summarize some instrumental takeaways.

[1]http://www.investopedia.com/articles/financialcareers/10/georges-doriot-venture-capital.asp.
[2]2015 NVCA Yearbook: http://nvca.org/research/stats-studies/.
[3]https://www.preqin.com/item/2015-preqin-global-private-equity-and-venture-capital-report/1/10599.

J.G. Wang and J. Yang, *Financing without Bank Loans*,
DOI 10.1007/978-981-10-0901-3_9

9.1 What Is Venture Capital?

Venture capital (VC) is generally defined as a type of equity financing that addresses the funding needs of entrepreneurial companies who are unable to obtain capital from more traditional sources such as public markets or banks for reasons of insufficient size, insufficient assets, or an inchoate stage of development.[4] Venture capital investments are generally made as cash in exchange for shares and an active role by VC members in the funded company.

Venture capital differs from traditional financing sources because venture capital typically focuses on young and high-growth companies. VC firms invest equity capital rather than debt funds, take higher risks in exchange for potentially higher returns, and have a markedly longer investment horizon than does traditional financing, since actively monitoring portfolio companies via board participation, strategic marketing, governance, and capital structure all fall within the potential purview of a venture capital firm following the investment.

Venture capital for these new and emerging businesses typically comes from high net worth individuals such as angel investors or venture capital firms. Since these investors usually provide capital unsecured by assets to young start-ups with the potential for rapid growth, venture capital inherently carries a higher degree of risk. As a "patient capital", however, it allows start-ups the time to mature into profitable companies.

Venture capital is also an active rather than a passive form of financing. Venture capital investors seek to add value, and not merely capital, to the endowed companies in order to encourage the company's growth and achieve, for themselves, a greater return on the investment that was made. As a result, venture capital investors typically require the endowed company to allow them active involvement in the business operations of the company, and almost all venture capitalists require, at a minimum, a seat on the board of directors.

While VC investors are committed to a company for the long haul, however, they don't usually plan to stay with the invested companies indefinitely. The primary objective of equity investors is to achieve a substantially high rate of return through the eventual and timely disposal of investments. Venture capital investors all consider potential exit strategies from the moment the investment is first presented and considered.

Venture capitalists, typically, only invest in companies who have innovative products and are in the early stages of development, endowing investments amounts of about $1 million to $10 million. However, as competition intensifies, the scope

[4]https://www.sba.gov/content/venture-capital.

of venture capital appears to be expanding towards other equity investment fields as well. In order to reduce risk, venture capitalists are now less likely to invest the full amount of their funds at once, instead preferring to space out their investment in batches.

9.2 Venture Capital Investment in China

The earliest example of a venture capital firm in China can be traced back to 1986, when a state-owned VC called China New Technology Investment Corporation was established.[5] Since then, venture capital and private equity firms, such as High Tech Investment,[6] Dinghui,[7] and Hongyi,[8] just name a few, mushroomed in mainland China. At same time, many well-known international equity investment firms, such as IDG, KKR, Blackstone, Goldman Sachs, Kalley, and Sequire, also entered into Chinese market. In the year 2014, there were 258 newly-established private equity funds in China. The total amount of investable capital was estimated at USD $19 billion, distributed over 1917 projects. The total number of exits tallied to 444; among them, 172 were conducted through IPOs.[9]

Venture capital and private equity funds typically take the form of a Limited Partnership (LP). Currently, there are three major types of LPs: domestic LPs, foreign LPs, and joint ventures of domestic and foreign LPs. Foreign LPs started to enter into Chinese market in the early 2000s. While the investment strategy of these foreign firms has become increasingly conservative due to the slow-down market and the restrictions for foreign investors in China, volume wise, they are still the dominant players in the market. Domestic LPs, on the other hand, primarily obtain funds from wealthy individuals and families; they have maintained a faster growth rate in recent years compared to their foreign counterparts, and is gradually becoming an important driving force in this emerging market.

The 1917 projects undertaken by VC in 2014 covered 24 primary industries. Among them, 503 were invested in internet, 338 in telecommunications, and 181 in the IT industry. In terms of total investment value, Internet ranked highest with $3.6 billion, followed by telecommunications with $2.9 billion, and semiconductor in third with $1.56 billion.[10]

---

[5]http://zgxinchyetouz.net114.com/.

[6]http://www.szhti.com.cn/.

[7]http://www.cdhfund.com/.

[8]http://www.honycapital.com/#.

[9]http://research.pedaily.cn/201501/20150116377077.shtml.

[10]Ibid 9.

9.3 The Procedure of Venture Capital Investment in China

9.3.1 Exploring Investment Opportunities and Selecting Investment Projects

Because the typical investment targets of venture capitalists are high tech projects, VCs, by nature, take on a higher level of risk. As a result of this risk level, it becomes of critical importance for VCs to select the "right" projects, and whether or not a proposed financing project is "right" is largely determined by the initial assessment of the project.

The primary factors that venture capitalists focus on when assessing a proposed investment project include the technical feasibility of the innovation, the net present value of future cash flow that the project can potentially bring in, and the qualification and competence of the management team. The priority order of the factors usually comes from person, market, technology to management.

A start-up's innovation (or product) is at the core of the venture capital investment, and it is the key component that venture capitalists will scrutinize when deciding whether to invest. Does the new innovation represent the future development of the industry, and can it provide some unique value that its competitors cannot? Can the technology be engineered into a physical product and commercialized within a functional time frame and with affordable financial support? Can the new product be readily protected by patent or other entry barriers, so as to not be easily replaced by other innovations? All these questions have to be adequately addressed before an investment decision is made.

In addition, because the technology or the proposed product of a VC investment is typically still in its nascent stage of development, incurring a high level of uncertainty, the qualification and competence of the entrepreneur who leads the project become critical to success. Abilities of the most successful entrepreneurs include but are certainly not limited to: acute insight regarding industry trends and developments, the ability to engineer a technical idea into a physical product, the ability to commercialize the innovation that is produced, and familiarity with various financing channels. Of course, the assessments of these qualifications of the entrepreneur team vary from VC to VC, and are subjective, personal judgments rendered by the venture capitalists.

Market potential is another critical factor that venture capitalists have to think through when considering a project. If the technology or innovation presented indeed becomes a success, then the scope of the potential market will determine the ultimate potential of the investment return—with high investment return being the main criterion that justifies the tremendous risk that the VC undertakes. Regardless of whether or not the start-up will be operating in an existing market or a brand new market, the overall market potential for the new products, the competitive advantages of the new products and resulting potential market share of the company will fundamentally influence the VC's initial investment decision.

The competence of the management team is another factor that would be carefully assessed by venture capitalists. Engineering and commercializing a technology is not a task for a single person, but rather a product of considerable team work and joint efforts. It would take the effective operation of a cross-functional and well-integrated team to make the product a success, including strong R&D, financing, and market development teams. Without able personnel in each of these critical positions, the success of the venture would become less likely.

9.3.2 Evaluation

A start-up seeking capital will submit a prospectus that addresses all possible concerns the VC may have, as well as projected future financials. If the VC assesses the prospectus favorably, they will then subject the start-up to an exhaustive series of questions regarding all areas critical to the applicants' business, and require detailed explanations for any concerns.

9.3.3 Term Negotiation

There are four major issues that need to be resolved through negotiations with the participation of attorneys, accountants and financial advisors: (a) the total funding amount and share distributions, including the valuation of intangibles or technologies the start-up may possess; (b) the positions that will be held by each party; (c) the use and limitations of the investors' rights; and (d) the method of exit by the venture capitalists.

9.3.4 Fund Transfer into the Venture

When the agreement is signed, the funds agreed upon by both parties will be transferred into start-up's account, and the joint venture will be initiated.

9.3.5 Rock and Roll

Once funds are transferred and received, the firm will be able to start or continue operations. Several important issues require the collaboration and contribution of both parties, including strategic development planning with industry selection and market positioning, appointment of a fully functional board of directors, the engagement of external experts such as attorneys, accountants and consultants, and the finding of new investors which may bring in not only new funding, but also new management concepts, new networks, and new profit potential.

9.3.6 Exit Strategy

The "patient" nature of venture capital allows venture capitalists to stay longer with the venture firm compared to financing counterparts such as short-term commercial bank loans and other short-term financing. However, venture capital is not industrial capital that targets controlling shares in a corporation, and the ultimate goal of VCs is to exit with impressive returns. In order to ensure such returns, it becomes imperative for firms to determine a time and method of exit that will maximize returns on these risky capital investments. Typically, there are four ways that a venture capital can exit: through an initial public offering (IPO), through merger and acquisition, though equity buy-back, or through liquidation. Financially speaking, an IPO is regarded as the most ideal result, while liquidation is considered the least preferable.

IPOs are generally considered the preferred method of exit for venture capitals because the shares are sold through a public bidding process, and therefore the chance for the value of the venture firm to be better assessed and priced would usually be higher. This, of course, in turn, will provide venture capitalists with a higher return on their initial investment when they ultimately decide to cash out. Meanwhile, venture firms generally also prefer the exit of venture capitalist through an IPO because the management team will typically stay intact when a company is listed publicly. In addition, the reputation that comes along with being a publicly traded company may bring the venture firm additional business opportunities that may not be as readily accessible for non-publicly traded firms. However, the downsides of the IPO, such as the higher listing cost, and more stringent regulations on operations, should also be considered by venture firms, since these could largely increase the firms' operating cost. More importantly, the possible "lock-up" period on sales of the firm's shares, which are owned by the major shareholders, may prevent venture capitalist from receiving the cash immediately after the IPO, which, for venture capitalists that needs cash immediately, may not be ideal.

Management buy-out is another way a venture capitalist can exit the invested company. When the start-up grows to a point when it begins to have relatively stable cash flows month-on-month and improved credit scores, there may come to the point at which the venture capitalists would like to exit and the management would like to take over. Although the price of the sales of the company's shares might be lower for the VCs with this method than in an IPO, the relative ease of operations in terms of time, expenses, and process may well justify the deal. Financially, since the firm's assets are the collateral, the leveraged buy-out will enable the management to use commercial bank debt funding to acquire and replace the equity shares previously held by the venture capitalists, allowing a smooth exit for both the VC and the company.

Merger and acquisition is another option that VCs may consider. When the start-up grows to certain stage, and a large amount of additional capital is needed to continue the growth, selling the firm to interested contenders may not be a bad choice if both the venture capitalists and the entrepreneurs are working towards an exit. The likely price of the shares tends to be the key for getting the parties to agree on the deal; this price usually depends upon the market position of the start-up. Finding more potential buyers could help the seller gain a more advantageous position, and allow venture capitalists to exit with higher rate of return on their investment.

Liquidation, fortunately or unfortunately, is another possibility for exit. When the venture doesn't grow as expected and turnaround seems unlikely, liquidation and bankruptcy may be the rational solution in order to mitigate losses. Terminating a venture project that clearly isn't working can still be considered an optimized solution for a given restricted conditions, and is consistent with common practice of the "real option" in corporate finance.

9.4 The Influence of Venture Capitalists on the Venture

As a high risk, high stakes investment, venture capital is not only a "patient" capital but also an "active" capital and a "value added" capital. Taking typically 30 % or more equity in the start-up and possessing substantial business knowledge and operating experience, the venture capitalist often plays multiple roles in multiple areas of the start-up's operations. In addition to merely providing finance, the VC has a hand in everything from strategic and operational plans, market positioning and marketing strategies, financial operations to the hiring of important employees.

The primary influence of venture capitalists on the start-up can be observed in several areas through their participation in board activities, their participation in the distribution of voting rights, and their control of additional investment channels.

As mentioned previously, most VCs require a seat on the board of directors upon investing. The board of directors is the highest decision-making body in a company, both in determining the direction of the firm and in resolving all critical issues regarding the way the firm is run. Participation in the board will not only allow the venture capitalist to best understand the day-to-day activities of the start-up and monitor its operations but also enable the VC to fully exert its influence on the invested firms. As a result, VCs typically hold board member positions in the companies in which they invest, and in many occasions have the final say in major management decisions.

The voting rights of board members depend on the type of equity stock that they hold. Only common stock shareholders possess voting power. Many VCs, however, hold convertible preferred stocks, in such a manner that it allows them to balance the risk they are undertaking while giving them voting rights when needed.

As shareholders of preferred stock, venture capitalists are able to receive fixed dividend income regardless of rain or shine, which reduces the risk of their venture, while the "convertible" nature of their equity allows them to "convert" their options from "risk control" to "decision making" in a timely manner when they consider it necessary or appropriate. The existence of financial vehicles such as convertible preferred stock provides VCs with a convenient method of balancing the risk and return on their investments.

In addition, the venture capitalists can exert influence by helping obtain new funding sources for the start-up. Through the networks that successful VCs have established through years of operating in financial and real sector industries, VCs can help companies locate new funding sources if and when the VCs themselves may choose to stop investing in the company. In addition to funding, VCs can also contribute industrial experience, management skills, and other non-financial resources.

9.5 The Challenges Facing Venture Capital in China

The importance of the private equity fund, in general, and venture capital, in particular, is gradually being recognized in China, and VC's role as an alternative method of equity funding to the traditional commercial banking system for SMEs, especially tech start-ups, has proven to be irreplaceable. In China, however, where it is a new market yet without adequate regulation, the venture capital industry faces tremendous challenges.

First is the issue of funding sources. Currently, the primary funding source of venture capital is the funds from individuals in the private sector. Typically, individual VC investors prefer short-term investments with high returns but with high risk. Number wise, there are a lot of these types of investors, but the capital each individual can invest is relatively limited. When it comes to the capital requirements for investments of relatively longer duration, these funds from individual investors will likely prove insufficient.

In addition, the financial tools that VCs use to facilitate the investment transaction are also currently inadequate. For example, the high yield-bond that is commonly used by venture capitalists in leveraged buy-outs in developed countries is not well developed for venture capitalists in China. As a result, finding sustainable funding sources for venture capital appears to be a critical issue that needs to be resolved in order to ensure the healthy development of the venture capital market in China.

The second challenge to VC growth is exit outlets. Not only are the exit options currently quite limited, the Chinese equity market is also not well developed. The high entry barrier to going public may discourage the active participation of VCs from engaging in the funding of early start-ups, given the interconnection of the primary market and pre-IPO markets such as PEs and VCs. From 2006 through June 2013, there were a total of 14,244 venture capital investments. However, there

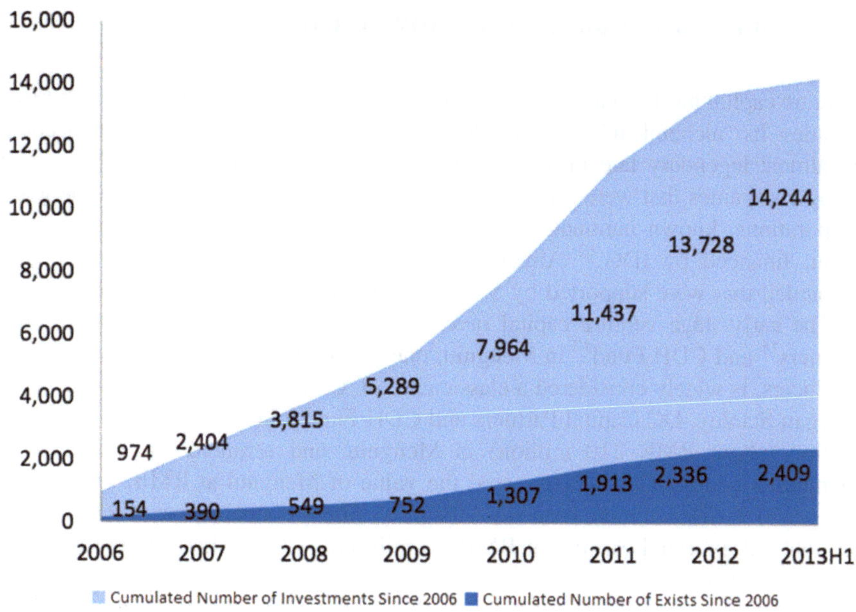

Fig. 9.1 Ratio of investment/PE from 2006 to 2013 H1. *Data Source* Qingke Research Center (http://research.pedaily.cn/201501/20150116377077.shtml)

were only 2409 exits (16.9 %) during this 7.5-year period of time.[11] As more and more private equity funds and venture capitalists approach maturity in their investments, insufficient exit from start-ups could critically deter the growth of these firms (Fig. 9.1).

The third challenge is insufficient regulation of the venture capital market. Because VC is still in its early stage of development in China, there are significant discrepancies between what the market needs and what actually exists by way of regulations. As a result, the transactions in the VC market are exposed to an unnecessarily higher level of risks.

The fourth challenge is a lack of experience across the board, from venture capitalists to the start-ups themselves, due to the nascent nature of the industry. As a specialized profession, the market always requires seasoned VC investors who possess adequate knowledge in finance, economics, and management, in addition to valuable experiences in the industries in which they're investing; however, because the market is so young, seasoned VC investment professionals with long-running experience tend to be short in supply. Meanwhile, the start-ups in which the VCs invest are typically run by their founders, who sometimes lack the adequate knowledge or background to run a publicly traded (or pre-publically-traded) firm. Professional management personnel with adequate training and extensive industry experiences sometimes aren't quite in place yet.

[11]Ibid 9.

9.6 Some Case Studies of VC Investments

Venture capital has been a notable player in China's financial market in the past two decades. Its "alchemical" ability to "touch a stone and turn it to gold" has become an almost legendary tale inside and outside the financial markets in China, and many companies that were initially financed by venture capital have become giant corporations, known nationally and internationally, such as Baidu, Tencent, and Sohu, financed by IDG,[12] Alibaba invested by Softbank,[13] and Jingdong and Paipaidai, that were supported by Sequoia,[14] and that's just to name a few.

The early-stage venture capital investment by Morgan Stanley,[15] DC Capital Partners[16] and CDH Fund[17] in Mengniu, one of the largest Chinese dairy products producers, is widely considered a classic case of VC investment in China. In 2002, Morgan Stanley, DC Capital Partners and CDH Fund jointly invested USD $25.97 million (about RMB 210 million) in Mengniu, and acquired 49 % shares of Mengniu's equity. The VCs assessed the value of Mengnui at RMB 400 million using a 10 % discount rate, based on Mengniu's after-tax net income of RMB 33.44 million and expected earning of RMB 40 million in 2002. The resulting PE ratio was about 10 times.

Since the investment was incredibly high risk, mitigating the risk during the fund transfer from the VCs' accounts to the account of the company became the key to success. After the investment fund had been received, actual performance of a venture ended up being way off what was promised by management team, especially when measured against standards in China then, but that was not uncommon. In the end, VC required that the shares held by the management team will only receive 10 % of the earnings of the investors' shares in the first year. Until the promised target was hit, the shares held by Mengnui's management team could not receive the earnings as other common stock shares. Luckily, Mengniu's management team survived and hit their mark.[18]

In 2003, these three venture capitalists, again, jointly invested an additional USD $35.32 million (about RMB 290 million) in Mengniu's overseas parent company. With a cumulative investment of RMB 500 million, the VCs held 34 % of total shares with a market valuation of RMB 1.4 billion and a PE ratio 7.3; the decrease in PE ratio came from the consideration of increased risk that the venture capitals were undertaking as they put more eggs in the same basket. As a result, the valuation of the invested company was relatively lower.

---

[12]http://www.idgvc.com/.

[13]http://www.softbank.com/.

[14]http://www.sequoiacap.cn/en/.

[15]http://www.morganstanley.com/what-we-do/investment-management/merchant-banking/private-equity-asia/.

[16]http://www.cdcgroup.com/.

[17]http://www.cdhfund.com/.

[18]http://www.rztong.com.cn/newshtml/201010/ns68974.shtml.

In June 2004, Mengniu successfully went on to IPO on the Hong Kong Stock Exchange. With sales of 350 million shares, Mengniu collected HK $28 billion, with a PE ratio of 19. Through this IPO, the three venture capitalists cashed out for HK $392.5 million with sales of 100 million shares combined. The initial venture equity investment of USD $61.2 million (or HK $477 million) by the venture capitalists earned them HK $392.5 million cash and 31.1 % of outstanding shares of Mengniu, and, after converting the convertible bonds, a market value of HK $1.9 billion.

This case proves, if nothing else, that the rate of return on a venture capital investment is remarkable if the investment is successful. The founder of the Mengniu, Niu Gensheng, maintained 4.6 % of the firm shares with a market value about HK $200 million when the IPO was completed.

9.7 The Future Development of Venture Capital in China

Financing, investment, management and exit are widely considered the four basic functionalities of private equity funds, a category which includes venture capitalists. Though venture capital is a newly developed market, and progress and improvement in every area are needed, exit could become a major focus in the near future, a forecast supported by the fast growth of national and regional equity exchange centers such as the New Third Board, a national equity exchange system. As of the end of 2013, about 30 national high-tech zones issued supporting policies such as local government subsidies and tax refunds to promote New Third Board listing, and over 600 companies are already listed on the New Third Board. In particular, the launching of the market maker system effectively vitalized the market, and activated the equity transactions (Fig. 9.2).

Meanwhile, as new players such as commercial banks, trust funds, and security firms also enter into this market through asset management and other channels, the competition in the pre-IPO market is likely to become increasingly intense. Since venture capital may not have much advantage over these late-comers in terms of volume of funding and operational experience, venture capital may have to focus their investment targets on companies in the very early stage of development—namely, start-ups—which gives venture capital their market positioning as "value creators."

Of course, despite being an early stage investor, VCs must be aware that the function of post-investment management and value added services may also become critical. Such services could directly impact the probability of the venture's survival, the time that the venture capital has to stay with the firm before exiting, and, of course, the return on their investment upon sale of the equity. Given the vast amount of choices in companies and the relatively limited expertise in terms of the industry coverage, VC collaboration with third party experts in terms of post-investment management for the venture may become a feasible and ideal solution for many VCs (Fig. 9.3).

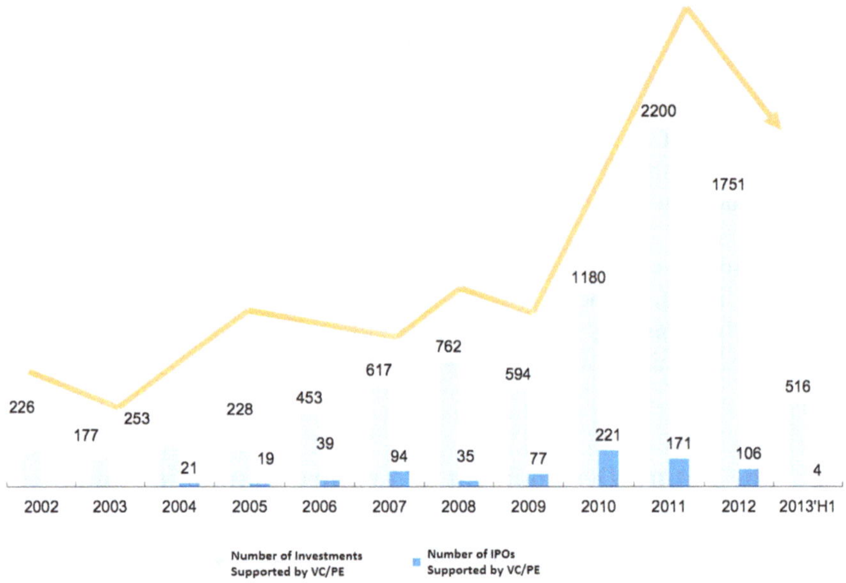

Fig. 9.2 Number of IPOs supported by VC/PE from 2002 to 2013 H1. *Data Source* Qingke Research Center

Fig. 9.3 Exit via M&A from 2008 to 2013 H1. *Data Source* Qingke Research Center

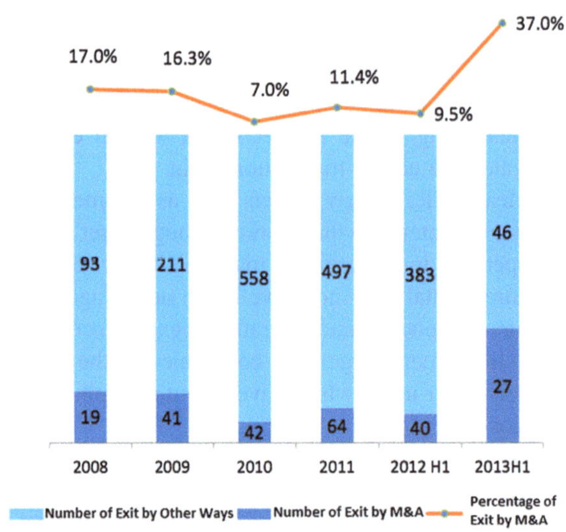

It may be worth noting that merger and acquisition supplanted IPO as the leading exit method in 2013, which may or may not signal a transitional phenomenon. When China's SEC ordered a temporary abeyance of IPOs, merger and acquisition flourished, as it provided VCs with an alternative exit method. Even though China's M&A market is far less than mature, and the valuation of venture firms could also be much lower than that through IPO, without other more attractive selections and with pressure to exit, VCs, for a while, didn't have a choice. It can be expected that, as the IPO is reinstated and the New Third Board and other regional equity exchange centers are launched, the percentage of venture capitalists choosing M&A as an exit outlet will accordingly decrease.

Chapter 10
All Roads Lead to Rome—Reverse Merger Financing

Reverse Merger, also known as reverse takeover or reverse IPO, refers a way of financing that a private company acquires a majority of the shares of a public company or "shell company" with relatively low market value by injecting its own assets into the shell company, and then uses the shell company as a vehicle to make the parent company go public.[1] In general, the shell company may change name after reverse merger. As an important "detour" to convert a private entity into a public company, reverse merger takes the advantages of relatively high efficiency and low cost to go public, and circumvent the high IPO requirements to obtain the access to the capital market for the SMEs with urgent financing needs in China.

All roads lead to Rome. No matter it is the well-known classic case for reverse merger, such as GOME Electrical Appliances Holding Limited (Hong Kong Stock Exchange Code: 493)[2] and Haier Electronics Group Co., Ltd (Shanghai Stock Exchange Code: 01169),[3] or the relatively recent event of Geely Holding Group (Hong Kong Stock Exchange Code: 175)[4] that caught the last train right before the toughened rules for reverse merger was issued, their successes set up great examples for other companies, even though they may not be duplicated exactly. The rules and regulations about reverse merger in China have been changed a lot, and a stricter standard and more complicated procedures were finally placed. In September 2013, following the new regulations, Beijing Zhongchuang Telecom Co Ltd lifted its veil on restructuring, and it was probably one of the most interesting cases of reverse merger in the history of A-share market in China.[5] This chapter will discuss reverse merger as an alternative way of financing for SMEs in China, and

[1]http://www.investopedia.com/terms/.
[2]GOME Electrical Appliances Holding Limited is one of the largest privately owned electrical appliance retailers in Mainland China and Hong Kong. http://www.gome.com.cn/.
[3]Haier Group is a Chinese multinational consumer electronics and home appliances company. http://www.haier.com/.
[4]Geely Holding Group is a Chinese multinational automotive manufacturing company. http://www.geely.com/.
[5]http://e.chinacqsb.com/html/2013-09/30/content_381657.htm.

J.G. Wang and J. Yang, *Financing without Bank Loans*,
DOI 10.1007/978-981-10-0901-3_10

use Zhongchuang's case as example to show how private companies go public through reverse merger, and what are the benefits and risks associated with reverse merger.

10.1 Why Take a Back Door?—The Motivations for Reverse Merger

The financing is always a challenge facing the SMEs worldwide, but it is especially true for the SMEs in China, as discussed in other chapters of this book. Obtaining public equity, apparently, is one way to resolve the issue. In general, there are two basic approaches for a private company to get access to the domestic stock market: initial public offering (IPO) and reverse merger. In China, there were 279 private companies successfully going public through reverse merger, out of the totally 410 public listed companies, up to the end of year 2007, which was about 68 % of total listed companies.[6] In 2014, about 52 firms took reverse merger, increasing 3 times comparing with 15 firms in 2013.[7] The statistics reflects that reverse merger has become a major pathway for private firms, especially for SMEs, to access the equity market in China, with the relatively larger scale and lower cost.

Comparing with IPO, reverse merger represents several distinct advantages, in terms of simplified reviewing procedures, reduced cost of intermediaries, shortened process time, and much less strict financial threshold. As the shell companies are typically the ones without operations or on the verge of bankruptcy, the acquiring private companies can often easily become the controlling party of the new, merged firm. It is, indeed, a convenient detour for the private firms, especially SMEs, to get access to the public equity market, compared to conventional IPO.

If we look back the history, it can be seen that the development of reverse merger for private companies in China has experienced three major stages: The first one is the initial start-up stage (1992–1999). In the year of 1994, Hengtong Corporation purchased 12 million shares of state-owned Lengguang Industrial Co. at the price of RMB 4.3 yuan per share to hold 35.5 % of total equity of Lengguang, which initiated reverse merger for private companies in China.[8] However, restricted by the multiple factors, such as the understanding of the reverse merger concept, policy stance towards the reverse merger, stock market quota, and some other factors, at the time, there were very few private companies that actually went public through either IPO or reverse merger during that period of time.

The second stage can be described as a spur growth stage (2000–2013). Since 2000, China has adopted an approval-based IPO system to replace the previous quota system, and also launched the new policy to allow the listed company to issue

[6]Peng (2011).

[7]http://stock.10jqka.com.cn/20141208/c568830838.shtml.

[8]http://guba.eastmoney.com/news,600696,50496426.html.

new stocks one year after the reorganizations. As a result, the reverse merge became a popular financing tool and developed rapidly. In the year of 2013, there occurred a wave of reverse merger in China, and many reverse mergers came out at this time. This wave of reverse merger was truly policy driven, and also significantly influenced by "auditing storm" and the expanded shut-down of IPO window in A-share market by China's SEC.[9]

The third stage is the maturity stage (2014-present). China reopened IPO in 2014, and the registration-based system, instead of approval-based system, for IPO was proposed and implemented.[10] In addition, China Securities Regulatory Commission (CSRC) issued a stricter regulation for reverse merger, and raised the standards for back door listings as almost same as IPO's.[11] As a result, the market expectation tends to consider that the shell resources will move into a long way of depreciation.[12]

The motivation for SMEs to undertake reverse merger as an alternative way of financing can be further categorized and analyzed as follows. Comes first is to gain better financing opportunity. With listing through reverse merger, the acquiring company will have better access to the capital markets in the form of issuing additional stock through seasoned new issue or share allotment. The cost of seasoned new issue is usually lower, compared to IPO, and the pace of the issuance is also faster. According to present regulations, the listed company could issue share allotment up to 30 % of total equity,[13] and such equity financing could help lower down the firm's debt ratio and improve the company's repayment ability for the outstanding debt. In particular, the acquiring company could improve the management and enhance the stock price through the reorganization and restructuring of the shell company after the reverse merger is completed. This is an important reason why so many private companies prefer reverse merger.

The second motivation is the simplified listing process. In general, the reverse merger doesn't need to go through all those review process as did by IPO, either under approval or registration process. As a result, the time needed to complete the reverse merger would be much shorter. In addition, the financial disclosure required is also much less.[14]

The third one is the increased company's reputation, brand image, and better advertising effect. The public traded companies typically enjoy greater popularity in the market with increased awareness and recognition among market participants. Apparently, reverse merger can help private companies, especially SMEs, extend the influences and gain faster growth through the "augmentation" effect of publicly traded companies. For instance, several Chinese SMEs, such as Yorkpoints and

---

[9]Ibid 5.

[10]http://money.163.com/special/xgfxgg2013/.

[11]http://www.cs.com.cn/ssgs/gsxw/201312/t20131210_4239450.html.

[12]Ibid 8.

[13]http://www.csrc.gov.cn/pub/newsite/zjhjs/zjhnb/200904/P020090423500392960851.pdf.

[14]http://research.pedaily.cn/201108/20110831229618.shtml.

TCO, Powerise Information Technology Co, Sichuan Topsoft Investment Co., and Chengdu Unionfriend Network Co.[15] were all less-known regional companies. After reverse merger, however, they quickly received name recognition nationwide. As a result, their businesses were greatly boosted.

Finally, it comes to the change in the company type and governance structures. Through reverse merger, private companies are changed into publicly listed companies. As a result, the structure of ownership is changed, and the external shareholders are introduced. Correspondingly, a modern enterprise will be established, and the corporate governance structure will be improved, which, in long run, will greatly benefit the company's sustainable growth. In particular, in China, going public may also help the acquiring company to obtain more supports from local government.

10.2 No Free Lunch—The Cost and Risk of Reverse Merger

There is no free lunch in this word, as is often said, and so is reverse merger. While it is a convenient short cut for private company to gain public status, there are also, and always, risks associated with it. Among all these risks, comes to the first is the risk to fail in the debt restructuring of the shell companies. One of the keys for success of a reverse merger lies in a fact that the acquired shell is a "clean" one. "Clean" shell means that the acquired shell company doesn't contain undisclosed debts or other pending liabilities stemming from sources such as litigation or guarantee responsibility, which will significantly reduce the value of the shell company. Many merger and acquisition failed due to the overpayment of the acquired companies. The risk comes from the difference between acquiring company's perception or expectation about shell company and the real financial conditions of shell company. In China, the validity of financial and accounting information, even for the listed companies, is not strictly monitored and audited. Many debts or liabilities were not accurately recorded on company's book, which made the degree of asymmetric information even more severe. Apparently, without the successful handling the original debt and liabilities of shell company, the acquiring company would encounter tremendous risk, and the reverse merger may fail finally.

The second risk comes from the failure in reorganization and restructuring of the shell company, when the original owners of the shell company still have stakes in the post-reverse-merged firm. According to a research report from Shanghai Stock Exchange,[16] the entire performance of the listed companies through IPO are much

[15]http://www.szse.cn/szseWeb/FrontController.szse?ACTIONID=15&ARTICLEID=1377&TYPE=0.

[16]Lu and Zhang (2004).

better than the average performance of all listed companies in Shanghai and Shenzhen Stock Exchanges, while the listed companies through reverse merger generally performed poorly. One of the primary reasons is the difficulty in the successful integration of the acquiring company and shell company into an efficient and well performed entity, when the shell company is not just a pure "shell". The acquiring company and shell company could be different in many aspects, including management style and corporate cultures. As a result, the possible conflict between two parties may hinder a successful restructuring and consolidation of the newly merged firm.

The third risk could be the overpayment of the shell company. Like buying a stock at higher price than true value may lead to loss of the investment, the overpayment of the shell company may cause the failure of the reverse merger. Due to the scarcity of the shell resources from time to time, the price of a shell firm may become very expensive and over-priced at certain time point. In particular, if the acquiring company wants to execute a takeover through the secondary market, it may raise anti-takeover objection, which will result in a brutal war and kill the cash flow enormously. Therefore, if acquiring company didn't pick the right deal time and cut the deal with right price, the post-reverse-merged company may face liquidity issue and un-favored market valuation of the firm, and cause difficulties for the firm to refinance in the secondary market, which is typically the real goal of reverse merger.

Another possible risk is the failure to pass the review process. Reverse merger in China deals with multiple regulation agencies and must go through a required reviewing process. It can be finally launched only after all the required reviews and scrutiny are passed. Failure to pass any one of reviews will lead to delay the entire process, and even may cause the failure of reverse merger. Therefore, the acquiring company and the shell company must communicate timely and efficiently with the reviewing agencies during the whole process. In particular, the shell companies, as the very few listed firms in China, are often the previous star companies in the local area, regardless if it is state-owned, and received much attentions and support from local government even when they went down. Therefore, acquiring companies, especially for those nonlocal acquiring firms, need to fully communicate with local government for many issues that could be sensitive locally.

In order to mitigate the risks, there are several strategies that can be taken by acquiring companies during reverse merger. Comes first is the thorough due-diligence on shell company. Pick up an appropriate shell could be the most important step in the entire reverse merger process. A clean shell and its intrinsic value are closely related to the purchasing price of the shell to acquiring company, and the quality of shell may determine the final result of reverse merger. Therefore, it requires the acquiring firm to fully understand the impact of the shell company selected, and search for the shells with desired ownership structure, no or less pending liabilities, so as to purchase a shell with expected value.

The second is to compare the cost and benefit of a reverse merger, and make a prudent decision. The costs of reverse merger include the cost of the shell, reorganization, injection of the acquiring firm's asset into the shell after reverse merger, and operations of the post-reverse-merged firm. The benefits of reverse merger will include the revenue earned by sales of the asset of shell company, and the proceeds received in the following seasoned new issue and share allotment in the stock market. A careful benefit and cost analysis should be conducted before the decision about the reverse merger is made.

The third one is to make an effective financing and reorganization strategies. Because a reverse merger usually involves in a large amount of asset transfer, an appropriate financing schedule needs to be well prepared. Typically, the assets in loss or inconsistent with business direction of the post reverse merged firm should be sold out to repay the possible debt incurred by financing the reverse merger. In addition, a complete reorganization and restructuring strategy should be planned and implemented, which include the adjustment of operations and the placement of human resources and various assets.

10.3 A Successful Reverse Merger Case in A-Share Market

In China, reorganization is an eternal issue for all corporations, especially for those ST stocks that are facing the risk of termination of listing.[17] Meanwhile, for those private companies, especially SMEs, that are unable to get access to the public equity market, reverse merger undoubtedly is a favorable choice to circumvent the strict review requirements, save the processing time, and improve the financing efficiency. The regulations on restructuring of eight key industries including steel, cement, automobile, and others, issued by central government in 2012,[18] provoked a storm of reverse merger.

In September 2013, one of the largest reverse mergers arose in A-share market in China. Beijing Zhongchuang Telecom Company, a listed shell firm with market value of RMB 1.17 billion, announced the reorganization plan that an acquiring company, Beijing Xinwei will purchase Zhongchuang as a shell company through a seasoned new issue of total RMB 30 billion in value plus assets injection into the shell company. The transactions included that Zhongchuang, as a public shell firm, would issue around 3.13 billion shares to purchase 96.53 % of Xinwei's equity amounting to the value of 26.88 billion yuan. Meanwhile, Zhongchuang planned to issue additional shares worth of 4 billion yuan in the secondary stock market. Xinwei's revere merger case was widely considered as "an elephant swallowing a snake".[19]

---

[17]ST stands for Special Treatment. The stock exchanges take "special treatment to warn the risks of termination of listing" and mark "ST" in front of the company abbreviation to differentiate it from other stocks. (source: Finasia, a Division of Taiwan Economic Journal).

[18]http://www.miit.gov.cn/n11293472/n11293832/n15216906/n15217002/15218043.html.

[19]http://www.chinadaily.com.cn/hqgj/jryw/2013-10-10/content_10285781.html.

This is a case for a much bigger company back door listing through a small shell company, and the market responded vehemently. Since the announcement and Beijing Zhongchuang resumed trading in the market, its share price continuously rose in the following eight consecutive days, accumulatively, up by over 95 %. In just a few days the market value of the shell company surged by RMB 1.1 billion, almost doubled its initial market value. After reverse merger, Mr. Wang Jing, CEO of Beijing Xinwei owned about 1.2 billion shares of the post reverse merger firm that were amounted to 31.66 % of total 3.78 billion shares,[20] and became the controlling shareholder of Beijing Zhongchuang.[21]

After the reorganization, the major business of Zhongchuang was turned into the systematic solution and technical support for broadband wireless communication industry and Internet Service Providers (ISP). With a joining of a proficient technical team in research and development in 4G broadband wireless communication system, the post-reverse-merger company will greatly enhance its competitiveness in product design.

The key question is why Beijing Xinwei choose reverse merger to gain the listing company status? Beijing Xinwei, established in 1995, was a subsidiary of state-owned Datang Telecom Technology and Industry Co. Xinwei abandoned GSM, the 2nd generation of mobile communication technology which was developed by Europe for 15 years, and invented its own SCDMA communication system. Since China's Ministry of Industry and Information allied with ISP to start the project of extension of radio and TV broadcasting to every single village in 2003, SCDMA system had been put in massive production, and Xinwei once achieved the annual output value of 2 billion yuan at that time.[22] In 2006, Xinwei submitted its IPO application to Shenzhen Stock Exchange. However, the request was denied by CSRC due to various reasons. Until 2009, when Wang Jing reorganized Xinwei to become a private firm, Xinwei resumed its process of going public.

As time goes by, however, the market for SCDMA withered gradually as China would issue 3G licenses. In just several years, the sales of Xinwei plummeted to less than RMB 100 million, and the total number of employees dropped from 2800 to about only 400. The total loss reached almost RMB 400 million, and obviously, its IPO request then was rejected again.[23] Meanwhile, Datang Group agreed Xinwei to become a privately owned firm. Mr. Wang Jing then invested 95 million yuan to receive 41 % of Xinwei stock, and thus became the biggest shareholder of the firm. In the subsequent years, Datang Group gradually reduced its holding in Xinwei

[20]The Reorganization Report issued by Beijing Zhongchuang, the full report is available: http://www.cninfo.com.cn/finalpage/2014-03-15/63679897.PDF?COLLCC=2084428101&.

[21]Nicaragua's Congress granted Mr. Wang's Cayman Islands-registered HKND company a 50-year concession to develop the canal in 2013. The plan is to build a canal to connect the Caribbean with the Pacific Ocean in Nicaragua and the total cost of canal is estimated to be around USD $40 billion. Source: http://baike.baidu.com/view/2092513.htm.

[22]Financing and Accounting Report in Beijing Xinwei Prospectus, full report is available: http://stock.jrj.com.cn/share,600485,ggcontent.shtml?discId=00000000000000r2fz.

[23]Ibid 22.

from 43 % to currently 6 %, and faded out finally from the firm's decision making.[24]

There are several reasons for why Xinwei chose reverse merger to go public. In the year of 2012 and 2013, the major business income of Xinwei came from the sales of communication equipment and relevant software to foreign customers such as those in Cambodia and Ukraine. The total business income of Xinwei in 2012 was 900 million yuan, and this number climbed to 1.99 billion yuan in the first half of 2013.[25] However, large chunk of these revenues were accounts receivables, which amounted to 555 million yuan in the end of 2012, and surged to 2.49 billion yuan on June 30, 2013, which means 85.8 % of Xinwei's business income during this period of time came from accounts receivables.[26]

The issue was that most of Xinwei's foreign customers were in those less developed countries, which cannot provide any basic collateral for financing these projects, and also, would not be willing to sell their domestic resources or open key fields for trade to exchange for financing. On the other side, Xinwei was in a rush to spread its communication network overseas, and thus, even further provided guarantee for these deals. For example, just for Cambodia project, Xinwei offered 2 billion yuan guarantee. As a result, Xinwei was holding large amount of accounts receivables with high default risk, and may not get pay back for many years. Shortage of cash will become a natural consequence.

Another issue is the cash out of private equities (PEs). Back to 2010, the price of Xinwei's share was only 1 yuan, after nearly 10 rounds of PE financing, however, Xiwei's share price surged to 50 yuan with the highest bid reaching 79.2 yuan. It was these equity financings from PE made Xinwei's net asset increased by almost 4 billion. However, while PEs were looking for exit to cash out their investments, Xinwei's money was running out in the projects such as these in Cambodia and Ukraine. As a result, Xinwei needs to find a short cut to quickly get access to the public equity market.

The third reason for Xinwei to rush to back door listing might be the emergence of 4G market. Xinwei needs funding to seize this huge market before the 4G era actually comes. But the long waiting period of time for IPO in China made it impossible for Xinwei to timely receive the funding it needs. Since October 2012, CSRC closed the door for IPO, and the companies on the waiting list were counted up to 774 in 2013, while many firms cancelled their IPO applications.[27] Therefore, the action taken by Xinwei to pursue the reverse merger was apparently a workable alternative.

In addition, the shell company Zhongchuang's major businesses were the monitoring and maintenance system of communication network as well as the testing machine of communication network, which is exactly the downstream business of Xinwei. As a result, if Xinwei acquired Zhongchuang, it not only received the status of

---

[24]http://tech.sina.com.cn/zl/post/detail/t/2013-09-27/pid_8435367.htm.

[25]Ibid 20.

[26]Data come from Zhongchuang reorganization report—financing and accounting report.

[27]The numbers here are quoted from Flushing Financial Information.

public company, but also gained supply chain advantages. Zhongchuang's resources, including both physical assets and human resources, could be directly and conveniently integrated into Xinwei's assets portfolio. Meawhile, Zhongchuang was a quite clean shell, and it had small market value, not sophisticated internal structure, and the largest market share in machine and monitoring areas, all of these factors made Zhongchuang a good target to be chosen.

10.4 How Far Could Reverse Merger Go in China in the Future?

The private companies, especially SMEs, in China have gone through a fast growth period of time in the past years, and they have been gradually becoming a vital component of Chinese economy. However, the financing difficulty is still the biggest issue facing the SMEs, and the reverse merger provided an alternative path for these firms to break the ice and obtain the access to the capital market. However, the reverse merger has been proved to be a double-edged sword for SMEs, and there are pros and cons, as analyzed earlier, associated with the reverse merger. While timely seizing the opportunity of obtaining equity financing through a back door, the private SMEs should fully identify the possible risk of reverse merger, and exercise prudent risk controls.

For the privately-owned SMEs, how to find a desirable shell to conduct a successful reverse merger could be a challenge. One possible way is to search from the well-developed industries aiming at the firms taking reorganization and restructuring. Another one is to focus on those firms with Special Treatment (ST) on their stocks with explicit expectation on reorganization and restructuring. For investors who are interested in stocks with reverse merger firms, they should consider about the quality of injected assets, and fully understand the fundamentals and financials of the post-reverse-merger firms. Two types of shells can be considered, one is the company which previously failed in reorganization or reverse merger, because it is generally a better shell resource, and thus more attractive; another one is the firm in the industries with excessive capacity such as steel, aluminum, cement, which is more likely to look for reorganization.

Also, regulations will play an important role for reverse merger and risk control. Reorganization and restructuring has become one of important channels for capital market to allocate resources since China basically completed the dual-share-structure reform in 2006.[28] As an alternative to IPO, reverse merger once got overheated and even causing concerns about the possible speculation bubble.[29] As a response, CSRC issued "The Announcement to Strictly Implement IPO Standard for Reverse Merger Review", stating clearly that the stricter IPO review

[28]http://stock.cngold.org/school/c2882560.html.

[29]http://news.cnstock.com/news/sns_yw/201312/2828589.htm.

standard should be applied to reverse merger cases, and no reverse merger is allowed in Growth Enterprise Board.[30] Such an action from regulators undoubtedly raised the bar for reverse merger, and prevented the speculations on penny stocks. As a result, it should be reasonably expected that higher quality assets will be filled into the shells through reverse merger, and the speed of growth for reverse merger could gradually be slowed down, but a quality market will emerge for the years to come.

References

Lu, X. and W. Zhang. 2004. *The study of developments of private companies listed in stock market in China*. Shanghai Stock Exchange Research Report.

Peng, X. 2011. The condition, motivation and suggestion for reverse merger in private companies in China (in Chinese), *Finance and Accounting Monthly* issue 4.

[30]http://www.csrc.gov.cn/pub/newsite/flb/flfg/bmgf/ssgs/bgcz/201402/t20140218_243967.html.

Chapter 11
An Equity Market for SME Start-Ups—New Third Board

The year 2014 marked a new milestone for the development of China's multi-level capital market when China's National Equities Exchange and Quotations (NEEQ) system was officially launched.[1] As it was different from the previous "Old Third Board", an Equity Transfer System which was set up in 2001 and only undertook the exiting firms from the main boards such as Shanghai and Shenzhen Stock Exchanges, and some other equity shares owned by "legal persons",[2] the NEEQ was called "New Third Board", because it adopts the new comers of the equity market, such as start-ups, as well. For the SMEs in China, especially for these tech-oriented start-ups, the New Third Board provided a new alternative to access the equity capital from general public. As it can be expected, listing on the New Third Board has been keenly sought after by SMEs since its inception. Therefore, what is exactly the New Third Board and what is new about it? What is the nature of its unique business model, and what kinds of advantages and risks for SMEs using the NEEQ? This chapter is intended to provide the answers to these questions.

11.1 What Is New Third Board?

In China's financial industry, there are three layers of equity markets or boards. The first layer or the "First Board" is composed of the "main boards" such as Shanghai Stock Exchange and Shenzhen Stock Exchange, including its SME (Small and Medium Enterprises) Board. The second layer or the "Second Board" is the Growth Enterprises Board for the smaller enterprises with growth potentials. The listing requirements on these boards all include financial performance metrics such as earnings and market cap.[3] In contrast, a market that were composed of some

[1]http://www.neeq.cc/.
[2]http://stock.hexun.com/2013-11-27/160053534.html.
[3]http://finance.ifeng.com/a/20150612/13773482_0.shtml.

J.G. Wang and J. Yang, *Financing without Bank Loans*,
DOI 10.1007/978-981-10-0901-3_11

regional equity exchange or share transfer centers with much less strict terms for listing for these exiting firms from main boards back in early 2000 was called the third board, or the "Old Third Board". In January 2014, when the NEEQ was officially launched in Beijing's Zhongguancun Science and Technology Park, the "New Third Board" was formed and was successfully put into operation on May 19, 2014.

The origin of this new market can actually be traced back in 2006 when China's financial administration piloted a quotation system for enterprises in China's four high-tech parks in Beijing, Shanghai, Tianjin and Wuhan. Afterwards, the China's State Council released the *Decision of the State Council on Issues Related to the National Equities Exchange and Quotations* (NEEQ) in December 2013.[4] The *Decision* clearly specified that NEEQ will be a national equity trading platform to primarily provides financial services for the development of innovative, entrepreneurial, or growth-oriented micro, small and medium-sized enterprises. All qualified domestic companies may apply for a quotation on the NEEQ for the purpose of public transfer of shares, equity and debt financing, and restructuring of firms. Very soon, the pilot project was expanded out of the four parks to the entire nation.

As of the end of 2015, over 5000 companies have been listed on the New Third Board, comparing to less 3000 firms on the main boards. The scale has overtaken both the GEM (Growth Enterprise Market) and the SME boards that were focused on the smaller and growth oriented firms.[5] Companies on the New Third Board have carried out over 500 additional targeted share issuances since 2010, and 401 such issuances from January 2014 to November 2014 alone. In terms of financing scale, one billion Yuan was financed on the New Third Board in 2013, RMB 13 billion in 2014, and 61 billion over the first half of 2015, as disclosed by some financial information and security firms.[6]

The value of the NEEQ lies in its functionality and ability to provide equity financing for SMEs, especially for these tech-oriented startups. The tremendous difficulties and high cost of financing for SMEs in China are widely acknowledged. Despite a history of over 20 years, the two major security-trading-exchanges in Shanghai and Shenzhen only listed 2828 companies, which meant that only about 100 companies were listed, on average, every year.[7] It was estimated that there were about 70 million SMEs of various types in China,[8] so the number of the listed companies, percentage wise, was extremely small. Therefore, it was very insufficient to only rely on the two primary security-trading-exchanges to improve or significantly improve the ratio of direct financing for Chinese companies, especially for SMEs.

---

[4]Ibid 1.

[5]Ibid 1.

[6]WIND and Guotai Junan Securities: http://www.wind.com.cn/, http://www.gtja.com/i/.

[7]http://money.163.com/15/1226/06/BBO8PNDM00251LIE.html.

[8]Wang, J., deputy director general of small business administration, MIIT, China, http://business.sohu.com/20150713/n416677759.shtml.

Meanwhile, there are also increased number of private equity investors, including angels and venture capitals, that provide equity funds. While these funds are willing to take higher level of risk, they are also seeking high returns when the proper way of exits is set up. As a result, the launching of the NEEQ was a timely response to the market need for the exit channels for private equity funds, which, in turn, will help improve the financing of SMEs in China.

11.2 What Are New About the NEEQ?

There are several distinct features of the NEEQ in comparison with the main stock exchanges. From the perspective of listing requirements, there are fundamental difference between the NEEQ and the main boards including SME and GEM boards, even though all NEEQ, Shanghai, and Shenzhen Stock Exchanges are national equity trading venues. In Shanghai and Shenzhen Stock Exchanges, the listing firms must meet some basic financial requirements, such as net income over RMB 10 million for two consecutive years for GEM board, and cumulative net income over RMB 30 million for three consecutive fiscal years for main boards and SME board, in addition to some other requirements in terms of equity value, business scope and corporate governance.[9] In contrast, the NEEQ is primarily dedicated to providing financial services for innovative, entrepreneurial and growth-oriented start-ups, and there is no financial threshold at all for listing, which perfectly match the status of the start-ups that typically don't have cash inflow at the moment but with tremendous growth potential in the future and need equity capital investment.

From the perspective of investors, the Shanghai and Shenzhen exchanges are characterized by a large number of individual investors. Over 85 % of the transactions on the equity exchanges were conducted by these individual investors.[10] In contrast, the investors of NEEQ are pretty much institutional ones. As the majority of the companies to be listed are start-ups with higher risks, the NEEQ requires a higher threshold, such as legal entities with a registered capital of over RMB 5 million or individuals with financial assets of over RMB 5 million, for investors to participate. Therefore, the NEEQ is basically an equity market for institutional or wealthy individual investors, because they, in general, have better risk identification ability and higher risk tolerance level.

From the perspective of listing procedures, there is also distinct difference between main boards and NEEQ. While the companies to be listed on all main boards including SME and GEM boards are required to obtain an approval from China Securities Regulatory Commission (CSRC), the companies to be listed on

[9]China Securities Regulatory Commission: http://www.csrc.gov.cn/pub/newsite/flb/flfg/bmgz/fxl/201012/t20101231_189708.html.

[10]Securities Times: http://news.stcn.com/content/2012-06/27/content_6051682.htm.

NEEQ only need to "file" with the exchanges, given that the listing conditions are satisfied. The primary requirements for listing include two consecutive years' continued business operations, stable operational ability, distinct core business, and with growth and innovation potentials.[11] As a result, the process becomes much simpler and the time of listing becomes much shorter, decreasing from more than 6 months to about 5–50 work days.

From the perspective of information disclosure, under the requirements of listing on the NEEQ, the primary issue for the listing-company-to-be is the standardization of the firm's financial and accounting information. The financing firms need to adjust and report their financial statements in compliance with the generally accepted accounting principles (GAAP), and set up an effective internal control system to guarantee the validity of the company's information. In particular, the NEEQ requires the disclosure of information of the listing firms specific to their particular industries, regions, and stages of business development, which will help facilitate the selections of the listing candidates by professional investment institutions.

From the perspective of the ways of transactions, the NEEQ offers multiple choices for the ways of share transfers while all the main boards only take one way, the centralized auctions, to conduct equity exchanges. At NEEQ, one option provided is to trade the shares by mutual agreement, through which both parties can transfer shares at mutually-agreed-upon price and quantities. Another option is through a market-maker system, where trading parties rely on one or several intermediary entities, "market makers", to maintain the liquidity and activeness of the market. When one side of trading is missing, the market maker will have the responsibility to buy or sell the shares to complete the transaction, and maintain an active market and pricing. The third one is a centralized auction system which can help the listing firms with sound financial conditions to switch to the main boards or the GEM board.[12] These three systems run in parallel, and the listing firms can make choices according to their needs.

It is worth mentioning that the NEEQ, or the New Third Board, is the first stock exchange in mainland China that takes the form of for-profit-corporation[13] that is similar to these world major exchanges such as New York Stock Exchange and Hong Kong Stock Exchange. In contrast, all the main boards in China were classified as non-for-profit legal entities, and organized as an affiliation of China Securities Regulatory Commission (CSRC). NEEQ's taking the form of for-profit independent corporation indicates the progress in China's financial industry, and the intentions of Chinese government to run the NEEQ in a more effective, efficient, for-profit, and business way, instead of less effective, less efficient, non-for-profit, and administrative way. This change may also provide a reference for the further reform of China's Shanghai and Shenzhen Stock Exchanges in the future.

[11]Ibid 1.

[12]Ibid 1.

[13]Ibid 1.

11.3 What Did the New Third Board Bring to MSME?

The value of the NEEQ, as mentioned earlier, lies in its functionality and ability to provide equity financing for SMEs, especially for these tech-oriented startups. The characteristics of start-ups of high risk, no immediate cash inflow, and lack of credit history, among others, made it tremendously difficult to obtain debt financing from traditional commercial banks, and the NEEQ timely fill a critical gap by providing the badly needed equity capital for start-ups. However, the benefits that NEEQ can bring to the SMEs, in general, and start-ups, in particular, can go far beyond that. Some primary values or benefits may include the following:

(a) Improved corporate governance

An effective and efficient corporate governance is a prerequisite for SMEs to gain access to public financing, and a foundation for the sustainable development of SMEs. The start-ups, however, are typically strong in technology, but deficient in business management and corporate governance. In this case, listing in NEEQ can help bring external helpers to improve the corporate governance of start-ups. During the process of listing, the professional intermediaries such as security firms, law firms and accounting firms can help the listing companies to set up a modern corporate governance structure, standardized operating procedures, and effective internal control mechanism in compliance with the requirements of Chinese regulators.

(b) Additional exit for early-stage investors

Financial investors, typically, are not life-time partners of the listing firms. They need proper exits, at certain point of time, to cash their stakes and receive the returns on their investment. A convenient exit for early investors are critical for the start-ups to attract adequate angel and venture capital or even PE funding for their projects. As a result, the launching of NEEQ provided such a widely needed outlet for the early equity investors, which, in turn, will provide stronger motivation for them to invest in the start-ups.

(c) Value identification and determination

Through listing on the NEEQ, the market value of the listing firms will be fully identified through share transfers and trading among the buyers and sellers or through market makers. As a result, the complete value and growth potential will be more thoroughly and effectively explored through market mechanism. In practice, many listing firms received higher valuation by investors, partially due to increased liquidity and clear way of exit.

(d) Open the door to full direct financing venues

The features of "smaller-scale, faster speed and on-demand financing" for SMEs to be listed on NEEQ will not only enable the listing firms to get access to the common stock type of equity capital, but also open the door to other forms of financing products such as corporate bonds, preferred stock and other financial products.

(e) Credit enhancement

As publicly traded companies, the listing firms on NEEQ may also gain the credit enhancement through listing. Audited financial statements, required information disclosure, revealed growth potential and market-priced value all increase the credibility of the listing firm. So, when they also pursue the indirect financing such as commercial bank loans, they may be able to receive better credit ratings and reduced financing costs. In addition, the increased credibility may also help their product sales in the market.

(f) Lowered barrier to enter into equity market

In comparison to GEM and SME boards, the NEEQ has less rigorous listing requirements. Only two years' business continuity is required without financial performance metrics, and the qualification of listing firms are left to the security firms for determination.[14] As a result, NEEQ lowered the barrier for the start-ups to get access to the equity market.

(g) Shorter period of listing time

Since the approval from the Securities Regulatory Commission for listing is not needed, and the security firms can decide whether to recommend the listing of the firms, the listing process and the time required becomes much shorter, which can typically be completed within 60 days in the NEEQ, comparing with over 9 month process time for listing on the main boards. Convenient procedures will save much time and effort for start-ups to be listed.

11.4 What Did the New Third Board Bring to the Early-Stage Investors

The benefits that the NEEQ can bring to the market are not only for start-ups and MSMEs, as mentioned earlier, but also for early stage investors such as angles, venture capitals (VC), and private equities (PE). As the early-stage investors, what they most concerned, in addition to finding valued investment targets, is how they can exit smoothly and profitably with decent rate of returns from their early investment. Or, in other words, the early-stage investors could weigh "prudent exit" over "good start". One of the issues facing VCs and PEs earlier was the failure of the listed start-up and MSMEs in the "Old Third Board" to switch to the GEM, SME and other main boards. When the board switching fails, the exit of the early-stage investors could become difficult, even though it is not totally impossible. Therefore, the launching of the NEEQ will significantly increase the

[14]Ibid 1.

opportunity of "prudent exit" for the early-stage investors, which, in turn, will greatly increase the motivation of PE and VC investments on start-ups and MSMEs.

Statistics showed that until May 2014, nine companies on the NEEQ had been successfully switched to the main boards or the GEM board, including Century Real Technology, Beilu Pharmaceutical, Join-cheer Software, Bohui Innovation Technology, Thunisoft Corporation, Jiaxun Feihong Electrical, Kyland Technology, Guangdong China Sunshine Media, raising a total of RMB 4.417 billion through IPO. Among them, Beilu Pharmaceutical and Century Real Technology have brought huge returns for VC/PE institutions that have invested in these firms.[15]

It is worth mentioning that the better chance of exit of investors brought more technology-oriented start-ups, such as Internet-related firms, to the NEEQ, which helps the early-stage investors to conveniently explore and select the investment targets. The collection of the tech-oriented start-ups within one "showroom" helps greatly the investors facilitate their search of investment targets, and reduce their search costs. In addition, comparing with the start-ups that are not listed on either NEEQ nor other boards, the degree of transparency of these firms listed in NEEQ is much higher. As a result, for the early-stage investors such as VC and PE, investment on companies listed on the NEEQ will take less risk.

11.5 The New Third Board: Issues and Risks

Sometimes, people may mistakenly equalize the quotation in the NEEQ to the listing in the main boards, and assume the quotation on the NEEQ will secure a large amount of equity financing like IPO. In fact, it is not the case. Quotation in the NEEQ simply means that the previous non-listed-companies can receive independent and individual inquiries from potential investors for their shares, but does not guarantee that the listing companies can actually acquire the expected equity financing and obtain the needed liquidity. Because of the higher risk of the listed firms and relatively less investors, the actual funding that the listing firms are able to receive may be less than expected, at least, at the beginning. As a matter of act, the lack of liquidity is one of the major issues for the companies listed in the NEEQ, as evidenced by the low transaction volumes.

Several policies and actions have been taken by the regulators since 2014 to solve the liquidity issue of the NEEQ. On August 25, 2014, China Securities Regulatory Commission officially introduced the market-maker system, and 43 listing companies became the pilot firms using market-maker.[16] It was expected that market-maker system will be gradually extended to other companies on the NEEQ

---

[15]"In-depth Case Study of New Third Board", Forward-looking Investment Consulting Co., Ltd.

[16]http://finance.sina.com.cn/roll/20140829/182220164067.shtml.

as well, and become one of major ways for the trading in the NEEQ, which will significantly improve the liquidity of the Board.

Another way of trading adopted in NEEQ is the collective auction mechanism, which may also help eradicate the issue of liquidity. The collective auction mechanism will be operated by the principle of "price priority and time priority", which intends to provide the continuous auctions for the listed firms in the NEEQ, and prevent any possible price manipulations by either parties.

Regulators also indicated publicly to launch a pilot board-switching project of the NEEQ around the year end of 2015, with a main purpose to open up a pathway for NEEQ listed firms to switch to the GEM board, where the market is much more liquid. So, if companies that have achieved the standards of full-fledged enterprises through development in NEEQ need more liquidity, they can be upgraded to the GEM board or the emerging strategic industries board on the Shanghai Stock Exchange.[17]

Apparently, the current threshold on investor side for participation are indeed high, and was formulated to prevent disorder and avert risks at the early stage of the development of NEEQ. While this regulation may help make a change in the structure of the investors in China's equity market, which, currently, is primarily composed with individual investors, the further development of the NEEQ may reduce the threshold to allow smaller investors to enter, and increase the liquidity of the market.

Every coin has two sides. While the lowered threshold is easier for SMEs and start-ups to be listed on NEEQ, it also represents higher risk for the investors. It is fully understandable that the "new born" of the start-ups is accompanied by many "deaths" of existing listed firms. Only very few SMEs could survive and succeed, especially, within a short period of time. More specifically, there are several issues related with the "hidden" risk inherited in the NEEQ.

The first one is the "massive" entry of the firms with lowered qualifications. In the "Old Third Board", the NEEQ was pretty much a "showroom" for all listed companies with good financial performance, and nearly half of which actually met up with listing conditions of the GEM Board. After the New Third Board was launched, however, lowered entry barrier attracted more firms to enter, and most of which were actually less qualified firms with higher probability of bankruptcy. As a result, the risk that were encountered by the investors increased significantly

The second one is the higher likelihood of failure to be transferred to the GEM Board. The strongest motivation for investors to invest on the NEEQ is the exit through public issuance of shares after transformation from NEEQ to the GEM Board. However, with the lowered entry barrier in the New Third Board, higher percentage of the listing firms would not be able to be transferred to the higher

[17]Deng Yingling, "National Equities Exchange and Quotations (NEEQ), New Third Board and SMEs Development Forum", at "2015 China SMEs Investment and Financing Fair", July 2, 2015, http://www.sme-ifex.com/site/smeifex/othersecond/info/2014/611.html.

boards, which may lead the NEEQ more towards "Pink Sheet" market with many risky "penny stocks", instead of "NASDAQ" as many have expected.

The third one is the higher degree of information asymmetry. As the NEEQ requires less disclosure and scrutiny of the listing firms, the degree of information asymmetry was significantly increased. The external investors will face higher degree of uncertainty with the listing companies for the issues such as the firm's operations, financial performance, and the future development potentials. As a result, they will become more vulnerable for the changes in the listing companies and less protected.

The fourth one is the stock trading. The shares of the companies that are listed on the main boards, the SMEs board, and the GEMs board all can be traded continuously within the specified trading hours in the five trading days every week. Therefore, except for the cases of the price hitting the ceiling or floor limits, shares are always available or salable. However, the shares listed on the NEEQ are traded through auction in a discontinuous way, which created a risk for the investors for not being able to buy or sell shares when they need.

11.6 JD Capital: A Case Study of NEEQ Listing Firm

In April 2014, JD Capital started to be quoted on the NEEQ and became the first PE firm listed on The New Third Board.[18] As WIND data showed, by December 29, 2014, 1534 companies were quoted on the NEEQ with a total revenue of RMB 12.64 billion, of which JD Capital took up RMB 4.549 billion, accounting for 36 % of the total revenue and ranking the first place.[19] Since the announcement of listing on the NEEQ, JD Capital remained at the top position for a long period in terms of stock turnover. Any secrets are behind?

11.6.1 JD Capital—"Listing Workshop" of SMEs

The Kunwu JD Capital Co., Ltd (JD Capital) is a professional investment firm specializing in equity investment and management. As a benchmark firm of China's PE industry, JD Capital was selected as a classic case of the Harvard Business School due to its unique "JD Model" for "customized listing". According to Zero2IPO's ranking of China's Private Equity Investment Firms, JD Capital ranked first among "China's Top 50 Private Equity Companies" in 2011 and 2012, and received the "Award of China's Best Private Equity Investment Company".[20]

[18]http://www.jdcapital.com/.

[19]http://www.wind.com.cn/.

[20]http://www.zero2ipo.com.cn/en/.

Since its inception, JD Capital has revealed its uniqueness in many ways. For example, most founders of other famous PE firms in China have overseas working experience and seek funds from the largest and most well-known LPs (limited partners) in Europe or North America. In Comparison, JD Capital is much more local, but both its founders and many employees have working experience in China Securities Regulatory Commission. Therefore, from the very outset, JD Capital has sought out its own operational way with "Chinese style", which is to concentrate on finding companies that are most likely to go public in a relatively short period of time in China. The top secret of the repeated investment success of the newly-founded JD Capital is to keep the simplicity of investment. They did not give much thought on the industries, strategies, R&D and management skills of the target company, instead, they focused on which deal will allow them to exit fast. Therefore, JD's transactions were aimed at making profits though the huge value arbitrage between public market and private market, that is, the capital appreciation from the difference between PE's buy-in price and expected IPO exiting value.

Another secret of JD's success lies in JD's segmentation and capture of a group of firms that were usually ignored by PE firms. A simple and clear JD investment philosophy is that the total number of China's listed companies will likely be expanded to 8000 in 2020, but there are only over 2000 right now. Among these remaining over-5000 firms, JD expected there will be 400 large companies or state-owned enterprises (SOEs), in addition to about half of the companies with decent size. What left then will be the world of SMEs. Among these SMEs, if JD Capital can capture only 10 %, then, you talk about several hundreds of billions of RMB. Therefore, JD Capital focused at a specific segment—the large group of SMEs.

In addition, JG developed a "JD Model" to convert the invested firm to investors in a standardized way. JG serves as the "listing factory" to offer tailored packaging services for SMEs' public listing. In JD's "factory", the listing qualifications are the product standards. Huge amount of capital and corporate resources will flow into the "factory" for the selected firms, and the chosen SMEs will be forged into standardized "list-companies-to-be" in this PE factory, ready to be sent to the IPO application process. This model is of a great appeal to the large group of SMEs in China, and interlocks the industrial chain and snowballs bigger and bigger. Under this investment model, JD Capital has invested in over 200 companies, among which there are over 60 listed and to-be-listed companies.[21]

11.6.2 *Why JD Capital Chose to Be Quoted on the NEEQ?*

The way of PE operations in the capital market has been changing quietly in the past years. In comparison to the earlier business model of investing in companies

[21]PE Daily Data: http://zdb.pedaily.cn/company/%E4%B9%9D%E9%BC%8E%E6%8A%95%E8%B5%84/.

first and exiting through invested company's listing, PEs in China have made some remarkable changes by listing PE firms themselves in the capital market to obtain additional funding. JD was the first PE firm to take listing in the NEEQ, which greatly enhanced its own brand value. Before JD, there was no precedent of Chinese domestic PE firms ever doing that.

One of the reasons why JD Capital didn't choose to be listed on the main boards directly lies in the obstacle from policies and regulations. PE companies were generally founded in the form of limited liability company. According to the Partnership Law in China, "No wholly state-owned company, state-owned company, listed company, non-profit or social organization may become a general partner." If a PE firm becomes a listed company on main boards, it will no longer be entitled to be a general partner of the firm. Therefore, to be listed on the main boards, the business form of company must be changed, and a parent company or an affiliate company must be established in compliance with the regulations to circumvent the restrictions of policies and laws. As a result, before being quoted on the NEEQ, Beijing Tongchuang Jiuding Investment Capital Holding Co. Ltd. (the former full name of JD Capital) was changed to Beijing Tongchuang Jiuding Investment Management Co., Ltd. to satisfy the requirements of regulations.

Another reason is that, even if all listing conditions are met, it is still needed to wait in a long queue for listing, which deters some PE firms to go public. After being listed on the NEEQ, required information disclosure can help improve the transparency, allowing investors to know more and better about the company and make more reasonable value assessment. Apparently, the better assessment will also offer a reliable reference for value assessment in future board upgrading or switching.

However, one of the major reasons why JD Capital chose to be listed on the NEEQ this time was due to the increased exit pressure from some old Limited Partners (LPs) of the fund. In 2012, the capital market underwent a sudden change, as China Securities Regulatory Commission unexpectedly cut down the number of IPO applications, and shut up completely the IPO window in October 2012. With sharply reduced exit opportunities, PE firms encountered a harsh winter with dwindling incoming funds. Right before being listed on the NEEQ, JD Capital already had many un-exit investment projects, so many of its LPs were expected to became anxious.

In its Public Transfer Prospectus, JD Capital disclosed all current projects it invested with its equity fund. There were 185 projects under its management with initial total value of RMB 14.26 billion and evaluated value of RMB 25.1 billion. By October 31, 2013, JD Capital Management Fund was further expanded to RMB 26.4 billion and invested in 209 projects in consumer goods, services, medicine, agriculture, materials, equipment, new emerging industries, and mining, adding up to RMB 15.43 billion investment value. In terms of exit, however, JD Capital had only 24 projects exit with total investment value RMB 1.17 billion, and exit value RMB 2.7 billion.[22] The data above shows that since its establishment in 2007, JD

[22]http://www.jdcapital.com/info.

Capital had only 11.48 % of all its invested projects exit, with exit value accounted for only 7.58 % of its entire investment value. The "old" JD Capital primarily made profits through IPO of their invested companies, and with the announcement of CSRC, there were huge uncertainties about IPO exit of their un-exit invested firms in the future. As a result, JD needs badly an outlet to allow some early LPs exit with decent returns.

Another reason of JD Capital landing on the NEEQ is to increase liquidity. The firm used to focus on the traditional PE business, and began to step up efforts in mergers and acquisition after the IPO channel was closed. JD would also be possible to engage in alternative asset management or even investments in other financial institutions in the secondary market in the future. As a result, source of funding became critical. Due to restrictions on exit, however, it would be difficult for JD Capital to come up with a lot of money through the traditional way, and it would be a wise choice to explore new financing channels with the aid of capital market.

11.6.3 JD's Innovative Solutions of Listing on the NEEQ

JD's listing on the NEEQ has created a new exit channel for investors of JD Capital. The nature of JD Capital's listing is "LP Exit by Share Swap", that allows management firms to replace company stocks with LP shares, a preferred solution to the urgent need of exit for LPs.

Before listing on NEEQ, JD Capital had announced its incremental fund raising program, and proposed issuing 5.798 million shares to 138 targeted shareholders (including 131 new ones) at the price of 610 yuan per share with a targeted fund raising of RMB 3.537 billion. This fund raising was mainly targeted at old LPs of JD Capital, who could come up with an estimated basic value of all their holding shares and replace them with shares of JD Capital. All these shares were added up to three billion Yuan.[23] This was equivalent to standardize some fund shares, whose liquidity would be hugely enhanced in terms of share trading. For LPs who are in need of cashing out, shares after replacement would be more convenient for exit and could be disposed at any time in the NEEQ. LPs that choose to keep the holding shares can continue to enjoy returns on their investment through dividends or other means. This new model of LP share replacement carves out a new exit channel for investors, and help facilitate the future fund raisings of JD Capital.

In summary, JD Capital had seized the opportunity of the launching of NEEQ, and paved a new way to its financing channels. Very soon, many PE firms followed JD in pursuing the listing on the NEEQ. PE firms, such as CSM Group, Reach Holding Group, Zhejiang Thinking Investment Management, have disclosed their

---

[23]The Public Transfer Prospectus, released by JD Capital before being listed on the New Third Board.

Public Transfer Prospectus, while many other PE firms are advancing on the quotation issues in NEEQ. Under the context of IPO shut down and long queues, PE firms can get access to exit channels through share transfers on agreement, market-making trading, mergers and acquisitions, and other ways on the NEEQ. This new PE development model is indicating a new attempt of the New Third Board to offer financing services for SMEs and start-ups.

11.7 The Future Development of the New Third Board

As analyzed in the previous sections, the future of the New Third Board or NEEQ largely depends upon the quality of listing firms, liquidity of the NEEQ, and its transferability to the main boards. Among them, the quality of the listing firms may become a key. Only when the quality of the listing firms are significantly improved, the confidence of investors in these firms will be improved. As a result, the liquidity of these shares will be improved, and main board transfer will become easier. However, the improvement of the quality of the listing firms may need the improvement of the overall capital market environment in China, which may require the regulatory agencies to shift their primary focus from on financing for companies to protection of medium and smaller investors by more severely penalizing the listing firms with false financial information disclosed. It can be expected that the NEEQ, with required improvement in place, can take a important position in China's multi-layer capital market in the future.

Chapter 12
"Born to Serve the Small": Crowdfunding for SMEs

Since ArtistShare's launch in 2003, crowdfunding has emerged as a prominent alternative method of financing, especially for fundraisers and investors dealing in smaller quantity funding. In 2014, global crowdfunding was estimated to have raised USD $16.2 billion for various initiatives, up by 167 % from the $6.1 billion raised in 2013. In 2015, the entire industry is, once again, projected to grow to more than double its current size, reaching $34.4 billion.[1] In Asia, the highest growth in crowdfunding volumes was 320 %, reaching an aggregated value of $3.4 billion, and Asia became the second-largest region for crowdfunding worldwide, ahead of Europe ($3.26 billion) and trailing only North America ($9.46 billion).[2] As the fastest growing country in Asia, China has also caught onto the crowdfunding trend. As of the end of 2014, there were 128 crowdfunding platforms in 17 provinces, raising a total of over RMB 1.5 billion funds and financing over 3000 projects.[3] In this chapter, we would like to discuss the development of crowdfunding in China, and the features and issues related to this "another" alternative way of financing SMEs.

12.1 What Is Crowdfunding?

Crowdfunding is typically defined as the use of small amounts of capital from a large number of individuals to finance a new initiative.[4] Capital obtained by crowdfunding contributes to projects such as the development and production of entertainment products such as movies or albums, free software development,

[1]Massolution's 2015 CF Industry Report: http://www.crowdsourcing.org/editorial/global-crowdfunding-market-to-reach-344b-in-2015-predicts-massolutions-2015cf-industry-report/45376.
[2]Ibid.
[3]http://www.01caijing.com/html/zc/1439_8230.html.
[4]Investopedia: http://www.investopedia.com/terms/c/crowdfunding.asp#ixzz3pKi6MbDZ.

J.G. Wang and J. Yang, *Financing without Bank Loans*,
DOI 10.1007/978-981-10-0901-3_12

inventions development, scientific research, and certain civic projects. In general, crowdfunding can be classified into categories based on purpose and industry, such as rewards-based crowdfunding, equity crowdfunding, debt-based crowdfunding, litigation crowdfunding, and charity crowdfunding.

Reward-based crowdfunding allows fundraisers to provide non-equity returns on the funds received from fund providers, and can be further classified into two sub-groups: Keep-it-All (KIA), in which the financing entity sets a fundraising goal and keeps the entire amount raised regardless of whether or not they meet their goal; and All-or-Nothing (AON), in which the financing entity sets a fundraising goal and keeps nothing unless the goal is achieved. In contrast, litigation crowdfunding gives individuals the opportunity to invest in legal disputes taking place globally by allowing them to take a stake in the claim that they choose to fund. Litigation crowdfunding allows those in need of litigation to obtain funds from their peers worldwide, and if the case succeeds in court, the investors will get higher returns, thus benefiting both investor and those in need of legal counsel. Another type of crowdfunding, charity crowdfunding, is the collective effort of individuals to help finance certain charitable causes. Finally, there is debt-based crowdfunding, also known as "peer to peer lending" or "P2P", which was discussed in the previous chapter.

One of the most important types of crowdfunding, however, is equity crowdfunding, which can be used as an alternative way of financing SMEs. In general, equity crowdfunding is considered the collective effort of many individuals to fund a project or venture by a SME by providing small amounts of monetary contributions, typically via the internet, in exchange for equity in the firm. The entities involved in this crowdfunding transaction include (1) the project initiator (a SME) who lists a project or idea of theirs onto a crowdfunding platform with product specifications, funding terms, amount of funding, and expected rate of return, (2) the individuals or entities who financially support the selected ideas or projects through the crowdfunding platforms; or in other words, the investors, and (3) a moderating entity or platform that reviews and presents the projects, provides intermediary services, and brings the related parties together.

Just like in other types of equity investment, there is no guarantee in crowdfunding that the principal of the investment will be paid back through either the distribution of dividends or the sale of the equity stake or both. As a result, the qualification of the investor for participating in the equity crowdfunding is sometimes restricted for protecting unsophisticated and/or non-wealthy investors from putting too much of their savings at risk. In the US, for example, who is allowed to fund a new business and how much they are allowed to contribute is regulated by laws such as the 2012 JOBS Act.[5]

[5]https://www.sec.gov/spotlight/jobs-act.shtml.

12.2 Crowdfunding in China

At the end of 2014, the Chinese SEC issued its "Guidelines on the Management of Private Equity Crowdfunding (Draft)". Even though the detailed regulations that were expected to follow up the guidelines are still not in place yet, in terms of legal status, crowdfunding in China's financial market is widely considered to be officially recognized. As of the end of June of 2015, there were 235 crowdfunding platforms in China, including many well-established business giants such as Alibaba, JingDong, Tencent, PingAn and Wanda who had all begun to enter into this emerging sector. Several crowdfunding platforms, such as TianShiKe and ZhongTouBang, had already received their A-round venture capital investment, while, at the same time, other third-party service platforms related to crowdfunding also emerged.[6]

Of the types of the crowdfunding platforms that are currently in operation in China, there are 98 equity crowdfunding platforms (46.45 %), 67 rewards-based platforms (31.75 %), 42 mixed (19.91 %), and only 4 charity-based platforms (1.9 %). Of the projects that were financed by crowdfunding platforms, 9830 were rewards-based, 4876 were equity related, and 2976 were charity related. Within these projects, only the rewards-based projects had managed to overshoot their initial targets. The funds raised by charity type projects only reached about 50 % of the original goal, and the funds obtained in equity-based projects ended up even further below the pre-established targets. However, if we look at performance from an efficiency perspective—which is to compare the percentage of total listed projects with the percentage of the received funding—equity-type projects appeared to be the most efficient, as they received about 60.69 % of total funding, with only 27.58 % of the total projects. It is followed by reward-based, and the charity type came as the least efficient.

Comparing the average funds raised per project among the crowdfunding types, equity-type projects tended to raise the most, at about RMB 2 million per project, followed by reward-based projects' RMB 165,000, while charity-type projects tended to raise the least, only about RMB 100,000 per projects. For the number of investors, however, the order is reversed. Charity projects have the most investors across all platforms in China, 6.03 million, followed by reward-based projects' 4.26 million investors. As the most risky type of crowdfunding, equity-type projects have attracted only about 28,000 investors in China. For the average investor per project, charity type also leads with 2025 investors, followed by 433 investors for reward-based, and trailed by only 6 investors for equity type crowdfunding projects.

In terms of the completion ratio of the projects, which is another important measure of success, charity projects see the highest percentage of success at 74.7 %, followed by a 60.19 % completion rate in rewards-based projects, and a mere 7.14 % completion rate in equity projects.

---

[6]http://www.wangdaizhijia.com/news/baogao/21251.html. The statistics in the following paragraphs also came from this source unless indicated otherwise.

That charity-based projects have such a high success percentage shouldn't come as a surprise, however, as indicated in the previous paragraphs, there are currently only 4 charity-type platforms in China, projects tend to have much smaller monetary-sum goals, and a large amount of investors are typically involved; it is usually easier for charity-type projects to reach their goals. In contrast, higher fundraising goals combined with higher risk and a fewer number of investors make it significantly more difficult for equity-type crowdfunding projects to achieve a higher completion-ratio. Apparently, since the characteristics of reward-based crowdfunding integrate characteristics of charity type and equity type projects, its completion ratio is also in the middle.

Geographically, crowdfunding platforms that are in normal operations are basically located in 19 provinces in China, with most in relatively-developed coastal areas. Although itself landlocked, Beijing, as the birthplace of crowdfunding in China, possesses the largest number of crowdfunding platforms with 58 platforms. Guangdong Province comes as the second with 49 platforms; 61.22 % of the Guangdong's platforms are equity-based ones. Another top-three-area is Shanghai, with 35 platforms. Out of top-3, Zhejiang, Jiangsu, Sichuan, Shandong, and Chongqing all have 5–15 platforms respectively, while Henan, Anhui, Tianjin and Fujian all have platforms being set-up.

Of the amount of funds that were raised in the first half year of 2015, RMB 4.67 billion was collected nationwide. Among China's regions, Beijing took the lead with a total amount raised of RMB 1.65 billion, Guangdong was second with RMB 1.3 billion, followed by Zhejiang (RMB 617 million) and Shanghai (RMB 589 million). It is interesting to note that the total funds raised by these top-four regions encompassed 89 % of the total funds raised nationwide. Or, in other words, the funds raised by the rest of the country were only about 11 % of the total funds raised by crowdfunding platforms.

12.3 The Business Model of Crowdfunding

The core intent of crowdfunding is to make use of the vast networks that are easily accessible through the internet in order to announce new business projects and attract investors. With its convenience and low threshold for entry, crowdfunding can significantly increase and encourage entrepreneurship through the establishment of start-ups and micro/small businesses, while at the same time enlarge the total pool of investments by introducing these smaller investors to others outside the usual circle of owners, relatives, and venture capitalists. Crowdfunding platforms, regardless of the type, all run on commission-based business models in which the platform takes a percentage (typically 4–7.5 %) from every successfully completed fundraising project on the platform. In some cases, crowdfunding platforms may have the option to take an equity-stake in the successfully-funded businesses if they so choose, but, in general, the basic business model for crowdfunding platforms is driven by transaction volumes and the associated commissions or fees. Naturally, the more projects that are launched and funded successfully on the platform, the more profitable that platform will be.

As crowdfunding continues to grow at a fast pace worldwide, the value and risk that this burgeoning industry brings to start-ups, investors, platforms, innovators, and the economy as a whole are becoming more apparently understood. At macro level, for example, crowdfunding was projected to create 270,000 new jobs in the US in 2014, and provide more than USD $10 billion for start-ups. It was also estimated that, for every $37,702 invested in a start-up, one new job can be created; and for every $1 invested, $6.36 in revenue can be obtained.[7] In a developing or emerging country such as China, however, the value of crowdfunding as an alternative financing method could prove to be even more profound.

First, crowdfunding is, and can become even more of, a valuable funding source for the SMEs in an economy with a limited number of legal funding possibilities such as China. This lack is especially egregious for technology-oriented start-ups, who may be able to benefit strongly from crowdfunding. Given the risky nature of many young tech start-ups and the relatively smaller amounts of capital they require, these start-ups are usually not on the radar of large state-owned commercial banks who typically focus on less risky, more well-established corporations with stable cash flows; in addition, if an idea or project is in a stage at which it may not be deemed "significant" enough, economically, it may not get picked up by any angel and venture capital investors either. However, the progress of a society is, indeed, made by all innovations, even those that at one point seemed "insignifiant". These smaller innovations, if successful, will still generate millions of new jobs, significantly improve the quality of life of citizens, and create wealth. Crowdfunding can effectively provide pre-A-round funding for "smaller" innovations or innovations at a more inchoate stage of development, and prepare these projects to receive future funding in their later stages, such as by venture capital or private equity.

Another important value of crowdfunding is its role as a provider of investment opportunities for smaller investors. Because the investible assets in China that deliver relatively higher returns, such as wealth management products, have a relatively high threshold of entry as well—typically RMB 1 million or more—smaller investors are usually limited to bank investments, an incredibly low-risk and low-return activity, or nothing. Crowdfunding is allowing even the smallest investors to pursue investment opportunities with higher returns, with entry barriers that are low both financially and technically. From a financial perspective, the low minimum investment amount, as little as RMB 100 on some platforms, makes it possible for investors with limited savings but higher level of risk tolerance to participate. On the technical side, the internet is able to facilitate these investments through crowdfunding platforms, which significantly reduces the information

[7] https://www.fundable.com/learn/resources/infographics/economic-value-crowdfunding.

search and transaction costs that previously prevented many of these smaller investors from investing.

Since SMEs typically make up the majority of the total number of companies in a country and represent the most vibrate component of an economy due to their drive to innovate, this new alternative method of SME financing, especially in the technology sector, is of important value for the entire economy. In particular, for a developing and emerging country such as China, where legal sources of loanable funds are quite limited, crowdfunding can play a significant strategic role in promoting sustainable economic growth.

On the other hand, however, the risk involved in crowdfunding activities is also significant. Crowdfunding is a financing tools that funds mostly young start-ups, which inherently involves much uncertainty, and most of the projects listed on crowdfunding platforms are by companies or individuals that are then unknown to much of the public. From an investor perspective, equity crowdfunding has no guarantee, internal or external, of the repayment of the invested principal, guarantees which are typically required in the case of debt financing. As a result, there is a chance that the investor may lose his/her entire investment if the financed project fails. Even though this is true for all equity financing, it would be much more likely to happen in the case of young start-ups, such as those listed on crowdfunding platforms.

Second, crowdfunding joins together the demand and supply sides of funding, but doesn't resolve the issue of asymmetric information between the two parties, as it usually occurred in the financial market. As a result, investors, typically, always know less about the start-ups or projects, in particular, for the risks associated with the projects to be financed. Given the higher failure rate of new technologies or start-ups, the negative impact of the asymmetric information could be amplified in the case of crowdfunding.

Third, there exists fraud risk in the case of project creators. Because many fundamental regulatory policies are still not in place in China, many investment contracts are not well-documented enough to sufficiently protect the interests of investors. Since equity investments don't mandate the repayment of principal, there is an increased chance of fund requesters deceiving investors. Even in the rewards-based crowdfunding, delayed or canceled deliveries of promised products are not uncommon.

This fraud risk could also negatively impact the platforms, especially if the platform takes on the responsibility of due diligence on the projects that it lists. If fraud committed by any of the platform's project creators is identified, there may be legal repercussions for the platforms as well as the company. At the very least, the reputation of the platform will be damaged.

Finally, since regulations on crowdfunding are not completely in place yet, especially in China, the legality of certain crowdfunding platforms may be in question; in addition, when the new rules are instated, many platforms may find the rules inconsistent with their current operating practices, and potentially have to change their entire platform structure or else shut down. Unlike in the US and UK, where regulators such as the SEC and the Financial Conduct Bureau have already been designated and the laws, such as JOBS, have already been enumerated, the laws and regulations governing the operation of crowdfunding in China have not yet been explicitly announced. As a result, investment through crowdfunding platforms entails some degree of legal risk.

Of the three parties involved in this game, the firms that petition for funds—whether a start-up or some other small business—are typically considered to bear the least risk; however, this doesn't mean that they are totally risk-free. For example, if a start-up picks a disreputable or inefficient platform on which to post its financing project, it may not be able to raise the needed funds within the required amount of time. It subsequently may not be able to carry out its innovation and, as a result, lose the first-comer advantage that it had expected to obtain.

12.4 Crowdfunding Case Studies

12.4.1 An Equity Crowdfunding Platform: Zhongtou8

Located in Shenzhen in Guangdong Province, Zhongtou8 was established on January 20, 2014. Its primary customers were companies that aimed to list or were already listed on the New Third Board. Investments on Zhongtou8 can take the form of either a "lead" or a "follow" investment. In the former case, investors take the lead in the investment, playing a role like a "general partner" in a Limited Partnership (LP). In the latter case, the investors "follow" the lead investor, playing a role like a "limited partner" in a Limited Partnership. Investable products cover areas such as mobile, energy conservation and environment protection, culture and media, new materials in manufacturing, new energy, bio-pharmaceutics, consumer services, and information technology, as well as other growing industries. In addition, investors can second-hand invest in the private equity funds of the venture capital firms that invest through crowdfunding. Zhongtou8 also helps facilitate private-investment-in-public-equity (PIPE) deals, such as in the case of Guangzhou Hengda Taobao Soccer Club. Investors get access to the platform via various channels, including a PC-based website, mobile apps, off-line New Third Board crowdfunding events, and other terminals. As of June 2015, Zhongtou8 has helped raise over RMB 500 million for over 100 projects, and have about 20,000 registered participants.[8]

Risk control is the key to success for crowdfunding platforms, and, for Zhongtou8, the most critical factors in risk control have been the quality of the project to be financed, the experience of the lead investors, and the effectiveness of post-investment management. Taking these into account, Zhongtou8 has set its

[8]http://www.zhongtou8.cn/, Zhu (2015). The statistics in this section came from these sources unless indicated otherwise.

basic listing requirements as such: in growing industries, such as mobile internet, health and consumption, new materials, and new energies, companies that want to list must have had two or more years of continuous operation, over RMB 10 million in sales revenue and over RMB 1 million in net income in the previous year, and over RMB 10 million as a minimum in the requested funding. Leading companies in an industry, firms with equity stake from institutional investors, and New Third Board listed (or those that reasonably anticipate being listed) may have priority in Zhongtou8's listings. The lead investors in any project are required to have at least two successful equity investment cases, ample resources in related industries, and a substantial ability to absorb risk. On the post-investment side, the lead investors are required to join the board of the firm they financed and push the firm to sufficiently disclose information on operations and financials. At the later stage of financing, Zhongtou8 would typically introduce the professional assurance firms into the process to help incubate and foster the firm, and accelerate the pace at which it can be listed on the New Third Board.

Currently, about 57.84 % of projects on Zhongtou8's platform are in the mobile internet industry, and include areas such social media, mobile games, vehicle online, the Internet of Things, mobile wealth management, take-out and delivery, and housing rental. Projects in consumer services, culture and media, information technology, and new materials all have more than 5 % share in the total number of projects listed; the single largest average project funded brought in RMB 12.725 million, and came from the new materials industry. In contrast, there has been little success in new energy and bio-pharmaceutical projects.

On average, the success rate of projects listed on Zhongtou8 is about 15.29 %. Taking into consideration subsequent B-round financing, the owners of projects typically give out limited shares. At Zhongyou8, over 50 % of project owners provided less than 10 % of shares to investors, while in 91.2 % of projects they offered less than 20 % of shares. The typical way that investors exit the project is through the project-creator company's buy-back of shares, though some also exit through a merger and acquisition.

12.4.2 A Rewards-Based Crowdfunding Platform: Taobao Crowdfunding

Headquartered in Hangzhou of Zhejiang Province, Taobao Crowdfunding went online on March 1, 2014. The mission of Taobao Crowdfunding was to help celebrities interact with their fans and allow them to sell their merchandise through the pre-booking system on Taobao Crowdfunding platform. The listed projects can be classified into the following categories: video, charity, books, entertainment, technology, design, animation, gaming, agriculture, and other miscellaneous categories. So far, over RMB 400 million have been raised by about 350,000 investors. The single highest project investment was over RMB 20 million. Rewards-based crowdfunding, to a large extent, mitigates the occasional lack of customization in the mass production age.[9]

Similar to equity crowdfunding, the key to success in rewards-based crowdfunding is risk control. At Taobao Crowdfunding, the project creators and fund providers are the sellers and buyers on Taobao's e-trading platform, respectively. The project creators launch their projects through Taobao and promise various forms of returns to potential investors. The platform then involves commercial insurance companies, and all funds provided through pre-booking will be guaranteed by the third-party. In addition, only projects that have delivered promised returns to investors can receive the full amount of funding; this delivery of returns must be confirmed by relevant investors.

Currently, there are over 1300 projects listed on the Taobao's crowdfunding platform. Over 50 % of the projects are in the industries such as technology and design. Agriculture, charity, movie/video and animation take up approximately 5 % of the total projects. On average, the requested funding amount for a single project in the technology category is about RMB 150,000, while the actual funds received per project is about RMB 560,000. The success rate has been as high as 97.29 % in the technology category, and about 95 % in the animation, charity movie/video, and agriculture categories. It is interesting to note that Taobao's crowdfunding platform is directly linked with Taobao's e-trading platform, and so the success (or lack thereof) of its crowdfunding segment could become an indicator of the future success (or lack thereof) of its e-trading platform—a project creator who had successfully funded a venture on Taobao Crowdfunding may then open a store on Taobao's e-trading platform in the later stages, and this expectation can, in turn, encourage financial supporters to fund the project. Meanwhile, since the platform aggregates so much data on successful projects, Taobao is able to gain experience and understand the kinds of projects that are listed online. A virtuous cycle is formed.

12.4.3 Charity Crowdfunding: Tenent's Charity (LeJuan)

Also located in Shenzhen of Guangdong Province, Tencent Charity was established by the Tencent Charity Foundation, and went online in 2014. As of the end of October 2015, Tencent Charity has raised over RMB 400 million, completing 1515 projects and involving 3796 investors in the process. The causes that listed on

[9]http://www.wangdaizhijia.com/news/baogao/21251.html, http://www.zczj.com/, https://izhongchou.taobao.com/index.htm?spm=a1z15.973.4467.17133&ad_id=100131995205a78ffb20&campaign_id=558688&jlogid=a09084137885b8. The statistics in this section are from these sources unless indicated otherwise.

Tencent included medical aid, education support, poverty assistance, disaster recovery, environmental and animal protection, and other social welfare activities. The Tencent platform is open to all verified individuals, private charity foundations, and public charity foundations. Initiators can list their projects, and, with the review and approval of the platform, raise the funds online. Investors can then choose the charity projects they prefer and donate the funds through Tencent's crowdfunding platform in an amount of their own selection.[10]

For risk control, Tencent charity platform set up a standardized fund transfer procedure. If the initiator is a public charity entity, the funds raised will be transferred directly into the recipient's Tencent "CaiFuTong" account, which would have been previously established. If the initiator is an individual or a private entity, Tencent would ask the public charity with which that individual or private firm is associated to help verify the validity and feasibility of the proposed project, and, if the vetting is successful, the funds raised will be first wired into the corresponding public charity's account. Then, the public charity will coordinate with the private initiator and further transfer the funds into the designated Tencent account. Initiators need to disclose the status of the implementation of the project periodically and in a timely manner, and also periodically release reports regarding specific funds use.

Among the projects that are funded through Tencent charity crowdfunding platform, medical aid projects take up the largest percentage (37 %) in terms of the number of projects, while education support takes the second place with about 29.7 %. Poverty assistance projects take up about 17.3 % of all projects, with environmental and animal protection constituting only about 4 %. On average, the success rate of fundraising on Tencent is about 57.68 %, with medical aid having the most success: 93 % of all projects are funded. Poverty assistance and disaster recovery, on the other hand, have the lowest success rates of about 40 %. Environmental and animal protection ranked in the middle at about 57 %, and education support followed at 49.2 %.

12.5 The Future of the Crowdfunding Sector in China

As a burgeoning industry in the internet age, crowdfunding has already revealed its potential for tremendous growth in China in only the last few years. The public policy document "Opinions on the Policy Supporting Massive Innovation and Entrepreneurship," published by China's State Council on June 16, 2015, expressed the Chinese central government's unambiguous support of crowdfunding in China, an approval which in itself portends a very optimistic future for the sector in the

[10]http://gongyi.qq.com/succor/index.htm, http://www.wangdaizhijia.com/news/baogao/21251.html. The statistics in this section are from these sources unless indicated otherwise.

years to come. As a result of this forecasted growth, several changes and developments in the sector can, therefore, be reasonably expected.

First, a larger amount of venture capital is likely to enter the industry, and at an accelerated pace. As policy risk further decreases with more explicit and enumerated support from the government as well as innovations in the crowdfunding business model, the number of standardized crowdfunding platforms, such as those with formal registrations or permits by government regulation agencies, can be expected to rise. For example, the crowdfunding platform "Ant Dake", a subsidiary of Alibaba's Ant Financial Services, recently obtained, in Shanghai, the first government license given to a crowdfunding platform. The Guangdong Provincial Free Trade Zone also announced that it will open the registration for equity crowdfunding platforms and companies with crowdfunded projects. In terms of new business models in crowdfunding, it can be said that crowdfunding platforms are becoming more explicitly and specifically classified. For instance, there has been the emergence of crowdfunding platforms chain such as ZhongChouJie and social crowdfunding platforms such as ZhongChouWo.[11]

Second, there is an idea of guaranteeing crowdfunding platforms. The current structure of equity crowdfunding is such that it depends heavily on the ability of the lead investors. As a result, the chance of a project failing can be relatively high, depending on who the lead investors are, and this significantly limits the potential for great growth in the crowdfunding sector. However, if a third-party firm or individual guarantee can provide additional assurance for investors, crowdfunding would be able to attract more capital and better finance projects. Zhou Hongwei, for example, the Chairman of 360, guaranteed the equity crowdfunding of QiKu cell phone in 2015.[12] However, policy risk also exists for guarantee firms and individuals, and it is possible that regulators may not approve of the guarantees offered by crowdfunding platforms.

Third, more specialized and customized crowdfunding platforms may emerge. As giants such as Taobao Crowdfunding and Jingdong Crowdfunding start to enter the industry, smaller platforms will begin to specialize further in order to find their niches and remain competitive. This effect can already be observed in the sector now. Currently, in China, many groups of specialized crowdfunding platforms have already begun to emerge, such as ARTIPO, which focuses on arts products, NoWorryHousing, which focuses on real estate purchase and rental, SingWorld (ChangJiangHu), a music-related platform, SunGethering for projects in new energy, and JuMi Finance, which focuses on internet-based movies and videos.[13]

Fourth, the entry threshold of crowdfunding might be lowered enough so as to allow more small-and-micro investors, such as those with extra investable income and the ability to bear a small amount of risk, to participate. A possible way that this can be achieved is allowing professional financial institutions to package

[11]http://www.wangdaizhijia.com/news/baogao/21251.html.

[12]http://www.wangdaiguancha.com/hulianwangjinrong/4676.html.

[13]http://www.wangdaizhijia.com/news/baogao/21251.html.

crowdfunding projects and then securitize the package. With this method, however, there is a chance that the legal risk may also occur if the collected funds are not "pooled" in a way consistent with laws and regulations.

Fifth, post-investment management could be further emphasized and the service chain could be extended. In addition to just providing a platform for raising funds for innovative projects, crowdfunding companies may also extend into marketing and other services such as suggestions on technological improvement, write-ups of business plans and prospectuses, and PR for charity projects. Furthermore, post-investment activities such as follow-ups on investment projects, information disclosure, and the execution of penalties on the violation of contracts would greatly benefit from the active participation of crowdfunding platforms.

Finally, the entire crowdfunding industry might see some degree of consolidation in the future. While weaker platforms that are unable to drive adequate volumes through their platforms begin to exit from the industry, stronger, larger platforms will have the opportunity to expand their market shares and grow their project/investor bases. Overall, we may see the establishment of an entire crowdfunding ecosystem that includes not only project initiators and platforms and investors but also providers of ancillary and peripheral services such as advisory, legal, and media production. This expanded ecosystem will greatly enhance the quality of crowdfunding services and enlarge the scope of the industry. It can be expected that, as more detailed laws and regulations are put into place and the business model of crowdfunding becomes more mature, an increasing number of smaller participants from both the real and financial sector, looking for funds and investments opportunities, respectively, will join the "crowd" in the years to come.

Reference

Zhu P. 2015. *Social mission of crowdfunding*. Presentation at Peking University.

Chapter 13
Inclusive Enough for "Neglected 80 Percent"?—Small Business Loans by Large State-Owned Commercial Banks

As the book title indicates, this is a book discussing alternative financing methods for SMEs that are unable to obtain traditional loans from state-owned commercial banks. However, as discussed previously, the lack of funding for SMEs in the first place actually originated from decades of large state-owned commercial bank being more or less the only financial institutions that were allowed to legally provide bank loans in the market, and their tendency to focus their services on large state-owned enterprises. These market conditions in turn triggered the development of alternative financing methods that loosened SME dependence on commercial bank loans. However, as the market evolves, large state-owned commercial banks, for various reasons of their own, have themselves begun to enter the SME financing market, a market which at one time they largely avoided due to the nature of the risk. In the last chapter of this book, we would like to uncover and discuss some of these recent developments, and the evolution of traditional bank loans provided by large, state-owned commercial banks in China.

13.1 Changing from Financing "20 %" to "80 %"?

Long before Jack Ma's remarks about financing the "bottom 80 %" on June 3rd, 2013,[1] the challenge of financing SMEs with justifiable profit margin and controllable default risk had been a quandary for large state-owned banks. As pretty much the only players in the loanable funds market who are legally allowed to provide commercial loans to borrowers, these bank's loan decisions had the ability to determine the fate of millions of companies, especially SMEs, regardless of which industry the companies were in. In prior years, when China's direct financing market, including both the bond and equity markets, was relatively under-developed, the commercial loans provided by these very few, very large state-owned commercial banks tended to be the last "legal" for external financing for a company. If a SME was not lucky enough to get

[1] http://money.sohu.com/20130604/n377910523.shtml.

J.G. Wang and J. Yang, *Financing without Bank Loans*,
DOI 10.1007/978-981-10-0901-3_13

funds from these limited number of banks, the only alternative left for the desperate company would be to obtain financing through illegal "shadow loans"—private, underground loans with annualized interest rates of as high as 50 %.[2]

The challenge that precluded most commercial banks from lending funds to most SMEs was the imbalance of risk and return in most SME ventures. It was quite often the case that the potential returns from lending to SMEs would not achieve the desired economies of scale. For commercial banks, the expenditure and input required for every individual loan is pretty much the same, regardless of the value of the loan. They must clear the firm for lending, a process which includes loan application review, credit assessment, comprehensive analysis, on-site investigation, final release of funds, and post-loan management; clearly, it is more economically advantageous for banks to target large loan amounts, given the greater potential returns and likely profitability. In general, the value of loans required by SMEs is much smaller than what banks need to achieve their targeted profitability.

On top of this, the risks inherent to SMEs further discourage the larger commercial banks in China from taking on SME loans. As is well documented in the literature of this subject, the higher degree of asymmetric information, non-standardized financial reports, lack of adequate collateral, insufficient credit records, and lack of internal auditing are among the top sources of SME risks,[3] and these risks make the imbalance between the risk and return of SME loans even more severe. As a result, it was mostly large, state-owned companies, which can provide high returns and entail low risk, that became the target clientele of large state-owned commercial banks—the "lucky 20 %," as denoted by Jack Ma.

However, the financial industry in China has been changing, even though the speed of changes may be considered slower than expected, at least, for the large commercial banks. The emergence of the internet, the mushrooming growth of small loan firms, guarantee companies, financial leasing firms, P2P online lending, and various bond and equity markets are all imposing tremendous pressures on large state-owned commercial banks. These market forces are pressuring them to think more deeply about the future, and how they should react to these irrevocable changes in China's financial industry. One way in which these banks are reacting is by issuing small business loans and expanding the scope of their business beyond just the top 20 %, and this is what we will discuss in the subsequent sections of this chapter.

13.2 Loan Products for SMEs

In recent years, the major state-owned commercial banks have all launched various loan products specifically designed to serve the increased financing needs of SMEs and expand the scope of their own commercial banking businesses. In general, there are several major types of commercial loans designed for SMEs.

---

[2]http://finance.sina.com.cn/g/20110801/071410237358.shtml.

[3]Wang and Yang (2014).

13.2.1 Working Capital Loans

Working capital loans are issued primarily to SMEs in the manufacturing and commerce sectors, as well as some other sectors, and include both short-term and medium-term loans for SMEs to finance their working capital and short-to-medium-term expansion. The operating income and other cash flows of the borrowing firms are considered the source of repayment for the loans. Using loan guidelines from the Industrial and Commerce Bank of China (ICBC) as an example,[4] the maximum amount of a single loan is RMB 30 million, and the term is typically no more than 3 years but could be as long as 5 years. The method of repayment is either mortgage-type payment or periodical-interest-and-principle-at-end-type payment. The qualification requirements for the application of the loans are very basic.

13.2.2 Credit Line Loans and Online Lending

Credit line loan is another debt product that is issued to SMEs for their financing needs. The targeted borrowers are SMEs with stable cash flows and adequate loan collateral, and require funds at high frequency and in the short-term. Within the quota and term limit specified in the contract, borrowers can borrow money multiple times and repay each loan separately, so that the quota can in essence be used repeatedly throughout the contracted period of time. The maximum loan amount can be as high as RMB 30 million for ICBC loans. As a deal that involved multiple loans but an only one-time contract, credit line loans can help reduce the financing cost for SMEs. In addition to off-line operations, the credit line loan can also be issued through an online banking system.

13.2.3 Collective Loans

A collective loan is a debt product designed for micro firms in certain sub-industries, geographical regions, or markets which produce similar products or services or have some similarity of operation. The lending process can be processed through an online banking system. The applicants need to provide either collateral or a guarantee with a credit rating of at least BBB/A-, depending on the products in question. For the ICBC, the maximum loan value varies from RMB 2 million to

---

[4]Industrial and Commercial Bank of China (ICBC): http://www.icbc.com.cn/icbc/%e5%85%ac%e5%8f%b8%e4%b8%9a%e5%8a%a1/%e4%bc%81%e4%b8%9a%e6%9c%8d%e5%8a%a1/%e4%b8%ad%e5%b0%8f%e4%bc%81%e4%b8%9a/%e4%b8%9a%e5%8a%a1%e7%bb%bc%e8%bf%b0/default.htm. All the statistics and product descriptions of ICBC are from ICBC web site unless indicated otherwise.

RMB 5 million, while the maximum value for loans provided by the China Construction Bank (CCB) is RMB 15 million.[5] The term of the loans is typically less than 1 year.

13.2.4 Trade Credit and Factoring

Trade credit is another product for SME financing and uses trade documents as collateral. The accepted collaterals include accounts receivable, inventories, and purchasing orders. In order to apply for trade credit, SMEs must meet the following qualifications: "stable business relationships" with its vendors and customers in the supply chain, sound credit record or sound credit of the firm's trading partners, a low default rate, and indisputable ownership of the goods used as collateral. Depending on the products, the loan amount from the ICBC can vary from 70 % to 100 % of the collaterals, and the term is typically short—only a few months. In addition, invoices can also be used as collateral; when using invoices, a SME doesn't need to transfer the ownership of the receivables. Needless to say, a letter of credit is a common financing tool for trading firms, and SMEs involved in trading are definitely among the customers of this banking service.

13.2.5 Asset-Backed Loans

Asset-backed loans are issued to SMEs that need to finance their expansion on fixed assets, such as real estate properties. The maximum value of loans could reach RMB 30 million, and the term of the loan is typically 3–5 years. The method of repayment is usually flexible, ranging from mortgage-type repayment to monthly interest payments with the principal payback at maturity. For ICBC, asset-backed loans also include loans for a SME's down-payment in the purchase of standardized factory buildings, such as those located in industrial parks. The maximum loan amount is also RMB 30 million, and the term is up to 5 years.

13.2.6 Special Purpose Loans

State-owned banks also provide special purpose loans such as "TV Loans" which are designed by the China Construction Bank. Applicants of these loans are TV series producers who can use the copyrights and accounts receivable generated by

[5]China Construction Bank (CCB): http://www.ccb.com/cn/home/product_svr.html. All the statistics and product descriptions of CCB are from CCB web site unless indicated otherwise.

their contracts with TV stations as collateral to borrow funds from CCB. The term limit for producers with higher credit-ratings, an A+ or above, is one year, while the term limit for the lower credit-rated firms is less than 6 months.

"Rental Loans" are another category of special purpose loan that are designed for small commerce firms or shops that are specifically looking to finance their space rentals in shopping malls. The maximum loan amount will be either the cost of one year of rental, RMB 3 million, or 20 % of the firm's sales revenue in the previous year, whichever value is smallest. The term of the loan is to be less than one year. The loan will be guaranteed by the shopping mall in which the rental is based, and the repayment guarantee fees are paid by the borrowers.[6]

The "Assistance Loan" (Zhu Bao Dai) is a loan designed by the CCB for micro and small firms in the selected "Micro and Small Firm Pool". The firms in the pool are one that has been singled out by local government to receive specific support. In order to receive this loan, the micro or small firm needs to provide a guarantee for at least 40 % of the loan value and receive government risk compensation fund support. Depending upon the credit rating, micro and small firms can receive "Assistance Loans" with a value of RMB 5 million to 20 million. The term limit of all the loans is less than one year.

The "Convertible Loan" is designed for SMEs that have been designated to have "growth potential" by the CCB. Convertible loans can be used to finance both working capital needs and fixed assets investments. These loans require third-party guarantees, and the maximum loan value is less than RMB 5 million. The term limit of the loan ranges from 1 to 3 years for working capital loans, and the term of fixed asset loans follows the CCB's general rules for loans.

A "Boat Mortgage Loan" is a loan designed for SMEs to finance their boat purchasing needs. The borrowing firms can use an existing boat or purchase of a new boat to be used as collateral, and the maximum term is less than 5 years.

13.2.7 Account Overdraw

The CCB also provides service for an SME's temporary financing needs by allowing cash overdraw for certain pre-specified bank accounts at a pre-specified amount and with previously agreed-upon terms. The use of overdrawn funds is limited to working capital, and the funds are not allowed to flow into areas such as the equity market, the futures market, or equity investment. The allowed term of the overdraw is less than one year, but the consecutive days between overdraws within that one year depends on the credit rating of the borrowing firms: for AAA-rated firms, the longest period of time is 90 days; for firms with a rating of AA− to AA+, the ceiling is 60 days, and the limit becomes 30 days if the firm has an A+ rating. The maximum allowed amount of overdraw is RMB 5 million.

[6]Ibid 5.

Overdraw service is also provided by China's Bank of Communication (CBC) for small business accounts.[7] If a firm's bank balance is not sufficient to cover the cost of the bill, qualified account owners are allowed to overdraw funds up to the limit specified in the contract between the CBC and the firm. Typically, qualified account owners are small firms with an existing CBC account that is over one year old and has a history of frequent daily transactions. The minimum amount allowed to be overdrawn is RMB 5000, and the maximum amount is RMB 1 million. Usually, the allowed overdraw period of time is 10 days, but the maximum time can be expanded to 3 months. The interest rate charged by the bank is usually a certain percentage above the basic rate. In addition, the bank charges a one-time fee for overdraws that comes up to 0.03 % of the total overdraw amount.

13.2.8 Micro and Small Loans

Micro loans are offered by CCB for the short-term financing of micro and small firms, for proprietorship, and for individuals looking to fund their working capital needs. The maximum loan amount is RMB 10 million, and the term is less than one year for firms, less than one month for individuals. The assets that can be used as collaterals include bank CDs, treasury bonds, guarantee certificates, bank notes, bank acceptances, gold, enterprise bonds, and other easily cashable assets.

For micro and small firms with sound credit rating, the CCB will also issue credit loans without collateral. However, the CCB requires that the spouse of the owner of the borrowing firm co-sign the loan contract as a co-borrower. The use of funding is highly restricted, and is designated solely to finance working capital. Funds cannot be used in the stock market or for equity investments. The maximum loan value, in general, is RMB 2 million or less, and can be extended to RMB 10 million if the borrower is an existing customer of the bank. The maximum term for the loans is 9 months.

In this credit loan category, the CCB will also "voluntarily" provide a credit line for a special group of customers. If a firm has a clearance account with the CCB that has been opened for more than 2 years, with more than 100 transactions and a total transaction value of RMB 2 million or more in the previous 12 months or an average daily balance of more than RMB 30,000 in the previous 12 months, then the firm will be entitled to receive a credit line of up to RMB 2 million. The maximum term is one year, during which the firm can borrow and repay the credit any time.

---

[7]China Bank of Communication: http://www.bankcomm.com/BankCommSite/cn/share/electron-bank/electron_bank_index.jsp?type=xqy. All the statistics and product descriptions of CBC are from CBC web site unless indicated otherwise.

13.2.9 Online Banking Products

As the internet "brutally" invaded the financial industry in China, not only in the private sectors such as P2P online lending and equity crowdfunding but also in the commercial banking sector, state-owned banks, either voluntarily or due to pressure, also jumped onto the internet and digital wagon. Providing financing for the SMEs through the internet is a notable point of progress in the traditional commercial banking industry. In this regard, the China's Bank of Communication (CBC)'s "e-loan" is a prime example of a remarkable internet-based innovation.[8]

An "e-loan" is an online service for the CBC's smaller customers, which they can apply for after they obtain loan quotas. Using the "e-loan", borrowing firms can use internet to withdraw cash, pay back the loan, and inquire about the loan's status. As a result, the firms' financing cost can be reduced, and the efficiency of lending process will be improved. Borrowing firms can now conduct their transactions anywhere, anytime.

13.2.10 The E-Debit Card

The "e-Loan Card" is a debit card issued by the CBC to small business owners for a value-added service that combines the functions of a debit card with lending and internet service, a three-in-one. In order to qualify, applicants must be small business firms that conduct frequent transactions in purchasing, office decoration, travel, catering, tourism, ticketing, rental payment, utility payment, or other related areas. The maximum credit allowance is RMB 1 million. The maximum term for the credit allowance is less than one year.

13.2.11 Insurance-Backed Loans

The CBC also provides short term working capital loans for domestic trading for SMEs with existing insurance. SME borrowers can use their insurance policy as collateral when applying for the loans. The maximum loan value is RMB 20 million, and the maximum term is one year.

---

[8]Ibid 7.

13.2.12 One-Stop-Shopping and Supply Chain Financing—Zhan Ye Tong

Another loan product provided by the CBC is called the Zhan Ye Tong, a one-stop-shopping supply chain financing product. Qualified borrowers include SMEs that are on the supply chain of a separate core company. The loan can be issued all at once but paid back in periods. The maximum term can be as long as eight years, and various tangible and intangible assets, such as real estate properties, treasury bonds, accounts receivable, commercial papers, and warehouse invoices can be used as collateral. The CBC also provides one-stop-shopping financing products for individuals, for their financing needs in real estate properties, car loans, renovation loans, student loans, and other wealth management products.

13.2.13 Start-up Loans—Chuangye Yi Zhan Tong

CBC also provides loans for the short term financing needs of start-ups. Qualified firms are those deemed to have "value creation potential." The maximum loan amount is RMB 5 million, and the maximum term is one year. The interest rates charged vary depending on the form of the guarantee. Because start-ups lack a long operating history, financial statements are not required for the applications of the loans. However, in place of that, CBC requires the primary owner or operator of the start-up to have at least 3 years of business experience and to have been a local resident for at least 2 years. In addition, the start-ups need to open an account in CBC and clear their transactions through their CBC account.

Similarly, the Bank of China also provides financing for start-ups in Beijing's Zhongguancun Technology Park. The applicants need to be on the list of innovative high tech firms of Zhongguancun Management Commission. If these requirements are met, the Bank of China can provide customized financing services across all the different stages of a firm's growth. The maximum loan value is RMB 50 million or less, and the firm's annual sales should not be more than RMB 500 million in order to qualify for the loan.[9]

13.2.14 Down-Payment Loans for Purchasing Fixed Assets

When SMEs purchase buildings in an industrial park designed to national standards, the Agriculture Bank of China (ABC) are willing to provide loans to finance the down-payment. The purchased buildings can be used as collateral, and the

[9]http://www.boc.cn/cbservice/cb8/cb81/201309/t20130912_2510061.html. All the statistics and product descriptions of BOC are from BOC web site unless indicated otherwise.

firm's operating income will become the source of loan repayment. The credit ratio for down-payment can be as high as 70 %, and the maximum loan amount can reach RMB 20 million; additionally, the maximum loan term could be as long as 10 years.[10]

13.2.15 Loans Backed by Intellectual Property Rights

The ABC's Guangdong Provincial Branch also provides short-term loans backed by intellectual property rights for SMEs in technology-related industries that are looking to finance their working capital needs, and get help for commercializing their intellectual property. Legal documents such as trademark certificates and patent certificates are required in the firms' applications, and the patent(s) that are used as collateral need to be new and applicable in practice, and they must be on the list of index reports published by the State Bureau of Intellectual Property.

13.2.16 Loans that Require a Risk Fund Pool—Hu Zhu Tong Bao

The Bank of China also provides loans for SMEs that agree to set up a fund pool containing mutual-risk-assistance-funds and risk guarantee funds; the pool is to be managed by a third party entity that works with the Bank of China. The fund pool is then actually used as collateral for the loan. The qualifications of the applying firm include annual sales of RMB 100 million or less, two consecutive years of operation, at least four years of business experience on the part of the firm's owner, as well as sound credit records.

13.2.17 SME Loans Issued by Tax Payment Records—Shui Kuan Tong Bao

The Bank of China's Guangdong Brunch also issues loans to SMEs with sound tax payment records, well maintained credit records and stable clearance records, as determined by the Bank of China. This loan would be a short-term loan. The qualifications for applicants are: annual sales less than RMB 100 million, taxable income between RMB 10 million and 150 million, two consecutive years of tax payment records, and 4 years of business experience for the owner of the firm.

---

[10]Agriculture Bank of China (ABC): http://www.abchina.com/cn/businesses/sme/. All the statistics and product descriptions of ABC are from ABC web site unless indicated otherwise.

13.2.18 *The Mezzanine Financing Product—Zhan Ye Tong Bao*

The Bank of China also provides a mezzanine level of packaged financing products to SMEs through both debt and equity financing. These products involve commercial bank loans, insurance, equity securities, leasing and wealth management products. The bank's target consumers are SMEs that are either in their early stage or stable-growth stage. The borrowers must also meet the following requirements: annual sales over RMB 5 million for early-stage firms and 50 million for stable growth firms, at least 4 years in operation for both, and well-maintained credit records for both. For approved customers, the Bank of China can provide a wide spectrum of products/services ranging from clearings, credit financing, wealth management, individual banking, insurance, and equity investment.

13.3 What's Next?

As indicated in the previous section, all the primary state-owned commercial banks, including the "Big Four"—the Industrial and Commercial Bank of China (ICBC), the China Construction Bank (CCB), the Agriculture Bank of China (ABC), and the Bank of China—and the "Distant Fifth",—the China Bank of Communication—have all stepped into the SME financing arena, developing a wide spectrum of financing products/services which covers mortgage loans, credit loans, special purpose loans, online products, supply chain financing, mezzanine products, and other financing services.

The entry of large state-owned commercial banks into SME financing may be driven by several factors. First are the changes in government policy towards SMEs in China. As the Chinese economy arrives at a crossroads after more than 30 years of high speed development, the traditional growth model that was characterized by overconsumption of non-reproducible energies, heavily polluted environments, and competition based solely on inexpensive labor is wide considered non-sustainable. As a substitute, an innovation-driven growth model was suggested, and SMEs, as the players in the economy with the strongest motivation and ability to conduct "creative disruption", are considered the linchpins in this new reality. As a result, supporting the growth of SMEs, especially financially, has become the primary focus of Chinese government. Consequently, as state-owned entities, these large commercial banks have no choice but to take the needed actions in order to implement these government policies.

However, the involvement of SME financing by state-owned commercial banks may not be entirely as a result of the "mandate" from the government administration. Changing market conditions may also be pressuring state-owned banks to explore new frontiers. As China's financial reform keeps moving forward—even though it may not be as quickly as many expected—the direct debt financing markets, such as the bond market, along with the equity market and other financial innovations and creations, begin to emerge. Since the prevailing market rate in the bond market in China is often lower than that in the commercial banking market, many decade-long customers of large state-owned commercial banks, those once deemed the "lucky 20 %," now turn to the bond market to finance their operations and investments. As a result of this shift and facing the new reality of losing these traditional "low-risk-and-high-return" customers, state-owned commercial banks are being pressured to explore new markets, even those with higher risk such as the SME market.

For both Chinese SMEs and the Chinese government, the movement of commercial banks into the SME financing sector is a welcome one; for one, it increases the supply of "legal" funding available to SMEs in the loanable funds market. The move is also advantageous for commercial banks, however. At present, large state-owned commercial banks still possess many competitive advantages in the market against smaller, privately-held commercial banks, and also against certain grassroots financial entities that also provide financing services for SMEs such as P2P online lending platforms. One of the major advantages these large banks has is their comparatively more abundant funding source. Compared to many smaller banks, and especially to financial entities such as P2P platforms that are not even legally allowed to take deposits or form a "fund pool", state-owned commercial banks are able to obtain and maintain an adequate funding source at the lowest financing cost, and are even able to become the funding source for some of their competitors. As a result, their leading position in the loanable funds market is hard to challenge.

Another primary advantage these large banks have is that they possess information on historical credit records of potential borrowers. These banks are among the few privileged parties that are allowed to access to the credit records database of China's central bank. These large banks can then use the information provided by the "big data" to better scrutinize and filter loan applicants, selecting only the ones with historically lower risks. Of course, the development of the internet and e-commerce makes it possible for private firms or financial entities to collect and generate a "private version" of big data, such as the databases created by Baidu, Alibaba, and Tencent (BAT), but this data is typically not available for free use by all private financial entities. Interestingly enough, this may indicate that though large state-owned commercial banks have entered the market for "the lower 80 %", they will likely only service the upper end of that 80 %.

Looking forward, the market in commercial bank loans for SMEs is likely to be segmented by the level of risk and the associated return. While large state-owned commercial banks will most likely take the juiciest but also safest part of the "eighty percent"—companies with relatively low nominal returns but which will also entail relatively lower risk, to compensate for the general increase in risk level that these large state-owned banks will be taking on across the board with SMEs. The other participants in the SME financing market, then, such as local banks, credit unions, and online lending platforms, will split the remaining market share, servicing the relatively risker SME customers and gaining higher upside potential as compensation. Needless to say, financing SMEs is “big game,” one which offers both strategic value to an economy and poses tremendous challenges for that economy, and will require the joint effort of all market players. Just as it does in all sectors of the economy, the government bears the ultimate responsibility to intervene in the case of “market failure” in SME financing—and so, as the primary executors of government policy, large, state-owned commercial banks have an obligation to shoulder their social responsibilities by participating in the SME financing market.

Reference

Wang, Jiazhuo G., and Juan Yang. 2014. Who gets funds from China’s capital market? Springer

MIX
Papier aus verantwortungsvollen Quellen
Paper from responsible sources
FSC® C105338

If you have any concerns about our products,
you can contact us on
ProductSafety@springernature.com

In case Publisher is established outside the EU,
the EU authorized representative is:
Springer Nature Customer Service Center GmbH
Europaplatz 3, 69115 Heidelberg, Germany

Printed by Libri Plureos GmbH
in Hamburg, Germany